JUDGES
AND
METHOD

JUDGES AND METHOD

New Approaches in Biblical Studies

Edited by
Gale A. Yee

FORTRESS PRESS
MINNEAPOLIS

JUDGES AND METHOD
New Approaches in Biblical Studies

Cover art: The Levite and his wife dining; the Levite yielding his wife to the wantons of Gibeah; the Levite's wife is wickedly abused; the Levite finds his wife dead at the door of his house. (Clockwise from top left.) From the Old Testament Miniatures, M.638,f.16. The Pierpont Morgan Library/Art Resource, New York. Used by permission.

Text design: Joseph Bonyata

Library of Congress Cataloging-in-Publication Data

Judges and method: new approaches in biblical studies/edited by
    Gale A. Yee.
        p. cm.
    Includes bibliographical references and index.
    ISBN 0-8006-2745-8 (alk. paper)
    I. Bible. O. T. Judges — Criticism, interpretation, etc.
2. Bible — Hermeneutics. I. Yee, Gale A., 1949–   .
BS1305.2.J83   1985
222'.3206'01 — dc20
                                                                95-14490
                                                                CIP

The paper used in this publication meets the minimum requirements of American National Standard for Information Sciences — Permanence of Paper for Printed Library Materials, ANSI Z329.48-1984

Manufactured in the U.S.A.   AF-1-2745

                3   4   5   6   7   8   9   10

CONTENTS

PREFACE

This book is the Hebrew Bible companion volume to *Mark and Method*, published by Fortress Press.[1] Like its New Testament counterpart, *Judges and Method* introduces a student audience to new developments in the field of biblical studies. Unlike *Mark and Method*, however, this volume includes chapters on structuralism and ideological criticism and excludes reader-response criticism. The distinctive choices of both volumes should alert the student that new approaches to the Bible exist beyond the ones discussed in the two works. For example, the psychoanalytic and New Historicist approaches that are emerging onto the biblical studies scene are not treated by either book.[2] All this is to highlight the fact that exciting and innovative methods are continually being applied to this important foundational text.

We would like to thank the University of St. Thomas, Augustana College, and the Perkins School of Theology for their financial support and release time needed to complete this work. We are grateful to Elizabeth Struthers Malbon, chair of the Society of Biblical Literature section on Biblical Criticism and Literary Criticism, for inviting us to present our work in one of her sessions at the 1993 annual meeting in Washington, D.C. Finally, we wish to thank the editors of Fortress Press — Marshall D. Johnson, Michael West, Cynthia L. Thompson, and former editor Charles B. Puskas — for all their help in the completion of this project.

This book is dedicated to the students we teach and who teach us.

1. Janice Capel Anderson and Stephen D. Moore, eds., *Mark and Method: New Approaches in Biblical Studies* (Minneapolis: Fortress Press, 1992).
2. Ilona Rashkow, *The Phallacy of Genesis: A Feminist-Psychoanalytic Approach* (Louisville, Ky.: Westminster/John Knox Press, 1993), and Mary Ann Tolbert, "The Gospel in Greco-Roman Culture," *The Book and the Text: The Bible and Literary Theory*, Regina M. Schwartz, ed. (Cambridge, Mass.: Basil Blackwell, 1990), 258–275.

1

INTRODUCTION:
WHY JUDGES?

Gale A. Yee

This book introduces the student and interested teacher to a variety of the newer methods of biblical interpretation currently being used by scholars: narrative, social scientific, feminist, structuralist, deconstructive, and ideological criticism. It not only presents the theory behind each method, the kinds of questions it asks, the presuppositions undergirding it, and its central characteristics, but also applies the method to the Book of Judges.

There are several reasons for choosing the Book of Judges as a testing ground for these methods. Its narratives are not as recognizable to students as those in the books of Genesis or Exodus. The stories of Adam and Eve or Moses and the ten commandments are more widely circulated than the deeds of the left-handed Ehud, the warrior-woman Deborah, the assassin Jael, or the indecisive Gideon. Less familiar as well is the tribal period of Israelite history that the book relates. One thus learns a new text in addition to new approaches to this text. Moreover, the Book of Judges contains some of the most absorbing and terrifying stories in the Hebrew Bible. The book is about murder, death, betrayal, and war. In contrast to other sections of the Hebrew Bible, it includes a number of stories involving women, the violence they inflict, and (much more often) the violence they endure.

Judges: The (Wo)men

Based upon the Latin *Judices,* the English title of the book, Judges, can be misleading. In present-day usage, the word *judge* carries a juridical denotation. One automatically thinks of magistrates dressed in black, sitting in mahogany-paneled courtrooms settling legal cases. In the biblical book, only Deborah functions as a judge in this forensic sense of the term. According to Judges 4:4, the Israelites came to her for judgment (*mishpat*). Nevertheless, we do not know how "official" Deborah's status was, and she certainly did not have a formal courtroom. The text describes her as sitting under a palm tree (4:5).

The designation "judge" translates the Hebrew participle *shophet*, which is derived from the verb *shapat*. *Shapat* has a broad range of meaning that is difficult to render into English: to decide (or judge), to govern, to vindicate, and to deliver. Indeed, most biblical "judges" rescued their people from the hands of their enemies. They functioned as military leaders during times of crisis. Moreover, many governed the land during the rest of their lifetimes.[1] However, except for the general, introductory description of the judges in 2:16-18, not one person in the rest of the book is actually called a *shophet*. So, why "judges"?

Another difficulty with the English title "Judges" from the perspective of the newer approaches discussed here is that it privileges men, their politics, and their wars as the foci of the book. Even though women like Deborah and Jael did participate and lead in the arena of war, when references to the judges recur in the biblical tradition, the spotlight is on the men.[2] Ben Sirach's admiration for the judges is set within his triumphalistic hymn "singing the praises of famous *men*" (Sir 44:1; 46:11–12). Samuel, the last judge of Israel, reminds the people that "the Lord sent Jerubbaal and Barak, and Jephthah, and Samson, and rescued you out of the hand of your enemies on every side" (1 Sam 12:11).

In its roll call of faith-filled individuals in Israelite history, Hebrews 11:32 highlights Gideon, Barak, Samson, and Jephthah. The selection of these four individuals is itself surprising. They are hardly the paragons of faith the Book of Hebrews would have us believe. Gideon (Jerubbaal) continually tested God (6:15, 17, 36-40). Barak was reluctant to fulfill God's oracle unless Deborah (a woman!) accompanied him in battle (4:8). Samson betrayed his nazirite vow for a woman. His exploits were conducted more on the personal than the military battlefield (15:4-8, 15-17; 16:4-31). Jephthah's own victory in combat came at the price of his daughter's life, taken to fulfill a rashly uttered vow (11:34-40). Although not a judge, Abimelech is said to have ruled Israel for three years (9:22). A usurper and tyrant, Abimelech achieved his rule through the slaughter of his fifty brothers (9:5). Fatally wounded by a woman, he orders his armor bearer to slay him, lest it be remarked that "a woman killed him" (9:53-54).

All pretense at heroism and glorious victory is abandoned in the last five chapters of Judges. This section culminates in the most atrocious events in the book. Cultic and social chaos reigns. A wife is betrayed, gang raped, and dismembered. A tribe is almost extinguished in a fierce civil war, and six hundred

---

1. Cf. 9:22; 10:2-3; 12:7, 9, 11, 14; 15:20; 16:31.

2. Judges 4–5; 9:53-54. See also Gale A. Yee, "By the Hand of a Woman: The Metaphor of the Woman Warrior in Judges 4," *Semeia* 61 (1993): 109–114.

women are seized and raped to restock this tribe. The explanation given is that "in those days there was no king in Israel; every man did what was right in his own eyes" (21:25, RSV).

Though ostensibly about the military and political adventures of male heroes, the Book of Judges is studded from beginning to end with the stories of women, which flicker in and out. Reading the book from their points of view unfolds a "countercoherence" that clashes with the apparently male emphasis on public politics, wars, and mighty deeds.[3] The narratives of women qualify any designation of "hero" for these male leaders by foregrounding their cowardice, betrayal, and brutality in their relations with women. Through these women's stories, the personal in the book becomes political; the private becomes public.

Judges: The Book

In light of the countercoherence of women's lives in the Book of Judges, one cannot simply outline the book, as is customary, according to the stories of these male leaders. While the narrative frame is oriented toward the male, women's stories appear at the book's most important junctures. In the outline below, their stories appear in boldface to underscore this interweaving.

Judges is structured in three parts. The first section summarizes the conquest and settlement of the Promised Land, revealing that not all the Canaanites are eliminated by the Israelite tribes. These Canaanites seduce the tribes into worshiping their fertility gods. God sends foreign oppressors to punish the tribes for their covenantal infidelity. In their suffering the tribes cry out to God, who empowers the judges to deliver them from their enemies. The second section — the body of the book — details the escapades of these judges. As the book progresses, the leadership and character of these judges deteriorate, so that by the end religious and social anarchy is rampant. The conclusion highlights the absence of a king (and the order he is thought to bring) by relating violent stories about the lawlessness of the period. These final chapters prepare for the establishment of the monarchy in the next biblical book, 1 Samuel.

Outline of the Book of Judges

  I. Introduction: The Conquest and Settlement of the Land (1:1 — 3:6)
     A. *The Military Problem:* The qualified success of the Israelite tribes in Canaanite territory (1:1-36)

3. See Mieke Bal, *Death and Dissymmetry: The Politics of Coherence in the Book of Judges* (Chicago: University of Chicago Press, 1988), for the most extensive treatment of the countercoherence of Judges.

  1. The three southern tribes: Judah, Simeon, Benjamin (1:1-21)

The future judge Othniel takes Achsah as wife (1:11-15).

  2. The six northern tribes: Manasseh, Ephraim, Zebulun, Asher, Naphtali, Dan (1:22-36)

 B. *The Religious Problem:* The tribes break their covenant with YHWH and worship the gods of "the inhabitants of this land" (2:1 — 3:6)

  1. The angel of YHWH prophesies that these gods will be a "snare" to the tribes (2:1-5)

  2. The apostasy of the new generation and God's punishment (2:6-15)

  3. YHWH raises up judges to deliver Israel from foreign oppressors (2:16-21)

  4. YHWH allows a foreign presence in the land to test the Israelites (2:22 — 3:6)

The Israelites intermarry with these foreigners and worship their gods (3:6).

II. The Lives of the Judges (3:7 — 16:31)

 A. *Othniel of Judah* (3:7-11)

In contrast to those who intermarried with foreign women, Othniel, who married the ideal Israelite wife, Achsah, is presented as the ideal judge.

 B. *Ehud of Benjamin* (3:12-30)

 C. *Shamgar* (3:31)

 D. *Deborah and Barak* (4:1 — 5:31)

Deborah urges Barak to defeat Sisera. Jael kills Sisera instead (4:1-24). Deborah sings of Sisera's execution by Jael and the imminent disgrace of his mother (5:1-31).

 E. *Gideon of Manasseh* (6:1 — 8:35)

Gideon has many wives, with whom he has seventy sons. He also has a secondary wife who bears him a son named Abimelech (8:29-31).

 F. *Abimelech of Shechem* (9:1-57)

Abimelech slays his seventy brothers, the sons of his father's primary wives. Jotham, the youngest of these sons, escapes and predicts Abimelech's death (9:1-21).

During battle, "a certain woman" crushes Abimelech's skull with a millstone. Abimelech orders his armor bearer to kill him, lest it be discovered that "a woman killed him" (9:50-57).

 G. *Tola of Issachar* (10:1-2)

 H. *Jair of Gilead* (10:3-5)

 I. *Reiteration of the Religious Problem* (10:6-17; cf. 2:1 — 3:6)

 J. *Jephthah of Gilead* (11:1 — 12:7)

Jephthah's rash vow results in the death of his only child, a daughter (11:29-40).

K. *Ibzan of Bethlehem* (12:8-10)

L. *Elon of Zebulun* (12:11-12)

M. *Abdon of Ephraim* (12:13-15)

N. *Samson of Dan* (13:1 — 16:31)

A barren woman gives birth to Samson and consecrates him as a nazirite. His affairs with women bring him in conflict with the Philistines.

III. Conclusion: "No King in Israel" — Cultic and Social Anarchy (17:1 — 21:25)

A. *Micah, His Idol, and His Levite* (17:1-13)

Micah's mother makes for him an idol of silver, which he sets up in his own shrine with his personal priest.

B. *The Levite and the Tribe of Dan* (18:1-31)

C. *The Levite and the Tribe of Benjamin* (19:1-30)

A Levite's secondary wife is raped. Her body is dismembered and its parts sent to the tribes of Israel.

D. *Intertribal War* (20:1 — 21:25)

Six hundred women are seized in a mass rape and given to the tribe of Benjamin (21:15-25)

Judges and Method

Historical Criticism: Judges as a Constructed Work

The modern study of Judges is influenced by the various kinds of questions that can be addressed to this book. Perhaps the foremost question asked in the early and middle decades of this century was, How was this book composed? The answer to this question determined the responses to other fundamental questions regarding the book: How credible was the book as a source of Israel's history, and how reliable was its author as a historian? The stories in Judges were important for the interpreter insofar as they were thought to yield accurate data that could reconstruct a more objective history of Israel's tribal period.

A number of biblical methods (tradition criticism, form criticism, and redaction criticism)[4] have been applied to the Book of Judges with these historical or historiographical questions in mind. These methods are generally subsumed under the rubric of *historical criticism*. Historical criticism distinguishes two types of questions in its analysis. The first deals with the historical situation(s) described in the text. The second considers the historical situation(s) that gave rise to the text — the circumstances that produced the work. The Book of

---

4. See the entries under Barton, Hayes, and McKenzie in the bibliography at the end of this essay for a more complete discussion of these historical critical methods.

Judges describes the historical period between the death of Joshua and the tribal bedlam before the birth of Samuel, the final judge in Israel (c. 1250–1020 B.C.E.). Nevertheless, it has become clear to modern scholars that the book did not originate during the tribal period, but was composed in stages (both oral and written) much later than the premonarchic era of Israel's history. Depending on which scholar one reads, the final written stage of the book's composition during the exilic or postexilic periods is more than four centuries after the time of the judges (c. 587–398 B.C.E.). Different historical critical methods examine the various phases of the book's development.

Tradition criticism asks questions about the earlier oral stages of the book. It investigates the places where oral traditions originate (cult centers, tribes, disciples, etc.), how they are transmitted in the various tradent circles,[5] and how they change over time until they are taken up by a redactor and put into written form. Tradition criticism of Judges determined that the book's core comprised an oral collection of stories and legends about the local heroes of various tribes who faced local enemies. For example, the judge Ehud probably was revered by the tribe of Benjamin, who was warring against the Moabites. The stories about Samson probably circulated among the tribe of Dan, whose central location near the coast put it into conflict with the Philistines.[6] The didactic cycle of apostasy, oppression, crying out, and deliverance connecting the earlier stories of the judges could have been imposed upon this collection during its oral stages. However, some critics think that the later deuteronomistic editor (discussed below) was responsible for adding this framework.

Form criticism inquires about the literary genres of pericopes (smaller literary units or sections) that make up a particular biblical work. Some biblical prose forms are sagas, myths, legends, short stories, historical writings, speeches, and letters. Several stories about the judges could perhaps be categorized as "historical romances."[7] Examples of poetic forms include fables (cf. Judg 9:8-15), hymns, psalms, victory songs (cf. Judg 5), and riddles (cf. Judg 14:14). These forms would have circulated orally before being put into writing. Form criticism analyzes the features or patterns that typically characterize a literary form. As an example one may take a present-day oral form: the joke. Although jokes come in different shapes and sizes ("Knock, knock" jokes, "dirty" jokes, ethnic jokes, "Did you hear the one about the . . . " jokes), every joke typically has a

---

5. Tradents are groups that circulate and hand down ancient traditions. They could be family groups; lineages; disciples; scribes; priestly, juridical, or wisdom schools; and so forth.

6. According to Judges 18, the tribe of Dan will migrate and settle in a region north of the sea of Galilee.

7. Robert G. Boling, *Judges: A New Translation with Introduction and Commentary* (Anchor Bible 6A; Garden City, N.Y.: Doubleday, 1975), 31.

feature known as a punch line. Form criticism, moreover, investigates the original oral setting(s) the form would have had within the life of the community,[8] such as a legal or a liturgical setting. Determining the form and setting of a particular passage helps one understand its literary intention. For instance, one assesses the meaning of the joke form and the settings in which jokes are circulated differently from those of religious sermons.

Redaction criticism investigates the process of combining smaller units of tradition and literary forms into larger wholes. It examines how later editors shape the final stages of the book's composition through the frameworks they provide for the smaller units; how they arrange (or rearrange) the smaller sections within the whole; the editorial remarks they make that modify, correct, and even contradict their sources; and the larger unts they compose, which add to and complete the work as we have it today. This method studies the religious, political, and cultural agenda of the different editors and how they inform the editors' task of reworking the tradition.

Redaction criticism is of particular interest to students of the Book of Judges. Biblical scholar Martin Noth detected affinities between the Book of Deuteronomy and the six biblical books that follow it: Joshua, Judges, 1 and 2 Samuel, and 1 and 2 Kings. In 1943 he published an influential study arguing that a major portion of these books was composed by one exilic author during the sixth century B.C.E. and formed a distinct literary complex. Noth labeled this complex the Deuteronomistic History, highlighting the theological relationship between the historical books and the Book of Deuteronomy, which introduces them.[9]

In the original history provided by this exilic author (whom Noth called the Deuteronomist), the period of the judges begins in Judges 2:6, immediately after Joshua 23. Joshua has just exhorted the people to remain steadfast to God's law and reject the worship of other gods. Judges 2:6-23 describes the actual conduct of the people after Joshua dismisses them. The Deuteronomist lays out a stereotyped pattern of apostasy that characterizes the tribal period, a pattern that would ultimately disintegrate in the book, as each generation behaves worse than its ancestors (Judg 2:19). For his account of the judges, the Deuteronomist combines two basic traditions: a collection of stories about regional heroes and their exploits and a short list of "minor" leaders (Judg 10:1-5; 12:7-15). The Deuteronomist transforms these local heroes from various tribes

---

8. The technical term for the life setting(s) of a particular form is *Sitz(e) im Leben*.

9. Martin Noth, *The Deuteronomistic History* (JSOTSup 15; Sheffield, Eng.: JSOT Press, 1981). A translation of *Überlieferungsgeschichtliche Studien* (Tübingen: Max Niemeyer Verlag, 1957, 2d ed.), 1–110. The first edition appeared as *Schriften der Königsberg Gelehreten-Gesellschaft. Geisteswissenschaftliche Klasse* 18 (1943): 43–266.

into liberators of all Israel and its tribes, fitting their stories into a framework detailing the nation's faithlessness.

According to Noth, the core of the Book of Judges in the original Deuteronomistic History comprises Judges 2:6-11, 14-16, 18-19, and 3:7 — 13:1. The present Book of Judges evolves through a series of postexilic editorial revisions and expansions upon this nucleus. These expansions include another introduction to the book (Judg 1) and the last five chapters, which recount the discord of the tribal period (17–21). Noth was not certain that the Deuteronomist incorporated the Samson stories (13:2 — 16:31) into his original history.[10] They could have been part of the core; they could have been added later.

Frank Moore Cross modifies Noth's work by positing two major editions of the Deuteronomistic History.[11] The first edition (Dtr 1) was produced in the seventh century B.C.E. by a Judean author supportive of King Josiah's religious reform policies. Dtr 1 blames the fall of the northern kingdom of Israel on the allegedly "illegitimate" cult practiced at the shrines of Dan and Bethel, which competed with the temple in Jerusalem. Dtr 1 climaxes its history with the reforms of Josiah, who tries to rid the country of its "idolatrous" cult objects and cult personnel (2 Kgs 22–23). The second edition (Dtr 2) was composed during the Babylonian Exile (587–539 B.C.E.). This edition brings the nation's history up to date to include the fall of the southern kingdom of Judah. Addressed to the Judeans in exile, this edition explains the traumatic time of uprooting theologically, by unfolding the people's history of idolatry and faithlessness in both the northern and southern kingdoms.

Cross's theory of the double redaction of the Deuteronomistic History is very influential for Robert G. Boling's important redaction critical analysis of the Book of Judges.[12] The Josianic Deuteronomist (Cross's Dtr 1) adds an introduction to the period and the people's apostasy (2:1 — 3:6) and a conclusion condemning the illegitimate cult of the northern shrines of Dan and Bethel (17:1 — 18:31) as a frame around an eighth-century collection of stories about the judges (3:7 — 16:31). The exilic Deuteronomist (Cross's Dtr 2) provides a second introduction about a fragmented and scattered people (1:1-36) and a

---

10. Noth, *Deuteronomistic History,* 42–53.

11. Frank Moore Cross, *Canaanite Myth and Hebrew Epic: Essays in the History of the Religion of Israel* (Cambridge: Harvard University Press, 1973), 274–289. See also Richard Elliott Friedman, *The Exile and Biblical Narrative: The Formation of the Deuteronomistic and Priestly Works* (Chico, Calif.: Scholars Press, 1981), and Richard D. Nelson, *The Double Redaction of the Deuteronomistic History* (Sheffield, Eng.: JSOT Press, 1981).

12. Robert G. Boling, *The Anchor Bible Dictionary* 3.1115-1116, idem, S. V. "Judges, Book of"; "In Those Days There Was No King in Israel," *A Light Unto My Path,* H. M. Bream, R. D. Heim, C. A. Moore, eds. (Philadelphia: Temple University Press, 1974), 33–48; idem, *Judges: A New Translation,* 29–38.

second conclusion about a people reunited in the face of a devastating civil war (19:1 — 21:25), creating a "tragic-comic framework" for the book.

The main focus of the various historical critical methods is the reconstruction of the historical world the biblical text describes and the different historical stages of the production of this text itself. We have seen that the redaction critical method has been particularly dominant in the study of the Book of Judges. The major complaint against these methods is that they fragment a work into its smaller units of tradition, literary forms, or redactional additions and expansions. The reduction and atomization of a text into its smaller elements fail to deal successfully with the meaning of the text as a whole. Dissatisfaction with the limitations of author-centered historical critical methods has expressed itself within the past twenty-five years in two major ways: with the shift to text-centered literary critical methods, and with the broadening of historical criticism to include social scientific approaches.

Literary Criticism: Judges as a Unified Work

Reacting against "the (historical critical) dissection of supposedly composite documents" that dominated the study of Judges, J. P. U. Lilley argues for a "fresh appraisal of Judges as a literary work, starting from the assumptions of authorship rather than of redaction."[13] He points to unities and coherences in the book that would be (dis)missed by historical critical investigations. Rather than view Judges 1 and Judges 2 as two conflicting introductions to the tribal era added by different redactors, Lilley sees 2:1-5 as a clear transition connecting Israel's inability to stamp out the all of the Canaanites (Judg 1) with its defection from God's covenant to worship Canaanite gods (Judg 2). Moreover, in the body of the book (3:7 — 16:31) Lilley observes a "gradual departure from stereotyped formula" and a steady deterioration in Israel's affairs. The narrative of tribal Israel's progressive disintegration reveals an artistic treatment of the source material that has not been previously recognized.[14] Finally, rather than consider the closing chapters of the book (Judg 17–21) as extraneous additions, Lilley thinks that a book about the moral failures of tribal Israel would be incomplete without these stories. The refrain ("In those days there was no king in Israel; every man did what was right in his own eyes") is a biting commentary on the prestate period as a whole and anticipates the establishment of the monarchy in the next phase of Israelite history.[15]

13. J.P.U. Lilley, "A Literary Appreciation of the Book of Judges," *Tyndale Bulletin* 18 (1967): 93–94.

14. Lilley, "Literary Appreciation," 98–99.

15. Lilley, "Literary Appreciation," 101.

Other literary critical reactions to the editorial splintering of the work point to its internal cohesion and thematic connections. Articles by D. W. Gooding[16] and Alexander Globe[17] detect chiastic[18] or ring structures that unify the book. Both regard the stories about Gideon as the center of the chiasmus or ring (6:1 — 8:32). By destroying an altar to Baal and building an altar to YHWH, Gideon embodies the moral integrity of the previous champions of Israel (6:25-32). Nevertheless, he makes an image out of gold taken as booty and leads the people back into idolatry (8:22-28). From Gideon onward, the behavior of Israel's tribal leaders (Abimelech, Jephthah, Samson) progressively becomes more questionable.

Gooding and Globe find thematic links between the two-part introduction (Judg 1, 2) and the two-part conclusion (17–18, 19–21). Judges 1 connects with Judges 19–21 by highlighting the tribe of Judah that YHWH sends first into battle (1:1-2; 20:18). The Benjaminites fail to drive out the Jebusites in Jerusalem (1:21). A Levite, reluctant to spend the night in Jerusalem with the Jebusites, is threatened with rape by inhospitable Benjaminites (19). In Judges 1, a Judean wife (Achsah) secures land with water for her husband (Othniel). In Judges 19, a Judean wife is raped and tortured when her Levite husband shoves her out into an angry mob. The amputation of a king's thumbs and big toes (1:6-7) contrasts with the dismemberment of the the the wife's body (19:29). Judges 2 is linked with Judges 17–18 in their common focus on an idolatrous cult. While Judges 2 insists that each successive generation behaves worse than the previous one in its apostasy, Judges 17–18 discloses that not only the people but the religious leaders themselves, the Levites, set up idolatrous places of worship.

A literary investigation of Judges is not limited to internal aspects of the book itself. Besides sorting out the thematic interconnections within the book and the tensions caused by the framework's disintegration, David Gunn explores the thematic links between the conclusion of the Book of Joshua (Josh 23–24) and the beginning of the Book of Judges (Judg 1–2). Gunn notes a chiastic structuring of their different episodes that emphasizes a pattern of

16. D. W. Gooding, "The Composition of the Book of Judges," *Eretz-Israel, Archeological Historical and Geographical Studies, Vol. 16: Harry M. Orlinsky Volume* (Jerusalem: Israel Exploration Society, 1982), 70–79.

17. Alexander Globe, "Enemies Round About: Disintegrative Structure in the Book of Judges," *Mappings of the Biblical Terrain,* V. Tollers and J. Maier, eds. (Lewisburg, Pa.: Bucknell University, 1990), 233–251.

18. A chiasmus is a literary device that structures words, phrases, sections of a work, and so forth by balancing them in an A B B′ A′ pattern. The artistic focus is on the center of the chiasmus; in this case, the B B′.

fulfillment/nonfulfillment. The theme of nonfulfillment and failure will characterize the Book of Judges.[19]

Literary critical studies of the Book of Judges have primarily appeared in articles.[20] However, two book-length investigations adopting literary critical approaches have recently been published. Barry Webb argues that Judges is a discrete literary unit, a book, in its own right, and not simply a work in which one finds traces of an original Deuteronomic subtext. Webb provides an "integrated reading" of the work, comparing its unfolding with a musical score. The Book of Judges contains an overture (1:1 — 3:6), variations (3:7 — 16:31), and a coda (17:12 — 21:25).[21] Using another perspective, Lillian Klein studies the literary convention of irony, which she sees as permeating the Book of Judges and providing its structural integrity.[22] Irony is particularly manifested in the judges themselves who are called to lead the nation: a left-handed secret agent (Ehud), a woman who commands a male warrior (Deborah), a coward (Gideon), a bastard (Jephthah), and a lover of foreign women who forsakes his nazirite vow (Samson).

This turn to the text underscores the aesthetic beauty of the biblical literature and the religious power of its rhetoric. One encounters the *text* firsthand and not simply the formative historical situations *behind the text*. Nevertheless, text-centered approaches are susceptible to certain problems in their analyses.[23] Severing the text from its author and history could result in an ahistorical inquiry that regards the text primarily as an aesthetic object unto itself rather than a social practice intimately bound to a particular history. Privileging the text overlooks the workings of ideology in the text. It disregards the fact that ideology is *produced* by a particular author who is culturally constrained by historical time, place, gender, class, and bias, among other things. The biblical texts were

19. David M. Gunn, "Joshua and Judges," in *The Literary Guide to the Bible,* Robert Alter and Frank Kermode, eds. (Cambridge: Harvard University Press, 1987) 102–121.

20. A complete survey of all literary critical studies of the Book of Judges is beyond the scope of this chapter. For a good start, see J. Cheryl Exum, "The Centre Cannot Hold: Thematic and Textual Instabilities in Judges," *Catholic Biblical Quarterly* 52 (1990): 410–431, especially the footnotes on the relevant literature.

21. Barry G. Webb, *The Book of the Judges: An Integrated Reading* (JSOTSup 46; Sheffield, Eng.: JSOT Press, 1987).

22. Lillian R. Klein, *The Triumph of Irony in the Book of Judges* (JSOTSup 68; Sheffield, Eng.: Almond Press, 1988).

23. For an analysis of the problems in author-, text-, or reader-centered approaches, see Gale A. Yee, "The Author/Text/Reader and Power: Suggestions for a Critical Framework in Biblical Studies," in *Reading from This Place: Social Location and Biblical Interpretation,* Fernando F. Segovia and Mary Ann Tolbert, eds. (Minneapolis: Fortress Press, 1995), 109–118.

not written to be objects of aesthetic beauty or contemplation, but as persuasive forces that during their own time formed opinion, made judgments, and exerted change. Moreover, in all its historical, cultural, and literary constraints, the Bible continues to be a powerful standard for present-day social, as well as religious, attitudes and behavior. Nevertheless, different readers inhabiting various social locations will understand the biblical text differently. The position of the reader with respect to factors such as gender, race, class, and ethnicity becomes determinative in answering the question, What does the text mean? Newer methods are needed to appraise such a foundational work as the Bible in light of its powerful (mis)use in the diverse religious and academic communities that have traditionally overlooked such factors.

New Approaches in Biblical Studies

The contributors to the volume present several of the methods that have recently come on the scene and which take biblical studies in new directions and address a number of the issues posed above. Each contributor will first introduce the approach by examining the presuppositions of the method: the particular questions it asks of a text and its central characteristics. The specific questions asked by the method will foreground its similarities to and differences from, in particular, the historical critical approaches. These questions will reveal the kind of information the method provides and what it does not furnish. The contributor will then apply the method to the Book of Judges, either to the text as a whole or certain selections. Brief annotated bibliographies will conclude each chapter.

Richard G. Bowman introduces narrative criticism, a method firmly located in the literary critical tradition. After presenting the various elements of narrative (narrator, direct and indirect discourse, repetition, structure, plot, setting, point of view, and character), Bowman singles out character for an exposition of the Judges text. The particular "character" he examines in the book is God, someone who is not usually regarded as a separate personality in the Bible. "God is the one who wrote the Bible. 'He' is not a character in the Bible." Bowman's analysis reminds us that depictions of God in the Bible are literary-theological constructions. They do not exhaust all that God is and may not impress or inspire every reader at all times and in all places.

Naomi Steinberg's essay addresses social scientific criticism, which broadens historical critical concerns to include the study of Israel's social origins, its customs regarding kinship and marriage, and its social and class structures. This method investigates the modifications and changes in these structures and practices during the course of Israel's history. This introductory chapter began by emphasizing that in spite of their displacement in the text women are important in the lives of the judges. Steinberg's analysis of Judges 9 reveals that the detail about the secondary class status of Abimelech's mother in Judges 8:31 is not a trivial or inconsequential one. Having the "correct" mother makes a big difference in one's social, political, and economic position within the community.

Except for the fact that she is a secondary wife and considered a "slave woman" by the offspring of the primary wives (8:31; 9:18), nothing more is known about Abimelech's mother. Feminist criticism raises questions precisely about the marginality or invisibility of women in androcentric texts. According to *J. Cheryl Exum*, feminist criticism employs a number of critical methods (historical, social scientific, literary) to recover women's lives that are obscured by male texts. It also provides subversive ways to read such texts "against the grain." Opting for a literary critical approach, Exum focuses on the prominent female characters in Judges: Deborah/Jael; Jephthah's daughter; Samson's mother, his Timnite wife, and Delilah; and the Levite's concubine of the concluding chapters of Judges. She names the nameless women in Judges and re-envisions the stories from their perspectives.

David Jobling organizes his essay on structuralism around the three major questions the approach asks of a text: What are the constant patterns that we find in different stories, and what is their significance? What do the differences that we find among similar stories mean? What general models are useful in analyzing the great variety of literary texts? While illustrating each question with an example from the Book of Judges, Jobling focuses his structuralist analysis on a reading of the "fords of the Jordan" incidents in the book (3:27-29; 7:24 — 8:3; 12:1-6).

Danna Nolan Fewell presents deconstructive criticism, an approach much maligned and misunderstood in critical circles today. Her analogy of the abstract blue painting and its various interpretations does much to make deconstruction accessible to the lay audience. Just as fluid undertones of red complicate and destabilize a painting that seems to be about the color blue, a literary text is a composite of dominant and submerged voices in dynamic tension with each other. Deconstruction is a strategy of reading that allows for all voices in the text to be heard. A text that seems to be about one thing to one reader can mean something else to another. Fewell's deconstructive reading of the deceptively simple story of Achsah in Judges 1:11-15 reveals how meaning in this text oscillates and depends upon the specific context of the reader.

In the final chapter of this book, I examine ideological criticism, which integrates sociohistorical and literary criticisms in order to investigate the twofold manifestations of ideology. Sociohistorical criticism uncovers, in an extrinsic analysis, the ideological circumstances involved in the text's production, such as the ideologies themselves, their social location in the dominant and subordinate power groups, the levels of cooperation or conflict among these groups, and so forth. A literary critical intrinsic analysis studies how ideology is reproduced in the text. It examines a text's absences and rhetoric to determine the relationship between the text and the circumstances surrounding its production. I apply ideological criticism to Judges 17–21, chapters usually discounted as postexilic appendices to the book. I argue that these chapters are integral to the first edition of the Deuteronomistic History (Dtr 1) as propaganda for Josiah's religious reform program.

We hope you will notice how very much these methods do interrelate, as well as how they diverge. For example, feminist and ideological criticism can employ narrative and social scientific criticism in their analyses. Structuralist criticism, as David Jobling points out, touches in some way upon all the other criticisms discussed in this book. We now invite you to explore these new approaches and the new ways of looking at a very old text.

Further Reading

General

DAVIS, Robert Con, and Ronald Schleifer, eds. *Contemporary Literary Criticism: Literary and Cultural Studies.* 2d ed. New York: Longman, 1989. A convenient anthology of essays by exponents of the newer literary critical theories. For more advanced students.

EAGLETON, Terry. *Literary Theory: An Introduction.* Minneapolis: University of Minnesota Press, 1983. An entertaining survey of the major approaches in modern literary theory. Reveals how each has an unconscious ideological agenda and argues for a politically engaged literary criticism.

SELDEN, Raman. *A Reader's Guide to Contemporary Literary Theory.* Lexington, Ky.: University of Kentucky Press, 1989. 2d ed. Offers a "crash course" in contemporary literary theory and theorists who have influenced biblical critics. Ranges from Russian formalism to Marxist, structuralist, poststructuralist, reader-response, and feminist theories.

WALHOUT, Clarence, and Leland Ryken, eds. *Contemporary Literary Theory: A Christian Appraisal.* Grand Rapids: William B. Eerdmans, 1991. Geared to introduce students and teachers in church-related institutions to the newer literary approaches, and assessing these approaches' relationship to Christian beliefs and assumptions.

Biblical

ALTER, Robert, and Frank Kermode, eds. *The Literary Guide to the Bible.* Cambridge: Harvard University Press, 1987. Different contributors analyze each book of the Old and New Testaments from a literary perspective. The editors consciously exclude from their project the more recent approaches, for example, ideological criticism, deconstruction, and feminist criticism.

ANDERSON, Janice Capel, and Stephen D. Moore. *Mark and Method: New Approaches in Biblical Studies*. Minneapolis: Fortress Press, 1992. The New Testament counterpart to the present volume.

BAL, Mieke. *Murder and Difference: Gender, Genre, and Scholarship on Sisera's Death*. Translated by Matthew Gumpert. Bloomington and Indianapolis: Indiana University Press, 1988. A provocative study that critiques the historical, theological, anthropological, and literary approaches that have been used to interpret Judges 4–5. Shows how these approaches have relied on "codes" that allow unconscious judgments to skew the interpretation of the text.

BARTON, John. *Reading the Old Testament: Method in Biblical Study*. Philadelphia: Westminster Press, 1984. Not only introduces students to the older and newer methods of Old Testament interpretation, but also tries to answer questions regarding the *purpose* of practicing these various methods.

THE BIBLE AND CULTURE COLLECTIVE. *The Postmodern Bible*. New Haven: Yale University Press, 1995. Consciously written to counter Alter and Kermode's *The Literary Guide to the Bible,* this book foregrounds what they omit, that is, the theory underlying the newer and more controversial approaches to the study of the Bible.

GUNN, David M., and Danna Nolan Fewell. *Narrative in the Hebrew Bible*. Oxford: Oxford University Press, 1993. Discusses narratology and the Hebrew Bible with special attention to reader-oriented criticisms, particularly the ideology of readers. Introductory level.

HAYES, John H., and Carl R. Holladay. *Biblical Exegesis: A Beginner's Handbook*. Atlanta: John Knox Press, 1987. Rev. ed. Familiarizes the student with the standard historical critical methods and with literary criticism, structuralism, and canonical criticism. Excellent bibliographies.

MCKENZIE, Steven L., and Stephen R. Haynes, eds. *To Each Its Own Meaning: An Introduction to Biblical Criticisms and Their Application*. Louisville, Ky.: Westminster/John Knox Press, 1993. Includes discussions of social scientific, structural, narrative, reader-response, poststructuralist, and feminist criticisms with applications to texts in either Genesis or Luke-Acts.

MCKNIGHT, Edgar V. *Post-Modern Use of the Bible: The Emergence of Reader-Oriented Criticism*. Nashville: Abingdon Press, 1988. A concise overview of biblical criticism, from precritical approaches (ancient and medieval methods) to historical critical and finally literary critical methods.

MORGAN, Robert, with John Barton. *Biblical Interpretation*. Oxford: Oxford University Press, 1988. Surveys the development of historical criticism during the past one hundred fifty years, as well as more recent social scientific and literary methods. Tries to bridge "the gulf between critical scholarship and religious faith." Includes an annotated index of biblical critics.

SCHWARTZ, Regina M., ed. *The Book and the Text: The Bible and Literary Theory.* Cambridge: Basil Blackwell, 1990. A collection of essays designed to complement studies such as Alter and Kermode's *The Literary Guide to the Bible* by engaging the more "controversial" approaches in literary theory, such as structuralism, deconstruction, semiotics, feminist criticism, ideological criticism, and psychoanalytic interpretation. For the advanced student.

SUELZER, S.P., Alexa, and John S. Kselman, S.S. "Modern Old Testament Criticism," *The New Jerome Biblical Commentary,* Raymond E. Brown, S.S., Joseph A. Fitzmyer, S.J., and Roland Murphy, O.Carm., eds. Englewood Cliffs, N.J.: Prentice-Hall, 1990, 1113–1129. A helpful overview from a Roman Catholic perspective of precritical and historical critical investigations of the Old Testament, as well as literary, social scientific, and feminist criticisms.

For the most up-to-date studies incorporating the more recent critical approaches to the Bible, consult the annual journals *Semeia* and *Biblical Interpretation*.

2

NARRATIVE CRITICISM: HUMAN PURPOSE IN CONFLICT WITH DIVINE PRESENCE*

Richard G. Bowman

A recent *New Yorker* cartoon[1] shows two ancient scribes, one peering over the shoulder of the other, who is seated at a writing table, pen in hand. The overseeing scribe has the stern, superior look of a self-assured lecturer, while the face of the seated scribe expresses surprise and incredulity. The seated scribe says, "You mean when I use a phrase like 'Pharaoh *dreamed* seven cows came up out of the Nile,' or 'God *remembered* Noah,' or David's wife Michal '*despised him in her heart*' — that's speculative journalism?"

For a narrative critical approach to interpretation such comments are not regarded as "speculative journalism." Instead they are understood as indications of the narrator's omniscient assessment of the events that are related through the story. As such, these comments are regarded as information that is essential for more complete understanding of the story.

This example illustrates only one feature of narrative criticism, which focuses on an analysis of the literary features of biblical texts. Narrative criticism seeks to discover and disclose the narrative's own intrinsic points of emphasis, thereby facilitating its interpretation and consequently helping to discriminate among various possible interpretations.

The basic presuppositions of narrative criticism are that (1) the final, present form of the text functions as a coherent narrative; (2) this narrative has a literary integrity apart from circumstances relating to the compositional process, the historical reality behind the story, or the interpretive agenda of the reader; and (3) an analysis of the literary features of this narrative will reveal an interpretive focus. The questions asked of the text follow from these presuppositions and

* The research for and writing of this essay was supported in part by a Research and Artist Fund Grant from Augustana College.
1. *The New Yorker* (September 20, 1993):106.

concern how the general elements of narrative are manifested in a particular narrative to yield a meaningful and meaning-filled story.

Assessment

No single reading strategy or interpretive method accounts for all the important literary or historical data, either textual or extratextual. Different methods approach the text with different presuppositions and for different purposes. As a result, readers ask various kinds of analytical questions of the story and seek a variety of answers. The asking of certain questions precludes the asking of others and consequently excludes obtaining certain information. No one method is, therefore, sufficient for a comprehensive interpretation of any narrative. Each approach has its own advantages and disadvantages. Often benefits of one method are limitations of another, and likewise weaknesses of one method are strengths of another. Here are what I regard as the inherent limitations as well as the essential advantages of narrative criticism.[2]

Advantages

The first advantage is that narrative criticism focuses on the present form of the text. Interpretations are based on empirically observable data within the text, not on the speculated intentions of the author, the hypothetical reconstructions of the historian, or the ideological agenda of the reader. By focusing on the narrative itself, the reader discovers the dynamics of the story itself. The division of the text into its component sources and the historical reconstruction of previous versions assist us in discovering issues important to earlier communities and in understanding the process by which the present form of the text was created. They do not, however, help us understand the final form of the story. The final form is as important as earlier versions, since it is the text that has been preserved for us and is the one most accessible to us.

A second advantage is that narrative criticism focuses on making constructive sense of the text. This method recognizes that a literary text cannot be completely consistent and free from all contradictions. However, instead of exploiting these inconsistencies in a deconstructive or ideological reading, narrative criticism chooses to explicate them in favor of constructive reading. It focuses on the constructive continuities of sense rather than the deconstructive discontinuities of nonsense.

2. For other assessments see Mark Allen Powell, *What Is Narrative Criticism?* (Minneapolis: Fortress Press, 1990), 85–98, and Tremper Longman III, *Literary Approaches to Biblical Interpretation* (Grand Rapids: Zondervan, 1987), 47–62.

Another advantage of narrative criticism is that it focuses on literary conventions inherent in Hebrew narrative. Identifying the conventions of composition is helpful in establishing and understanding the coherence and therefore the meaning of biblical narrative. An analysis of these conventions uncovers the dynamics of the story and signals the story's own internally generated emphasis. Through an understanding of these conventions the interpreter can show that the biblical narrative is not, to paraphrase Shakespeare, a tale redacted by an idiot, full of sound and fury, signifying nothing.

A final advantage is that it protects against overinterpretation[3] — the practice of assigning meanings to a story that exceed the possibilities generated by the data in the story itself. Since narrative criticism emphasizes textual data, it prevents the inclusion of extratextual information that alters the focus of the text in favor of the extraneous material.

One way in which narratives are overinterpreted is through the recent fascination with narrative gaps, that is, places in the story where desired information is missing and must allegedly be filled in by the reader's imagination in order to make sense of the story. Gaps are regarded as significant interpretive clues in that they provide evidence of inconsistencies and contradictions inherent in the narrative. (See the chapter on ideological criticism in this volume.) However, for narrative criticism, gaps are not hermeneutical invitations to speculate on the motivation of character, the meaning of events, or the concealed ideology of the author. Instead, they are indications of what is important to the narrator in the development and presentation of the story. What is omitted — that is, the missing material that creates the gap — is not important. Gaps are nonetheless of interpretive significance because they point to what is important — that is, the material that is included. Therefore, narrative criticism ignores rather than explores narrative gaps, thereby avoiding overinterpretation.

Limitations

The first limitation of narrative criticism is that it is not particularly concerned about the historical reality behind the text or in its reconstruction. Yet, narrative criticism is not in principle opposed to historical criticism and does not preclude the importance of historical information for an understanding of the present form of the text. Such information is extremely important in understanding certain features of a text and avoiding misinterpretation. An analysis of the literary dynamics of the story reveals when historical information is use-

---

3. See Umberto Eco, *The Limits of Interpretation* (Bloomington, Ind.: Indiana University Press, 1990), and Stefan Collini, *Interpretation and Overinterpretation: Umberto Eco* (Cambridge: Cambridge University Press, 1992).

ful and even necessary to clarify the meaning of the story. For example, an understanding of the procedure for conferring a blessing in ancient Israelite society adds an important interpretive dimension to the story of Achsah.

The second limitation is that narrative criticism does not specifically take into account the agenda of the reader. This is to be expected, since the method focuses on generating data from the narrative rather than on filtering it through political, social, or aesthetic convictions of the reader. Yet, narrative criticism is compatible with reader-oriented approaches, for example, feminism, since it does provide narrative data that can then be analyzed from the perspective of the reader.

A final limitation is that narrative criticism is not particularly sympathetic to deconstruction. Given its focus on the coherence and continuity of the story and the portrayal of its characters, it does not attempt to account for data that doesn't fit a consistent interpretive scheme. The method acknowledges ambiguities and even multiple meanings but attributes them to the complexities of character and the intricacies of events, complexities and intricacies that do not create unresolvable confusion and irretrievable significance.

The Elements of Narrative

A narrative, by definition, "requires a story and a story-teller."[4] The central elements of a story are plot, character, setting, and point of view. The storyteller is often referred to as the narrator. In developing the plot of a story and in presenting its characters, the narrator draws on a wide repertoire of compositional techniques, such as the use of narrated discourse versus direct discourse and repetition. These compositional techniques are integrated into the overall organizational structure of the narrative that the narrator supplies. This framework provides the story with coherence and thematic unity according to the conventions of ancient Hebrew narrative. In the following pages I shall offer a brief theoretical discussion of these elements and then give a more substantive interpretive illustration from Judges.

The Narrator

Narrators are usually either first-person or third-person narrators.[5] If the narrator is the first-person, "I" narrator, the story can be told only from the limited

---

4. Robert Scholes and Robert Kellogg, *The Nature of Narrative* (London: Oxford University Press, 1966), 240.

5. Literary critics often further distinguish between the narrator, the implied author, and the real author. In biblical narrative these usually merge into one figure, which I shall identify as the narrator. For a discussion of the three figures as they relate to biblical

position of what the narrator has experienced or observed. If, on the other hand, the narrator is an omniscient, third-person narrator ("he," "she," "they," or a person's name), the story can be related from any number of perspectives. The story can follow the actions of any of the characters; it can move from place to place and jump from a present time to a past or even a future time; and it can present the thoughts and feelings of any character or the narrator. Biblical narrators are usually third-person, omniscient narrators who reliably and accurately relate their stories, though not without an interpretive perspective.[6]

Narrated Discourse and Direct Discourse

The biblical narrator employs a variety of compositional techniques through which the narrative is conveyed and the thought of the story expressed. Central to the narrator's presentation of the story is the choice of narrated discourse (narration) or direct discourse (speech).[7]

Direct discourse or speech refers to occasions where the narrator reports the utterances of a character in the story. It usually occurs as part of a dialogue between two characters but occasionally appears as a monologue. In the development of the story, the use of direct discourse either as dialogue or monologue serves two functions:

(1) it develops the story by dramatizing significant aspects, and
(2) it emphasizes certain features through the dramatization.

Narrated discourse or narration refers to those occasions when the narrator speaks and relates aspects of the story. The use of the narrator's own voice to develop a particular aspect of the story serves four functions:

(1) it summarizes developments in the story instead of dramatizing them through direct discourse,

---

narrative see Elizabeth Struthers Malbon, "Narrative Criticism: How Does a Story Mean?" in *Mark and Method: New Approaches to Biblical Studies,* ed. Janice Capel Anderson and Stephen D. Moore (Minneapolis: Fortress Press, 1992), 27–28.

6. Some scholars disagree. See, for example, David M. Gunn and Danna Nolan Fewell, *Narrative in the Hebrew Bible* (London: Oxford University Press, 1993), 53–56.

7. The terminology is Phyllis Trible's. For examples see *God and the Rhetoric of Sexuality* (Philadelphia: Fortress Press, 1978), and *Texts of Terror* (Philadelphia: Fortress Press, 1984). For a seminal discussion of this topic see Robert Alter, "Between Narration and Dialogue," in *The Art of Biblical Narrative* (New York: Basic Books, 1981), 63–87.

(2) it provides necessary background information on events or characters through exposition or description,

(3) it allows the narrator's use of an omniscient perspective to reveal the internal thoughts and emotions of characters, and

(4) it provides the narrator with a means to comment on the story for explanatory or evaluative purposes.

The narrator's choice of either direct discourse, narrated discourse, or some combination of the two in the presentation and development of the story suggests important, internally generated points of emphasis. For example, the use of direct discourse interrupts what would otherwise have been a continuous narrative thread, thereby placing an organizational emphasis on the information contained in the speech. That an incident is dramatized through speech instead of summarized also indicates its significance within the organizational structure of the story, since it is presented more directly and with greater detail. Similarly, the narrator's use of omniscient perspective to acquire and report on the thoughts or emotions of a character provides important information on a character's motivation. This utilization of omniscient perspective in the narrated discourse portions also supplies contextual information necessary in understanding those portions of the narrative dramatized through direct discourse.

The biblical story of Achsah in Judges 1:11-15 provides examples of the alternating use of narrated and direct discourse. The narrative comprises two parts, which portray Achsah initially as object and subsequently as subject:

> Part I   Judges 1:11-13   Achsah as Object
> Part II   Judges 1:14-15   Achsah as Subject

The narrator begins the first part of the story with an expository narrated report that the Judahites were launching a divinely sanctioned attack against the inhabitants of Debir. Caleb, a leader of earlier preconquest ventures, is apparently commanding this exploit as well. The aging hero is not, however, personally going to lead the assault. Narrated discourse yields to direct discourse as Caleb issues an invitation for battlefield leadership: "Whoever attacks Kiriath-sepher [Debir] and takes it, I will give him my daughter Achsah as wife"[8] (Judg 1:12). This speech defines and even emphasizes the traditional roles of women as daughter and wife by its interruption of a narrated discourse sequence. It further points out an interconnection between the two: as a pos-

---

8. Unless otherwise noted all translations are from the NRSV.

session of the father, the daughter is a viable resource to be bartered in exchange for military conquest.

Having thus defined the accepted and expected status of Achsah, the narrator resumes narrated discourse to report Othniel's acceptance of Caleb's offer. In so doing the narrator uses omniscient perspective to further identify Othniel as the son of Kenaz, Caleb's younger brother. The marriage is thus between two Hebrews, thereby maintaining their ethnic integrity.

In vocabulary that repeats that of the invitation, the narrator further observes that Othniel "took" Debir, and that Caleb honored his commitment and "gave him his daughter Achsah as wife" (Judg 1:13). Through this repetition the narrator's report emphasizes the roles Achsah is expected to fulfill as the daughter of Caleb and the wife of Othniel. The subordinate status of Achsah is further reinforced because she is twice presented as the grammatical object of the verb "to give," initially in Caleb's speech and then in the narrator's subsequent report.[9]

At this juncture, however, the narrator, surprisingly, shifts the focus of the story. In the reorientation of the second part, Achsah becomes subject instead of object, active instead of passive, vocal instead of silent.[10] These changes are chronicled in encounters between Achsah and her husband and between Achsah and her father.

The story resumes with an encounter between Achsah and Othniel. The narrator uses narrated discourse to report, "When she came to him [i.e., Othniel], she urged him to ask her father for a field." The grammar of this sentence places Achsah as the subject of the verb. Contrary to traditional expectations, Achsah not only acts but acts assertively with her husband. However, without specifically reporting the result of this encounter or formally noting a change in setting, the narrator abruptly continues the story by reporting another encounter, this time between Achsah and Caleb.

Whereas the encounter between Achsah and Othniel was related in summarizing narrated discourse, the confrontation between Achsah and Caleb is presented in dramatizing direct discourse. The inconclusive nature of the encounter between Achsah and Othniel and contrasting use of direct discourse to report the encounter between Achsah and Caleb combine to stress the importance of the second encounter. The narrator conveys the climactic encounter as

---

9. Mieke Bal, *Death and Dissymmetry: The Politics of Coherence in the Book of Judges* (Chicago: University of Chicago Press, 1988), 26.

10. Achsah's assertiveness is also recognized in the literary analyses of Barry Webb in *The Book of Judges* (Sheffield, Eng.: Sheffield Academic Press, 1987), 87, and Lillian Klein in *The Triumph of Irony in the Book of Judges* (Sheffield, Eng.: Sheffield Academic Press, 1988), 26.

follows: "As she dismounted from her donkey, Caleb said to her, 'What do you wish?' She said to him, 'Give me a blessing; since you have set me in the land of the Negeb, give me springs of water'" (Judg 1:14-15).[11]

Achsah is again portrayed as making a request of a dominant male in her life. The grammar of the sentence again makes Achsah the subject. She is shown as acting and acting assertively a second time, here as the initiator in relationship to her father. She directly requests from him a blessing, a gift typically bestowed by the father upon the first-born son.[12] Achsah not only demands her own blessing, but she also continues her speech with a justification for her request. With this justification we probably learn in retrospect the result of Achsah's request of Othniel. It appears that her father had only halfheartedly complied with her previous appeal, giving only an arid portion of land. Achsah then circumvents male posturing and power plays and demands, under the aegis of the paternal blessing, springs of water so that her land might be productive and useful.

Narration concludes the story, reporting Caleb's compliance with Achsah's request: "And Caleb gave her the upper springs and the lower springs" (Judg 1:15). In this instance we learn immediately, albeit without elaboration, the result of her request. However, the narrator only reports Caleb's compliance and does not reveal his motivation. The absence of this information suggests that the narrator's stress is upon the assertiveness of Achsah and not the motivation for her father's compliance. The curious reader is left only to conjecture whether Caleb was persuaded by her presence, her argument, or both.

In part through the alternating use of narrated and direct discourse, the narrator portrays Achsah in unexpected relationships with both her father and her husband. The initial phase of the story shows her in a submissive role as the possession of her father. Her only option is to be offered as the wife of a warrior as compensation for a successful military campaign against the enemy. Yet, the final phase of the story portrays her differently. Once she becomes the wife of Othniel, Achsah assumes an assertive stance vis-à-vis her husband and her father. She asserts herself with her husband, asking him to acquire from her father a suitable plot of land to cultivate. When his effort apparently fails to achieve all she desires, she acts in his place and confronts her father directly, demanding arable land under the rubric of the paternal blessing. Thus, she is portrayed as the initiator of action in these relationships, a role inconsistent with the expected submissive postures of obedient wife and dutiful daughter. Instead of

11. My translation, following the RSV.

12. Achsah's request is not without precedent. See the request of the daughters of Zelophehad in Numbers 27:1-11; 36:1-13 and Joshua 16:3-6.

assuming these traditional stances, she expects her husband to heed her request and her father to fulfill his own bequest.

Structure

The narrator imposes order and coherence upon the recounted events through the organizational structure of the story. A description of the narrative structure, therefore, is central to discerning the narrator's internal, interpretive emphasis. Narrative structure can be determined on the basis of both form and content.

A three-part structure of Judges can be described as follows:[13]

> Part I   The Prologue — Judges 1:1 — 3:6
> Part II   The Era of the Judges — Judges 3:7 — 16:31
> Part III The Epilogue — Judges 17:1 — 21:25

The Prologue takes place "after the death of Joshua" (Josh 1:1) and relates various attempts to continue the conquest of the land. After a few initial successes, these attempts largely fail. Unifying this section of the narrative is a common content that centers around various attempts to take possession of the land (Judg 1:1-36) and subsequent explanations for the failure to do so (2:2 — 3:6). A formal feature of the narrative, which also serves to unify the section as well as thematically characterize it, is the tenfold repetition of the verbal phrase "did not/will not drive out" (1:19, 21, 27, 28, 29, 30, 31, 32, 33; 2:3).

The failure to drive out the inhabitants of the land inaugurates the Era of the Judges. This central section is further divided into six episodes, each of which is introduced by the thematically as well as structurally significant phrase: "the Israelites (again) did what was evil in the sight of the Lord" (Judg 3:7, 12; 4:1; 6:1; 10:6; 13:1). Each episode relates the career of a major judge, as follows:[14]

> Episode I   Judges 3:7-11   Othniel
> Episode II   Judges 3:12-31   Ehud
> Episode III Judges 4:1 — 5:31   Deborah
> Episode IV   Judges 6:1 — 10:5   Gideon (and Abimelech)[15]

---

13. Adapted from Webb, *The Book of Judges*, 81, 123, 181.

14. See Webb, *The Book of Judges*, 124–125.

15. Webb regards the Abimelech episode as a structural and thematic sequel to the Gideon episode. Space limitations prevent further consideration of this story. For a discussion, see Webb, *The Book of Judges*, 154–159.

Episode V   Judges 10:6 — 12:15   Jephthah
Episode VI   Judges 13:1 — 16:31   Samson

Again after some initial successes (Othniel, Ehud, and Deborah), the judges begin to show serious character flaws (Gideon and Abimelech, Jephthah, and Samson). As a result, Samson, the last judge in the sequence, is described as only "beginning to deliver Israel from the hand of the Philistines" (13:5).

The unsuccessful Era of the Judges in turn yields to an apparently leaderless time, which is recounted in the Epilogue. The formally distinguishing and unifying feature describing this period is the fourfold repetition of the phrase "in those days there was no king in Israel" (Judg 17:6; 18:1; 19:1; 21:25). The first and last repetition of the phrase is coupled with supplemental clarifying information: "all the people did what was right in their own eyes" (17:6; 21:25). The two stories included in this section, Micah and the Danites and the Rape of Levite's Concubine, suggest that what was regarded as "right" resulted in various murders and assorted mayhem.

The structure of the Book of Judges thus reflects a coherent literary unity. The narrator's use of repetition in each of the three parts presents an important thematic focus: the progressive deterioration in the relationship between the Hebrew people and God as well as among the Hebrews themselves.

Plot

Plot is similar to structure but refers more specifically to a sequence of events that are related in terms of their causes and consequences.[16] An analysis of the plot includes an identification of the tension motivating the action of the story and an understanding of the circumstances that resolve this tension. In assessing the dynamics of a story, it is often helpful to describe the conflict generating the story and to discern how the conflict is resolved.

Each episode of the central section follows, albeit with important variations, a fourfold plot schema that is conveniently outlined in the Prologue (Judg 2:6-19):

(1) Israel is unfaithful in relationship to God;
(2) Israel is consequently oppressed by her enemies;
(3) Israel petitions God for divine assistance; and
(4) God appoints a judge to deliver Israel.

This recurring sequence of actions illustrates another type of repetition and functions to emphasize the nature of Israel's relationship with God. The ten-

16. See Scholes and Kellogg, "Plot in Narrative," in *The Nature of Narrative,* 207–239.

sion that generates the action revolves around Israel's unfaithfulness to God and her consequent subjugation by external enemies. The plot climaxes when Israel repents and requests divine help. The conflict is finally resolved when God appoints a judge who defeats the enemy.

Each episode nuances this basic plot configuration in different ways. Whereas the episode involving Ehud presents a left-handed hero who deceptively assassinates the enemy king, the episode relating the story of Deborah turns upon friction caused by having a woman as judge. By way of contrast, Gideon doubts his own ability, Jephthah doubts the ability of God, and Samson overconfidently abuses his talents.

Repetition

As the preceding sections on structure and plot indicate, repetition is an important compositional technique used in organizing a story as well as in presenting and emphasizing its themes. The concept has been illustrated in these sections, but it would now be helpful to catalog the types of repetition and summarize their functions.

Several types of repetition are available to the biblical narrator: that of (1) words or phrases, (2) motifs or themes, or (3) a sequence of actions.[17] The first type is the most obvious and involves the repeated use of single words or phrases, for example, the phrases used to unify each section of narrative. The second is more abstract and involves the repeated use of images or the recurrence of central ideas, for example, the theme of irresponsibility in relationship to God. The final type represents a patterned sequence of actions, for example, the recurring components of the plot.

Three of the several functions of repetition in biblical literature are as follows:

(1) repetition indicates the structure of the narrative;
(2) repetition signals key themes; and
(3) repetition provides emphasis to central ideas.

An example of the first function is the division of the central section into six episodes, each of which begins with an introductory restatement of the evil committed by the people. The repeated reference to the failure of the Hebrews to drive out the inhabitants of the land in the first section is an example of the second function. The third function is exemplified by the reiterated lack of a king in the final section.

17. Adapted from Robert Alter's discussion in *The Art of Biblical Narrative*, 95–96.

Setting

Narratives take place in specific locales that are often significant for a more complete understanding of the story.[18] For example, much of the story about Samson, a man designated prior to birth as a judge, takes place not in Hebrew territory but among the Philistines in a variety of Philistine cities, as Samson pursues sexual liaisons with Philistine women. Such foreign settings reinforce the portrayal of Samson as an irresponsible judge who betrays his own heritage.

Point of View

Point of view refers to the perspective from which the story or portions of the story are told.[19] Even though a story is related from the vantage point of a third-person, omniscient narrator, this narrator can, on occasion, surrender this privilege and convey portions of the story from the more limited perspective of one of the characters. In so doing the narrator can show how a specific character understands certain events or how different characters have varying perceptions of the same event.

Seemingly contrasting accounts regarding the defeat of the Anakim and the capture of the Canaanite cities of Hebron and Debir provide an example from the books of Joshua and Judges. Included among the exploits of Joshua is the assertion that "Joshua came and wiped out the Anakim from the hill country, from Hebron, from Debir, from Anab, and from all the hill country of Judah and from all the hill country of Israel; Joshua utterly destroyed them with their towns. None of the Anakim was left in the land of the Israelites" (Josh 11:21). However, a subsequent account relates that "according to the commandment of the Lord to Joshua, he gave Caleb . . . Hebron. . . . And Caleb drove out from there the three sons of Anak: Sheshai, Ahiman, and Talmai" (15:13-14). Yet, in the Prologue of Judges, the defeat of the Anakim and conquest of Hebron is attributed to the tribe of Judah: "Judah went against the Canaanites who lived in Hebron; and they defeated Sheshai and Ahiman and Talmai" (Judg 1:10). Finally, a summary of the Hebrew conquests in Canaan notes that "Hebron was given to Caleb, as Moses had said; and he drove out from it the three sons of Anak" (1:20). Whether Caleb himself actually leads the assault on the city is questionable, since he had previously commissioned Othniel to attack Debir, and Othniel, not Joshua, is credited with its capture (1:12-13).

---

18. For a more extensive discussion of setting, see Powell, "Settings," in *What Is Narrative Criticism?* 69–75.

19. See Scholes and Kellogg's discussion "Point of View" in *The Nature of Narrative,* 240–282.

These ambiguities blur the historical issue of who defeated the Anakim, but they can be understood literarily when one realizes that the narrator is providing several different perspectives on these military escapades. From Joshua's point of view, he is the hero; from Caleb's point of view, he is the hero; from a nationalistic point of view, the collective tribe of Judah is the hero.

The alternating presentation of these points of view can be construed as demonstrations of the stereotypical male zeal for competition and exaggeration which is embedded within and integral to the various conquest stories of early Israel. These shifts in perspective thus present claim versus counterclaim in the quest for recognition. First Joshua, then Caleb, and finally tribal Judah are portrayed as contending with each other for the accolades of success by claiming victory in military campaigns against their enemies. Ironically, however, the goal of their claims and counterclaims appears to be elusive. Despite the militaristic posturing of Israel's leaders, their attacks upon the inhabitants of the land appear to have failed. This failure to drive out the inhabitants of the land then becomes the predominant theme of the Prologue of Judges. The dominant and evaluative perspective belongs to the narrator who presents each perspective, yet each stresses the repeated failure of Israel to achieve its military goal.

Character

What a narrative expresses is as important as the ways it organizes and conveys its story. An analysis of how a narrative is structured and which compositional techniques are used to relate the story provides clues to the narrative's own internally generated points of interest. Once these interpretive clues have been isolated, one investigates the information they disclose. A primary method through which this information is presented is the narrative portrayal of character.

Characters and their actions generate the conflicts which create the plot events of the story. Characters' speeches dramatize the events in which the characters are involved. Therefore, a character cannot be portrayed apart from events involving that character, and the events that involve a character cannot be separated from a depiction of the character. As a theoretician as well as practitioner of narrative literature, Henry James has rhetorically observed, "What is character but the determination of incident? What is incident but the illustration of character?"[20] His comment also applies to the biblical portrayal of character and event.

In biblical literature character is revealed in four ways:[21]

---

20. Cited in Scholes and Kellogg, *The Nature of Narrative*, 160.
21. Adapted from Robert Alter, *The Art of Biblical Narrative*, 117.

(1) through a character's own actions and his or her interactions with other characters,
(2) through a character's own speeches,
(3) through the speeches of other characters about a specific character, and
(4) through the narrator's specific comments about a character.

These techniques for characterization fall along a continuum of accuracy and dependability. Whereas a character's actions are ambiguous and subject to critical appraisal, the narrator's assessment of a character emerges from an omniscient perspective and is therefore more authoritative. Though less open to multiple explanations than a character's actions, a character's own speeches or the comments of other characters about him or her are still more problematic than the narrator's assessment. Because they occupy the center of the continuum, these speeches need to be the subject of careful evaluation.

In analyzing character it is also often helpful to distinguish between static and dynamic characters. Some biblical characters do not change over the course of the story, whereas others exhibit considerable change. Some show a single facet of their literary personality, and others reveal a complex array of traits.

Othniel, the first judge, is an example of a static, single-faceted character. In the brief, narrated discourse account of his tenure as judge, we learn only that he went to war against Aram and that he was successful in this venture.

Samson, by way of comparison, is a dynamic, multifaceted character. In the lengthy chronicle of his exploits, we learn that in spite of his prenatal designation as the deliverer of Israel from the Philistines, he spends his youth courting the Philistine women instead of conquering the Philistine men. Only after he is betrayed by one of his paramours does he gain insight into his mission and pray that God assist him in his campaign against the Philistines. Though he is given considerable talents, he uses them more for mischief and malice than for the vindication of his people and as the implementation of a vision.

Further illustration of the techniques for character portrayal will be discussed in the expository section that follows. Any one of the elements of narrative could have been developed at length, but I have chosen character, because it allows us to focus on an often neglected feature of biblical narratives — that is, the character of God.

Human Purpose in Conflict with Divine Presence

The Book of Judges offers characterizations not only of individual humans but also of God and the Hebrew people as a whole. The narrator portrays God and the divine involvement with humans in three ways:

(1) God intervenes to punish human transgressions;

(2) God appoints or somehow attempts to use human leaders to deliver the Hebrews from external political/military oppression; and

(3) God bestows the potential for human success but otherwise refrains from intervention, thereby allowing the exercise of human freedom but limiting the divine exercise of power.

Whereas the narrator offers a more nuanced portrayal of some of the judges and other characters, the storyteller characterizes both God and the Hebrew people more precisely and unambiguously. In contrast to Achsah, who is revealed through actions and speech, God and the Hebrew people are directly conveyed through the narrator's comments and evaluations.

God Portrayed as Punishing Human Transgressions

That God intervenes to punish transgressions is a major contention in the Book of Judges. The narrator relates the paradigm for this divine activity in an expository section toward the conclusion of the Prologue (Judg 2:11-15). The situation is one in which the people "did what was evil in the sight of the Lord and worshiped the Baals"; consequently, "the anger of the Lord was kindled against Israel." The narrator then describes the result of this divine anger in three ways: (1) God "gave them over to plunderers who plundered them"; (2) God "sold them into the power of their enemies all around"; and (3) "the hand of the Lord was against them to bring misfortune."

These three punishments are reported in detail in the second part the book which relates the Era of the Judges (Judg 3:7 — 16:31). The following chart summarizes for each succeeding episode the narrator's characterization of the divine response to the "evil" committed by Israel.

Divine Response to Transgressions

Judge	Divine Response to the People's Transgressions
Othniel	Sold into the hand of King Cushanrishathaim
Ehud	Strengthened Eglon, the king of Moab
Deborah	Sold into the hand of King Jabin of Canaan
Gideon	Given into the hand of the Midianites
Jephthah	Sold into the hand of the Philistines/Ammonites
Samson	Given into the hand of Philistines

In relating the specific instances that illustrate the general paradigm, the narrator reports three times that God "sold" Israel into the hand of its enemy.

This characterization of divine activity begins the sequence of six episodes and continues in an alternating pattern.

As the narrative episodes progress, the transgressions of Israel escalate. Prior to the tenure of Othniel as judge, the "evil" attributed to the people by the narrator is specified as the worship of the Baals and the Asherahs. By the time of Jephthah, divine anger is provoked by the people's worship of five other national gods as well as the Baals and the Asherahs. The divine response is likewise intensified, and the people are "sold" into the hand of two enemies instead of one.

Twice toward the end of the sequence, again in alternating fashion, God is portrayed as "giving" Israel into the hand of its enemy. Both reports are equally concise, although an intensifying of divine displeasure is implied by the length of time the Israelites are given over to oppression, which increases from seven to forty years.

In the second episode, the story of Ehud, the narrator cites the third divine-response option from the original paradigm. Rather than take direct action against Israel, in which the Hebrews are "sold" or "given" to their enemy, God intervenes indirectly against Israel by strengthening the power of its enemy.

Through the paradigm in the Prologue and through repeated illustrations of the paradigm in the episodes of the six major judges, the narrator portrays God as capable of intervention. This intervention is further portrayed as the divine punitive response to Israel's transgressions. These interventions specifically take the form of a transaction between God and Israel's enemies, in which God either strengthens Israel's enemy or "sells" or "gives" Israel into the hand of its foes.

God Portrayed as Delivering from Oppression

The narrator of Judges not only portrays God as intervening to punish transgressions but also as being involved in deliverance from oppression. Again, the paradigm is related in an expository section toward the end of the Prologue, when the narrator writes, "The Lord raised up judges, who delivered them out of the power of those who plundered them" (Judg 2:16). The paradigm suggests that the rescue process involves two phases: (1) a divine action by which God selects a judge and (2) a human action through which the chosen leader delivers the people.

A summary of the way the narrator specifically fills out the paradigm in each episode from the Era of the Judges is presented in the following chart.

Deliverance from Oppression

Judge	Divine Action	Human Action
Othniel	raised up	delivered (N)*

Ehud	raised up	delivered (N)
Deborah	was judging	gave into
	(use by God implied)	hand (C)
Gideon	negotiated with God	delivered (C, G)
Jephthah	negotiated with people	fight with/
	(use by God implied)	defeat (C, G)
Samson	God chose prior to birth	began to deliver (G)

Judge	*Result*
Othniel	Lord gave into hand (N)
Ehud	Lord gave into hand (C)
Deborah	Lord gave into hand (C)
	Lord routed; God subdued (N)
Gideon	Lord set every man's sword
	against his fellow (N)
Jephthah	Lord gave into hand (N)
Samson	Implied that God responded
	to a prayer for revenge (N)

˙N indicates that the narrator makes the comment, C that a character makes it, and G that God makes it.

As the episodes progress from Othniel to Samson, God is portrayed as taking a more active role in obtaining leaders. Whereas God initially "raised up" Othniel and Ehud, God uses existing leaders with Deborah and Jephthah, and finally the deity directly negotiates with Gideon and appoints Samson from birth.

Ironically, however, this progressive involvement seems to result in more limited success. The deliverances achieved by Othniel, Ehud, and Deborah are portrayed as unqualified successes. This is not the case with Gideon, Jephthah, and Samson.

Gideon is as successful as the previous judges. However, his success only encourages the people to make him their permanent leader. Even though Gideon rejects their offer for theological reasons, he requests the golden earrings of the spoil, which he fashions into an ephod. The narrator then observes that "all Israel prostituted themselves to it, and it became a snare to Gideon and his family" (Judg 8:27). His victory is thus compromised.

Jephthah is equally successful in his battle against the Ammonites. Yet, his success comes at the expense of his daughter's life, and it also leads to internal conflict with the Ephraimites.

Samson is successful in spite of himself. In seeking personal vengeance he inadvertently defeats a national Israelite foe. Even then his victory is not complete, but only partial. As the narratives in 1 Samuel show, Israel continues to battle the Philistine oppressors.

   In these episodes the narrator portrays God as capable of intervening in human affairs by designating a human leader to deliver the Hebrews from oppression. However, deliverance is contingent upon the action of these human leaders, actions that may or may not be consistent with divine intentions. As a result these episodes indicate that divine involvement does not necessarily guarantee overall success, and they hint that the divine power of intervention is constrained by the exercise of human freedom.

Human Freedom and the Limits of Divine Power

The limitations of divine power become more apparent in three other references to divine activity and involvement. These are: (1) the narrator's attribution of divine presence with someone, (2) the narrator's comment that the divine spirit is conferred upon an individual, and (3) a character's acknowledgment of the divine presence. The attributions of divine presence either by the narrator or by a character are conveniently summarized in the following chart.

Attributions of Divine Presence

Judge/ Character	The Lord Is With "X"	Spirit of God	Acknowledgment by Character
Judah	X		
Joseph	X		
Judges	X		
******			
Othniel		X	
Ehud			X
Deborah			X
Gideon	X (×2)	X	
Jephthah		X	
Samson		X (×4)	

   The phrase "The Lord is with [someone]" occurs primarily in the Prologue, but it is also used in relationship to Gideon. In the Prologue the narrator relates various incidents pertaining to the ongoing conquest of the land after the death of Joshua. As specified by divine instruction (Judg 1:1-2), Judah initiated the assault, whose success is attributed to God: "Then Judah went up and the Lord gave the Canaanites and the Perizzites into their hand" (1:4). After reporting a series of successful ventures, the narrator notes that "The Lord was with Judah" (1:19). The extent of the conquest by Judah is then summarized, "And he took possession of the hill country, but could not drive out the inhabitants of the plain, because they had chariots of iron" (1:19). Whatever the presence of God with Judah signifies, it apparently does not guarantee victory. The story thus functions to suggest the limitations of God's power to ensure success.

Also among the first to launch an attack upon the land was the clan of Joseph, with whom the narrator notes the presence of God: "The house of Joseph also went up against Bethel; and the Lord was with them" (Judg 1:22). As before, God's presence with the house of Joseph does not presuppose victory. God may be with them, but they nevertheless send out spies to reconnoiter the area, where they encounter a resident willing to betray his city. Covert negotiations with this man, not reliance upon divine strength, yield a successful assault upon the city. Even this success is qualified by the narrator's report that the betrayer moves to another locale, rebuilds the city, and names it Luz, after the one he betrayed. This story, too, hints at the limitations of divine authority insofar as it is represented by divine presence.

Another assertion of divine presence occurs toward the end of the Prologue in the paradigmatic statement that typifies the dynamics of the divine/human relationship in Judges. After recounting the formulaic disobedience of the people and God's anger with and punishment of them, the narrator writes, "Whenever the Lord raised up judges for them, the Lord was with the judge" (Judg 2:18). The narrator then explains the motivation for divine presence: "For the Lord would be moved to pity by their groaning because of those who persecuted and oppressed them" (2:18). From the statements made in this passage it would appear that divine presence guarantees victory. However, in the passage immediately following, the narrator reveals Israel's persistent transgressions and reports God's consequential decision not to drive out the remaining nations through a dramatizing, direct-discourse speech. In the speech God proclaims, "I will no longer drive out before them any of the nations that Joshua left when he died" (2:21). The narrator uses authorial omniscience to explain the significance of the action: "In order to test Israel, whether or not they would take care to walk in the way of the Lord as their ancestors did, the Lord had left those nations, not driving them out at once" (2:22-23). This speech and its explanation again suggest that divine power is constrained by the human response to it.

The final use of the phrase "the Lord is with [someone]" occurs in the Gideon episode. As part of the negotiations between Gideon and God regarding Gideon's assumption of the role of judge, Gideon is told twice that God would be with him (Judg 6:12,16). Initially Gideon is addressed by an angel of God as "a mighty warrior," and is assured that "the Lord is with you." Gideon responds with a skeptical question, "If the Lord is with us, why then has all this happened to us?" (6:13). His question reflects the perhaps prevailing notion that divine presence automatically guarantees success. However, the angel's original salutation, "mighty warrior," suggests that the basis of success actually resides in human abilities. Resuming the "mighty warrior" motif, God instructs him, "Go in this might of yours and deliver Israel from the hand of Midian" (6:14). This speech elaborates upon the importance of human abilities and suggests that possession by the divine spirit is not sufficient. Gideon must be willing to use his own skills if he is to be successful. God then reassures Gideon that "I will be with you, and you shall strike down the Midianites, every one of them" (6:16). However, such assurances and reassurances do not completely convince Gideon, who acts with extreme caution when he does act and who continues to seek repeated demonstrations of God's favor and authority.

These examples from the Gideon episode again suggest that divine presence only seems to confer the potential for human success; it does not confirm success as an inevitable result. Instead divine power is limited by the exercise of human freedom to obey or disobey God, to use or misuse human skills.

More common in Judges than the phrase "the Lord is with [someone]" is the bestowal of the divine spirit upon someone. It is first used in the Othniel episode, where the narrator writes that after God raised up Othniel as a deliverer, "the spirit of the Lord came upon him, and he judged Israel; he went out to war, and the Lord gave King Cushan-rishathaim of Aram into his hand; and his hand prevailed over Cushan-rishathaim" (3:10).

In this instance the conferring of the divine spirit seems to be associated with the activity of judging, which in turn is associated with the waging of war against Israel's enemies, a venture that on this occasion is successful. To whom the narrator attributes this success is significant. In part, the storyteller ascribes it to God: "The Lord gave King Cushan-rishathaim into his hand." Yet, Othniel exercised his own skill in achieving it as well: "And his [i.e., Othniel's] hand prevailed over Cushan-rishathaim." The brief story of Othniel thus presents the paradigm for successful divine/human interaction and cooperation. The presence of God confers the potential for human success, but faithful human action is also necessary to acquire that success.

The narrator does not explicitly state that the spirit of God is given to either Ehud or Deborah, the two succeeding judges. Yet, both successfully deliver Israel from the oppression of its enemies, and both voice their own conviction that God gave them their victories. Though divine involvement is not neglected in the portrayal, the narrator does emphasize the confident leadership ability and tactical skills of both human judges. Thus, Ehud is characterized as a clever assassin who uses his intelligence to outwit the Moabite king and then uses this success to summon support from the people. Likewise, Deborah is portrayed as an assertive female leader who is able to command male soldiers and success-fully lead them into battle against their enemies. Even though both of these judges credit God with the victory (3:28; 4:9), their stories stress the impor-tance and necessity of the human involvement in the achievement of success.

In the succeeding episode about Gideon, the narrator explicitly notes that "the spirit of the Lord took possession of Gideon" (6:34). Yet, as previously discussed and by way of contrast with Ehud and Deborah, Gideon doubts his ability to deliver, and twice demands additional signs of divine assistance. This episode continues to develop the theme that divine presence can be compro-mised by a limited human capacity to believe and to act upon those beliefs.

The subsequent story of Jephthah is similar to the story of Gideon. Both men possess the spirit of God and both negotiate additional assurances of suc-cess. After negotiations for a peaceful settlement with the Ammonites break down, the narrator writes that "the spirit of the Lord came upon Jephthah" (11:29) as he prepared militarily to confront the Ammonite oppressors. How-ever, immediately following the report of the conferring of the divine spirit and before the account of the battle is a scene in which Jephthah makes a vow to God. The narrator writes, "And Jephthah made a vow to the Lord, and said, 'If you will give the Ammonites into my hand, then whoever comes out of the doors of my house to meet me, when I return victorious from the Ammonites, shall be the Lord's, to be offered up by me as a burnt offering'" (11:30-31). As in the story of Gideon, the conferring of the divine spirit has limited effect. Jephthah still doubts his ability to be successful and makes an additional vow.

However, Jephthah's doubt and his consequent vow result in the victimiza-tion of his innocent daughter. Apparently following a custom for victory celebrations, Jephthah's daughter comes out "to meet him with timbrels and dancing" (11:34). Seeing her, Jephthah realizes the horror of the situation and makes a mourning gesture by tearing his clothes. However, he mourns not for his daughter but for himself. He berates her: "Alas, my daughter! You have brought me very low; you have become the cause of great trouble to me. For I have opened my mouth to the Lord, and I cannot take back my vow" (11:35). The speech not only suggests the extent of his daughter's victimization, since her father laments his own misfortune and not his daughter's, but it also sug-gests the belief that once initiated a human course of action cannot be altered, even by God.

The narrator's portrayal of the conflict in this story suggests that the father's act of self-preservation results in the death of his daughter. This human action is the cause of innocent suffering. When human freedom to act in destructive ways is exercised, God does not intervene and compromise the exercise of this freedom. Instead the deity allows divine power to be constrained.

The phrase "the spirit of the Lord" occurs four times in the climactic Samson episode. Initially it occurs in the narrator's summary at the conclusion of the narrative relating the circumstances of Samson's birth: "And the boy grew, and the Lord blessed him. The spirit of the Lord began to stir him" (13:24-25). At this point no action of any kind follows.

The second reference occurs during one of Samson's journeys to Timnah. The narrator reports that "Suddenly a young lion roared at [Samson]. The spirit of the Lord rushed on him, and he tore the lion apart barehanded" (Judg 14:5-6). In this instance the spirit of the Lord seems to allow Samson to defend himself against an attacking lion. However, the carcass of the lion later becomes the source of a riddle Samson uses to taunt the Philistines at his marriage feast. The riddle in turn becomes a source of conflict that eventually occasions the third use of the phrase.

After Samson's wife betrays her husband by telling her countrymen the answer to the riddle, the narrator writes, "Then the spirit of the Lord rushed on him, and he went down to Ashkelon. He killed thirty men of the town, took their spoil, and gave the festal garments to those who had explained the riddle" (Judg 14:19). In this instance the spirit of the Lord seems to facilitate Samson's revenge against the Philistines as well as his acquisition of the resources to pay off his lost wager. Once again, however, Samson's actions are motivated by concerns that are personal, not political.

The final conferral of the divine spirit also enables Samson to defend his personal safety. As the narrator recounts the incident, Samson sets fire to the Philistines' wheat fields because his wife has been given to someone else. When the Philistines respond by attacking Judah, the men of Judah persuade Samson to surrender himself. Samson is bound with "two new ropes" and left for the Philistines at Lehi. As the Philistines approach him, the narrator writes, "the spirit of the Lord rushed on him, and the ropes that were on his arms became like flax that has caught fire, and his bonds melted off his hands. Then he found a fresh jawbone of a donkey, reached down and took it, and with it he killed a thousand men" (Judg 15:14-15).

In these instances, possession of the spirit of the Lord seems to result only in the personal protection of Samson from a variety of threats, some of which are caused by his own antics. Granted, Samson kills several of the Philistine oppressors, but he does so only inadvertently as he pursues personal vengeance. Given the extensive preparations for the birth of Samson and the frequent references to his possession by the spirit of the Lord, such limited results seem surprising. It again appears that divine power is constrained by the exercise of human freedom, a freedom that on these occasions is used for personal protection rather than national defense.

Although the narrator of Judges portrays God as actively intervening in the life of the Hebrew people, the narrator shows God acting without constraint and with complete success only when authorizing punishment for human transgressions. The narrator's portrayal also shows God intervening to initiate a process of deliverance from oppression. The initial step in this process is the divine selection of a human leader. However, this exercise of divine authority is not unqualifiedly successful. Success depends upon the subsequent actions of the human leader.

This portrayal, furthermore, suggests that the presence of the God with the human leader or the leader's possession by the spirit of the Lord does not guarantee success. Divine success appears contingent upon an appropriate human response. Hence, the exercise of divine power is limited by the exercise of human freedom, the exercise of which frequently misuses and abuses human potential. Accordingly, the deity can influence but not command human actions; God will act to punish transgressions, but not to prevent them.

Whether these constraints on divine authority are inherent or self-imposed is beyond the purview of this essay, if not the parameters of the biblical literature. What this literary analysis of God's portrayal in Judges does emphasize, though, is that divine power is limited in its effectiveness by actions resulting from human freedom. Divine presence seems to confer only potential for success; it does not confirm success as an inevitable result.

Divine and Human Portrayals in the Epilogue

The Epilogue is usually regarded as a secondary, disruptive supplement to the Book of Judges. However, from a literary perspective, this section not only continues to develop themes from the Prologue and the Era of the Judges, but it also intensifies them.

Consistent with the emerging portrayal of a constrained divine authority, the narrator relates two stories that reflect the unrestrained exercise of human freedom. The narrator specifically and repeatedly notes that these stories take place when there was no king in Israel, a time when everyone did what was right in his or her own eyes. Not only is there an absence of human leadership during this era, but there is also a conspicuous lack of divine involvement.

In the first narrative, the story of Micah and the Danites (Judg 17–18), the process recounted in the section on the Era of the Judges is reversed. Instead of God's arranging for human leadership, human beings attempt to secure divine favor. An Ephraimite named Micah makes an ephod and teraphim, installs them in his personal shrine, and designates one of his sons as priest. When a Levite priest wanders by his house, Micah acquires his services for ten pieces of silver a year. Certain now that he has acquired for his personal worship an adequate facility and an appropriate functionary, Micah concludes, "Now I know that the Lord will prosper me, because the Levite has become my priest" (17:13).

Micah's manipulative attempts to acquire favor are not successful. When a band of Danite warriors seeking to acquire land of their own pass by Micah's house, they steal his icons as well as persuade the Levite priest to join them. Proceeding to the city of Laish, whose inhabitants the narrator describes as "quiet and unsuspecting," the Danites "put them to the sword, and burned down the city" (Judg 18:27). At this juncture the narrator makes the ironic comment: "There was no deliverer, because it was far from Sidon and they had no dealings with anyone" (18:28).

In situations where the exercise of human freedom attempts to manipulate divine favor, either through the manufacture of sacred objects and the purchase of priests or through the theft of another's icons and coercion of his priest, divine power is limited and constrained. In such circumstances there will be no deliverer, whether of divine or human origin. This story establishes a context for the following tragic story of the rape of the Levite's concubine (Judg 19–21).

The conflict that generates this story's action begins when the Levite's concubine "became angry with him, and she went away from him to her father's house" (Judges 19:2). The Levite "sets out after her," and the narrator explicitly states his purpose: "to speak tenderly to her and bring her back" (19:3). However, these intentions are not fulfilled, and their nonfulfillment results in the innocent victimization of the Levite's concubine.

On the return journey, the Levite seeks refuge for the night with an old man from Gibeah. During the evening, the men of the city, whom the narrator describes as "a perverse lot," demand that the old man send out his guest so they may sexually violate him. The old man counters by offering his own daughter and the Levite's concubine. When the men reject the offer, the narrator reports that the Levite "seized his concubine, and put her out to them. They wantonly raped her, and abused her all through the night until the morning" (Judg 19:25). The extent of the concubine's brutalization is revealed in the Levite's callous response to her the next morning. Seeing her "lying at the door of the house, with her hands on the threshold," he commands her, "'Get up, we are going'" (19:27-28).

The Levite's lack of concern for his concubine's well-being is further indicated by his own desire for personal revenge. He again disregards the sanctity of her person, this time by dismembering her body and sending the pieces "throughout all the territory of Israel" with the message, "Has such a thing ever happened since the day that the Israelites came up from the land of Egypt until this day? Consider it, take counsel, and speak out" (Judg 19:30). Thus summoned, the people of Israel seek and achieve vengeance upon the men of

Gibeah. The Levite is thus avenged for whatever indignity he believes he experienced, but the concubine remains forever victimized.

Like that of Jephthah's daughter, this story suggests that a human act of self-preservation results in innocent suffering. When human beings are irresponsible in exercising their freedom, God does not intervene. Instead God allows divine power to be constrained.

The Epilogue thus confirms and intensifies the emerging portrait of God in Judges, one in which the deity refrains from intervention in order to preserve the exercise of human freedom, even if that exercise results in innocent victims. It also confirms and intensifies the emerging portrayal of human beings as flawed in the exercise of their freedom. The narrator's portrayals stress human responsibility, not divine accountability, and emphasize responsible human interaction, not responsive divine intervention.

The Epilogue also continues to portray God as involved in the punishment of transgression. Following the rape and murder of the Levite's concubine, the people of Israel, from Dan to Beer-sheba, assemble to seek vengeance upon Gibeah. They decide to "go up against [Gibeah]" so that they might "repay Gibeah of Benjamin for all the disgrace that they have done in Israel" (Judg 20:9-10). When the Benjaminites decide to protect Gibeah, the tribes formulate their battle strategy by consulting God. They inquire of God, "Which of us shall go up first to battle against the Benjaminites?" (20:18).

The query is similar to one made at the beginning of the Prologue, where the people inquire of God, "Who shall go up first for us against the Canaanites, to fight against them?" (Judg 1:1). In the Prologue, however, the issue is not internal vengeance but external conquest. Also, there the people do not initiate the battle and then consult God, as they do in the Epilogue. On the contrary, God has sanctioned the assault prior to the people's inquiry about strategy. The circumstances surrounding the two consultations themselves portray the progressively deteriorating relationship between God and the people.

In both the Prologue and Epilogue, the divine response to the people's query is similar: "Judah shall go up (first)" (Judg 1:2; 20:18). However, in the Prologue, God adds, "I hereby give the land into his hand" (1:2). The narrator subsequently affirms that "Judah went up and the Lord gave the Canaanites and the Perizzites into their hand" (1:4).

In the Epilogue, however, divine assurance of success is missing. Accordingly, the Benjaminites inflict substantial casualties upon the assembled army. Before continuing the assault, the people consult God a second time: "Shall we again draw near to battle against our kinsfolk the Benjaminites?" (Judg 20:23). Again, the answer is, "Go up against them" (Judg 20:23). Once more, the Benjaminites inflict heavy casualties.

The tribes then inquire a third time, "Shall we go out once more to battle against our kinsfolk the Benjaminites, or shall we desist?" (Judg 20:28). God again responds affirmatively but this time adds the assurance of victory missing from the previous answers: "Go up, for tomorrow I will give them into your hand" (20:28). This time they are successful, and the narrator attributes the victory to God: "The Lord defeated Benjamin before Israel" (20:35).

Thus the narrator not only portrays God as punishing Benjamin but also implies judgment against the rest of Israel as well. By encouraging their attack without assurances of success, God, in effect, sets them up for defeat. Given the background description of the story as a time in which each person did what was right in his or her own eyes, and given the particular details of the story relating the brutal rape and murder of the Levite's concubine, the narrator seems to be implying judgment upon the people as a whole for allowing a climate of violence in which events such as these take place. What each person regards as right in his or her own eyes, especially as it involves interpersonal and even intertribal violence, is not, in fact, right in the eyes of God. Although God does not prevent the transgression, God does punish the transgressors.

Illustrating various concepts of narrative criticism, my reading identifies three central interrelated themes in the book of Judges: (1) the progressive deterioration of the relationship between God and the Hebrew people; (2) the limitations imposed upon divine power by the exercise of human freedom; and (3) the misuse and abuse of human freedom. Even so, this is only *a* reading of Judges, not *the* reading. Although there is no one definitive reading, mine is, I hope, a useful one. However, readings, like stories themselves, are received by the larger interpretive community according to the predisposition of the individuals who compose it. Some readings can hurt, some can heal. Whether an interpretation hurts or heals depends upon how the story and a particular reading of it is adopted by the individual, or even upon how the individual is forced to adapt to it. To paraphrase the narrator of Judges, there are in the contemporary reading environment no authoritative interpreters or absolute interpretations of the Bible; each reader interprets and appropriates interpretations according to what is meaningful in his or her own eyes.

Further Reading

General

BOOTH, Wayne C. *The Rhetoric of Fiction,* 2d ed. Chicago: University of Chicago Press, 1983. A classic study of the techniques used by writers in composing narrative literature. A knowledge of secular literature is helpful.

CHATMAN, Seymour. *Story and Discourse: Narrative Structure in Fiction and Film.* Ithaca, N.Y.: Cornell University Press, 1978. An influential study of the elements of narrative. Theoretical discussions illustrated with examples from secular literature and film.

————. *Coming to Terms: The Rhetoric of Narrative in Fiction and Film.* Ithaca, N.Y.: Cornell University Press, 1990. A helpful sequel to the previous book.

GENETTE, Gérard. *Narrative Discourse: An Essay in Method.* Translated by Jane E. Lewin. Ithaca, N.Y.: Cornell University Press, 1980. An advanced and technical discussion of narrative techniques in secular literature.

————. *Narrative Discourse Revisited.* Translated by Jane E. Lewin. Ithaca, N.Y.: Cornell University Press, 1988. A sequel to the previous book.

RIMMON-KENAN, Shlomith. *Narrative Fiction: Contemporary Poetics.* London: Methuen, 1983. A concise introduction to the techniques of narrative composition. A knowledge of secular literature is helpful.

SCHOLES, Robert, and Robert Kellogg. *The Nature of Narrative.* London: Oxford University Press, 1966. An excellent textbook introduction to the elements of narrative, including characterization, plot, and point of view.

Biblical

ALTER, Robert. *The Art of Biblical Narrative.* New York: Basic Books, 1981. A pioneering study on the elements of narrative as they occur in biblical narrative. Includes helpful examples as well as theoretical discussions.

————. *The World of Biblical Literature.* New York: Basic Books, 1992. A sequel to the previous book.

BAR-EFRAT, Shimon. *Narrative Art in the Bible.* Sheffield, Eng.: Almond Press, 1989. A helpful introduction to the concepts of the narrator, the characters, and the plot. Theoretical concepts are amply illustrated with biblical examples.

BERLIN, Adele. *Poetics and Interpretation of Biblical Narrative.* Sheffield, Eng.: Almond Press, 1983. A useful introduction to the concepts of character and point of view. Good examples and an insightful comparison of literary methods with historical critical methods.

BRICHTO, Herbert Chanan. *Toward a Grammar of Biblical Poetics.* New York: Oxford University Press, 1992. An advanced discussion of the compositional techniques of biblical narrative. Detailed explications of biblical narratives provide examples of the various techniques.

GUNN, David M., and Danna Nolan Fewell. *Narrative in the Hebrew Bible.* New York: Oxford University Press, 1993. A textbook introduction to the elements of narrative as represented in biblical literature. Lengthy examples illustrate the concepts. Excellent bibliography.

LONGMAN III, Tremper. *Literary Approaches to Biblical Interpretation.* Grand
   Rapids: Zondervan, 1987. A readable introduction to the literary study of
   biblical narrative. Brief discussions of interpretive theory and literary concepts are followed by helpful biblical examples.

STERNBERG, Meir. *The Poetics of Biblical Narrative: Ideological Literature and the
   Drama of Reading.* Bloomington, Ind.: Indiana University Press, 1985. An
   advanced and technical discussion of the compositional techniques of biblical narrative.

3

SOCIAL SCIENTIFIC CRITICISM: JUDGES 9 AND ISSUES OF KINSHIP

Naomi Steinberg

What Social Scientists Study

Many possibilities for misunderstanding arise when we seek to comprehend situations we don't understand. What typically happens is called projection—that is, interpretation based on the individual's own circumstances. Let me illustrate my point with two examples that come from personal experience in teaching about religion. One must know something about Judaism in order to understand why men, and sometimes women as well, cover their heads with a cap when entering a synagogue or why some men even keep their heads covered at all times. The reason is to show respect for God; covering the head is a way to demonstrate human awareness that there is a higher being. If, however, a person has no background in Judaism, he or she may draw conclusions about the significance of head covering that have nothing to do with religion and that are humorous as well. A student once told me that she believed Jewish men covered their heads because they were self-conscious about their baldness and tried to hide it by wearing a hat; she was under the impression that baldness was a genetic trait in all Jewish men. On another occasion a Jewish student expressed her belief that Christians worshiped money; while attending a Sunday morning church service, she noticed that after the collection plate was brought to the altar, the entire congregation stood and the minister offered a blessing over the money. With no comparable ritual from her Jewish background to help her understand this experience, the student misunderstood the significance of the blessing of the gifts by the church members for the work of the church.

Just as we must have a prior awareness of modern religious rituals in order to understand religious acts, so we must have knowledge of ancient social structures and institutions in order to fully comprehend the world depicted in the Hebrew Bible. Without such knowledge, we may wind up imposing contemporary Western models and attitudes onto an ancient society with a social structure different from our own. We call this way of thinking "ethnocentrism." To avoid ethnocentrism, scholars depend upon a number of approaches based in the social sciences.[1] Using social data, the researcher attempts to recover the dynamics of social organization in ancient Israel. The aim of this chapter is to identify some of the general presuppositions of social scientific study of the Hebrew Bible and to demonstrate the usefulness of this approach through an in-depth study of Judges 9.

The book of Judges recounts the story of the Israelites' escape from slavery in Egypt and their efforts to settle in the land of Canaan after wandering through the wilderness. Then, some process of social reorganization moved the tribes to form from what are reported to be loosely organized tribes a tighter social structure based upon a unified state organization. Can some theory of social change or a model of social organization shed light on how and why this transformation took place? Careful investigation of the narratives of Judges reveals that rather than being eyewitness accounts of Israel's early experience in Canaan, or the Promised Land, the texts were heavily edited at a later time (see chapter 1 of this volume). Specifically, after years of living in this land that Israel took over from the local population, foreigners entered and expelled the Israelites to Babylon. This expulsion prompted Israel to examine its past in order to try to explain why, in light of the treaty Israel had made with God at Mount Sinai, a treaty that promised Israel God's protection, Israel suffered military defeat at the hands of an enemy nation and was sent into exile. Judges simultaneously explains how Israel took possession of the land and why Israel eventually lost it.

Later individuals edited this material with the result that these possession stories repeat a pattern of God's people continually breaking their end of the covenant, such that God had no choice but to expel Israel for its transgressions. Given the double purpose that these narratives serve, how can the modern reader attempt to understand how Israel came to control a land of its own? Is it possible to move beyond the revision of earlier narratives in order to reconstruct the origins of Israel in Canaan?

Israel's Social Origins

Recently, scholars have come to recognize the value of turning to models provided by the social sciences for addressing the question of Israel's origins. Past

1. For a full introduction to the issues, see Robert R. Wilson, *Sociological Approaches to the Old Testament,* Guides to Biblical Scholarship series (Philadelphia: Fortress Press, 1984).

efforts by scholars to understand this process focused on questions of religion and history. Instead of asking about the dating of the Israelites' entry into the land, or when they first encountered their God, Yahweh, scholarship oriented toward sociology and anthropology now raises questions about the social structures and social circumstances that lie within the text, as well as those behind the text, that is, the ones in which the Israelites actually lived. This methodological approach shapes the questions asked of the biblical text. In the broadest sense, the methodology of the social sciences asks, "What social structures and social processes are explicit or implicit in the biblical literature, in the scattered socioeconomic data it contains, in the overtly political history it recounts, and in the religious beliefs and practices it attests?"[2] Yet the investigator must let questions arise from the issues raised by the biblical literature rather than imposing research agendas on the text that are neither relevant nor appropriate to the material. The comparative perspectives provided by the social sciences demonstrate that, in the case of ancient Israel, the answers to questions about social organization and social structure differ from those that arise out of our own Western, industrialized society.

The biblical tradition presupposes an all-Israelite conquest of the land, but the extent to which this perspective has been superimposed upon the texts by later compilers and editors must be addressed. Specifically, we must ask: Who migrated into the land and who settled there? What self-identity and religious unity existed among these tribes? Finally, how did the tribes come to occupy the land of Canaan?

The biblical texts themselves provide conflicting accounts of how this occupation took place. Some texts claim that a lightning campaign brought Canaan under Israelite control (Josh 10:40; 11:16-17), while other accounts (e.g., Judg 1) present a less glorified picture of what happened when Israel attempted to gain entry into the land. Scholarship suggests that the description of a swift, successful occupation comes from later editors while the earlier biblical traditions present the less glorified account.

Additional data on this issue come from archaeology. However, it provides inconclusive results if one aims to "prove" the Hebrew Bible. Sometimes the archaeological material lends support to the biblical account but at other times it actually conflicts with what the Bible tells us. One group of scholars argues that the archaeological evidence reveals a wave of destruction in the thirteenth and twelfth centuries B.C.E., which can be attributed to Israelite invasion of the land under Joshua. These scholars contend that there was indeed a conquest of Canaan by the Israelites. In contrast to this perspective, certain German schol-

---

2. Norman K. Gottwald, *The Hebrew Bible: A Socio-Literary Introduction* (Philadelphia: Fortress Press, 1985), 26.

ars working earlier in this century maintain that Judges 1 reflects what actually happened, that is, that there was a peaceful infiltration of the land over a long period of time. The occupation took place in two stages: nomads looking for summer pasturage for their flocks settled in Canaan, and then later expanded their control to other unsettled areas. Scholars of this line of thinking believe that the archaeological destruction attributed to the Israelite invasion actually reflects the incursion of the Sea People, or the Philistines.

More recently, several scholars have interpreted the biblical data in light of cross-cultural models that suggest the so-called conquest was actually caused by a decaying political system maintained by the upper classes in Canaan that weighed heavily upon the lower classes. A group of lower class individuals entering Canaan met people of similar economic status, to whom they brought a message of economic liberation. The groups joined forces and the locals rose up against their oppressive overlords. Thus the conquest was from within—an overturning of the hierarchical system of Canaanite overlords by the disenfranchised.

Many believe that the circumstances of Israel's origins are a combination of the conquest and the revolt models. A group of individuals came into Israel from outside the land and fused with sympathizers within, who willingly converted to this new message, thereby throwing off the old system of domination and oppression. The complex picture presented by archaeology indicates that the same conclusions cannot be drawn throughout Syria-Palestine. At some sites the local Canaanites were replaced by Israelites and at others by the Philistines. Different parts of the country experienced different patterns of occupation.

The means of conquest of the land can be directly related to the type of organization that ties one group of Israelites to another. In fact, the reader must continually ask what size group is being referred to when the name "Israel" appears in a text in Judges. We must be careful not to assume automatically that every reference to "Israel" should be read as including the twelve-tribe system that the biblical text later defines as normative.

The material in Judges provides no clear answer to the question of what unified Israel in its early occupation of the land. Were they in fact a unit, or merely separate tribes? Until recently the work of the German scholar Martin Noth provided the answer most accepted among biblical scholars. Basing his opinion on analogies from ancient Greece and Italy, Noth believed that early Israel was an amphictyony, "a community of those who dwell around" a sacred shrine. The amphictyony was a social unit linked to a common religious center where the tribes gathered for purposes of celebrating sacred festivals.[3] Recently,

---

3. Martin Noth, *Das System der zwölf Stämme Israels* (Stuttgart: W. Kohlhammer, 1930); idem, *The History of Israel* (New York: Harper & Brothers, 1958), 85–108.

biblical scholars have reevaluated the amphictyonic thesis and have rejected its theory of unification.[4] By carefully examining the biblical texts we see a lack of unity among the tribes prior to the existence of centralized leadership under David and Solomon (1000–922 B.C.E.).

Leadership in the tribes was typically local and, as currently edited throughout the texts, comes only through the inspiration of Yahweh. While Judges reads as a chronological flow from one leader to the next, the texts are believed to convey information about individuals who were originally unconnected to each other and who are of different personality types. These narratives were later edited together to present a picture of the divine spirit of God leading Israel in its time of need. Yet, Israel continued to follow other deities. So, we need to look at other models of social structure to help us better understand the social organization assumed in the texts.

Biblical scholar Norman K. Gottwald set the stage for a discussion of these issues by refuting the argument that early Israel was based on pastoral nomadism. Gottwald believes that early Israel has its origins within Canaan, as the disenfranchised peasants "conquered" the land from within by revolting against the hierarchical ruling structure, thereby achieving autonomy from it. Instead of city-states providing social organization, people were grouped in extended family systems that were concerned with economic self-sufficiency. Thus, he reconstructs the origins and so-called occupation of the land in a fashion quite different from earlier scholars. Gottwald relies heavily on social models of economic life for nomads and peasants, and on an understanding of the social processes of interaction between rulers and those who are ruled by them — in this case, bureaucrats ruling peasants, or the upper classes dominating and subjugating the lower classes. It is a model that interrelates religion, politics, and economics. Gottwald understands the religion of Yahwism as a message addressing concerns for equality among the disenfranchised. He concludes, "The name 'Israel' referred not merely to a religious community but to a sovereign retribalizing society concerned with fundamental issues of survival and the good life."[5]

The period of the formation of Israel can be understood as based on the tension between city-states and rural life, between hierarchical systems of taxation and kinship systems of social organization. The text under consideration here, Judges 9, can be analyzed from the perspective of power politics between

---

4. The data that form the basis of this critique may be conveniently found in John H. Hayes and J. Maxwell Miller, eds., *Israelite and Judaean History* (Philadelphia: Westminster Press, 1977), 299–308.

5. Gottwald, *The Hebrew Bible*, 284–88; idem, *The Tribes of Yahweh: A Sociology of the Religion of Liberated Israel, 1250–1050 B.C.E.* (Maryknoll, N.Y.: Orbis Books, 1979), 293–621.

the king and the assembly who put him into office. There appears to be tension between how much power the latter will allot the former, and how much the former expects the latter to sacrifice.

Kinship and Marriage

In order to better reconstruct the social organization of ancient Israel as reflected in Judges 9, we must first understand the kinship system. Ancient Israel traced kinship on the basis of patrilineal descent; that is, the social system connected generations through fathers and sons. Moreover, men were polygamous; one man could marry more than one woman (the reverse does not appear to be true) though the social standing of these different wives might differ depending upon the economic terms that initiated the marriage and on the offspring produced by it. In addition, the social system gave preference to endogamous marriages, or marriage within certain boundaries of the kinship system, as opposed to exogamous marriages, or marriage outside certain boundaries of the kinship system. Endogamous marriages functioned to perpetuate the lineage from father to son, rather than to form alliances between groups. Put another way, a preference existed for marriages based on patrilineal endogamy because ancient Israel's social structure depended for its continuance on a relationship between the choice of marriage partners and patrilineal descent as the function of such marriages. This particular pattern of marriage served to keep family inheritance within the lineage of the groom and his father.

Although monogamy is the type of marriage most familiar in our society, it may be a rather ineffective arrangement for perpetuation of the family due to various obstacles that may interfere with reproduction. In fact, historically, there have been several different options by means of which a family can address the problem of absence of progeny. Serial monogamy occurs when a man divorces a barren woman in order to marry a fertile one. Even more effective than serial monogamy for producing heirs is either polygyny or polycoity. Polygyny is defined as taking additional wives of equal status to one another, as opposed to polycoity, which is the addition of concubines or handmaids, that is, women of lower status than the primary wife, to the household.[6] An option other than adding women is for a husband to add a child or children

---

6. One notes that all of these labels categorize marriage from the male point of view. The expectation is for one husband to have one or more wives. When a woman is married to more than one husband, the marriage is labeled polyandry. The biblical texts typically consider the absence of progeny to be the fault of the wife; sterility of men is not addressed in the Hebrew Bible. The lack of data regarding male sterility may be attributed either to incorrect understanding of the process of reproduction or to male pride regarding the fathering of a child.

through adoption. The choice made among these options is determined by issues such as custom, economics (property considerations), and the ages of the parties to the primary marriage. In the case of the ancestral stories of the biblical book of Genesis, the relationship between these options and the designation of a family heir depended upon both the man and the woman, whether a primary or a secondary wife, being descendants of the Israelite lineage begun by Terah back in Genesis 11. With regard to adoption in the biblical texts, the adopted individual was required to be able to trace his lineage back to Terah in order to be a family heir.

In this scheme, a concubine was a woman whose continued presence within the family was not dependent upon economic arrangements. Typically, a concubine was a secondary wife, whose involvement with the husband represented a secondary union, both in terms of being an additional wife and of having a lower status than the legal wife. Her function was to provide sexual enjoyment in a situation where the man already had offspring by his primary wife. If he did not have a child by his primary wife, a man could take a secondary wife to produce a child.

A family unit can include both a wife and a concubine, or slave wife, and still be labeled a monogamous marriage. In fact, concubinage is typically associated with monogamy, not polygyny.[7] In a union between a man and a barren women, a concubine may be used to obtain an heir because she does not threaten the economic basis of the marriage. Her secondary status as a slave wife is separated from the status of her child, who is considered a legitimate heir to the biological father and to the primary wife.

Social Structure

It is important to discuss the place of the family within the structure of Israelite society. The smallest unit of society is the *bêt 'āb,* the family household. The family household refers to both social organization and residency; it fulfills both social and economic purposes, and is the locus for both production and reproduction. A family household is a domestic unit, or a group of persons living together who are related by birth or marriage (though servants may also be included in this unit), and who depend upon each other for economic survival. Although biblical scholars have attempted to better understand the organization of the Israelite household, the texts themselves provide conflicting evidence on this issue; even the archaeological data can be ambiguous. Whereas modern interpreters have information on how ancient homes were laid out and

7. Jack Goody, "Polygyny, Economy and the Role of Women," *The Character of Kinship,* ed. Jack Goody (Cambridge: Cambridge University Press, 1973), 180.

on how public buildings or utilities were placed, it is still difficult to be certain how the people who inhabited these spaces utilized them. Moreover, social scientists inform us that in any society no one form of household organization predominates. The biblical texts present information on a variety of household forms. Owing to the breakup of families, residential forms are never static but give rise to new configurations in the course of the evolution of the family household.[8]

The next distinct level of social organization in ancient Israel after the family household is the lineage, a descent group that is composed of a number of residential groups. The *mishpāḥâ*, or clan, is the enlargement of the kinship circle to include lineages related by marriage for purposes of protective association. On a daily basis, an individual in ancient Israel would be less directly affected by the *mishpāḥâ* and more acutely aware of his or her position within the *bêt 'āb*. Possibly the *mishpāḥâ* served protective functions in the time frame presupposed in the Book of Judges.[9] The social structure of kinship relates to the exercise of power within the larger social organization. The level of social organization above the *mishpāḥâ* would be the *shēbeṭ*, or tribe.[10]

Social Class

A consideration of social life in ancient Israel requires that we pay attention to economic matters. Increasingly, biblical scholars have come to recognize the interpretive value of economic status for the analysis of the biblical texts.[11] It is clear that social classes can and do change, hence the importance of studying issues of economic development over time and place. Attending to matters of wealth and power and the interconnection between these two dimensions of social structure raises the question, "Who gets what and why?"[12] Reconstruction of the economic dynamics of biblical texts helps the modern interpreter understand matters of power and social class. Yet these categories of social analysis need not be seen as separate from each other; in the case of Judges 9, a relationship appears to exist between how kinship structures social relations

8. A fuller discussion of these issues may be found in Naomi Steinberg, *Kinship and Marriage in Genesis: A Household Economics Perspective* (Minneapolis: Fortress Press, 1993), 5–30.

9. Gottwald, *The Tribes of Yahweh*, 292.

10. Gottwald, *The Tribes of Yahweh*, 338–41.

11. Norman K. Gottwald, "Social Class as an Analytic and Hermeneutical Category in Biblical Studies," *JBL* 112 (1993): 3–22.

12. Gottwald, "Social Class," 5, where he cites Gerhard Lenski, *Power and Privilege: A Theory of Social Stratification* (Chapel Hill and London: University of North Carolina Press, 1984), title of chap. 1.

and, particularly, how it legitimates power and can be invoked in the interest of accumulating wealth. The rules of social organization may require that specific behavior be displayed in recognition of kinship ties. An individual may be expected to provide hospitality, loyalty, economic aid, or assistance in military contexts based on kinship ties. Kinship links are most commonly stressed when an individual can gain something through the family connection. Economic obligations imposed through marriage—whether to a primary wife or a secondary one—are also relevant.

In order to investigate the complexity of these socioeconomic relations, cross-cultural models are potentially relevant for illuminating obscure aspects of social life. The modern interpreter must bear in mind that neither the ancient world nor the modern one can always be expected to conform to the rules; there are always exceptions, and we must recognize that the biblical text may preserve evidence of both the exception and the rule. Once we are aware that patterns of social structure are not consistently upheld, we can be careful not to impose a neat sense of order where the ancient Israelite may not have experienced one.

To demonstrate the benefits of social scientific methodology as a means of interpreting the Bible, we turn now to an extended analysis of Judges 9. The general outline presented above for interpreting the "conquest" based on economic concerns and a rejection of the hierarchical ruling structures dictated by Canaanite overlords provides the context for focusing on one particular text. How does analysis of Judges 9 shed additional light on the process of assuming economic independence from a power structure that disadvantaged the underclasses? Do economic concerns provide a context for understanding the dynamics of the text? Before we begin our work, let us remember that the methodological approach shapes the questions we may ask of the text. We are interested in what error, from the perspective of social organization, Abimelech committed, and in why it is an error.

Judges 9: Mother's Kin/Father's Kin— Does It Make a Difference?

Judges 9 relates the events that take place when Abimelech, a son of the prior judge Jerubbaal, decides to assume the responsibility of leadership over the city of Shechem at the expense of the lives of his seventy half-brothers, sons born to Jerubbaal by a woman who was a primary wife to him. By contrast, Abimelech's mother was his secondary wife (8:31).

Abimelech successfully seizes leadership over Shechem through the support of his mother's kin, who are from Shechem. Abimelech convinces his maternal kin to support him in his bid for rulership by arguing that the city will benefit from leadership by one individual within their family group, rather than suffering under the hand of Jerubbaal's seventy sons by another woman; the Shechemites believe that it would be to their advantage to be ruled by an insider, a kinsman, rather than by a group of outsiders, nonkinsmen (Judg 9:1-3). Abimelech hires an army and with them he kills his half-brothers. Having demonstrated his leadership abilities to the citizens of Shechem, Abimelech becomes king of the city (9:6).

Jotham, Jerubbaal's youngest son, survives the massacre and denounces Abimelech's actions. Jotham delivers his denunciation through a parable, or a speech made through the use of analogy, about trees seeking to appoint a king for themselves (Judg 9:8-15). Neither the olive tree, the fig tree, nor the vine is willing to take the position because, all three argue, they already serve a useful function and cannot abandon their responsibilities. Only the bramble, who seemingly has no special function, will agree to become king over the other trees, provided that the position has been offered to him in good faith. Jotham concludes by suggesting that the Shechemites did not act in good faith when they supported Abimelech's massacre of his half-brothers, because the father of all these men, Jerubbaal, is dishonored through this behavior toward his family (9:16-20).[13]

Despite the initial favor that Abimelech is offered by the Shechemites, their sentiments turn against him. The Shechemites station men on mountaintops who rob passing travellers (Judg 9:25). For reasons that are not made clear to us, this action appears to cause harm to Abimelech.

Introduced into the story at this point is the figure of Gaal, son of Ebed. Gaal takes up residence in Shechem, where the locals become sympathetic to his words against Abimelech. Specifically, Gaal questions whether the Shechemites owe their loyalty to Abimelech, and Gaal expresses his wish to organize the people under his own leadership so that they can overthrow Abimelech (Judg 9:28-29). Interestingly, the text tells us that Gaal has moved to Shechem with his kinsmen. Verse 31 repeats that Gaal and his kinsmen have moved to the area and that *they* are stirring up trouble against Abimelech. While Abimelech appears to want to rule not only Shechem but the surrounding area as well, Gaal appears satisfied with the idea of leadership over Shechem alone.

Abimelech is alerted by Zebul, the ruler of Shechem, to the fact that Gaal is stirring up the citizens against him. The text assumes Zebul's loyalty to Abimelech. Thus, Zebul informs Abimelech of the growing support for Gaal and suggests that Abimelech launch a surprise attack on Gaal's forces when they

---

13. In Judges 9:18, Jotham refers to Abimelech's mother as an *'āmâ* rather than as a *pilegesh*. The former word refers to a woman of secondary status, which describes Jotham's perspective — he is, after all, a son of Gideon by his primary wife.

come out of the city gate in the morning (Judg 9:32-33). Gaal spots the men of Abimelech waiting to ambush him and goes out against the enemy, but ultimately is defeated and forced out of Shechem by Abimelech. Meanwhile, Abimelech resides at Arumah, a city southeast of Shechem (9:41).

The following day, after learning that some of the citizens of Shechem are working in their fields, which lay outside the city gate, Abimelech attacks and kills these people. To finish off the city completely, Abimelech burns it to the ground (Judg 9:42-45).

Leaders from Shechem's tower hear of these events and come together in an attempt to overthrow Abimelech. Abimelech reacts to this challenge to his leadership by instructing his followers to do as he has done: to cut some firewood in order to burn down Shechem tower and kill the people who have taken refuge within it. The success of Abimelech's plan results in the death of approximately one thousand citizens (Judg 9:46–49).

Abimelech's final battle is fought against the city of Thebez, inside of which is a fortress where all Thebez's citizens are gathered. The people move onto the roof of the fortress, a vantage point from which they are able to see Abimelech attempting to burn down their city. A woman throws a millstone, or a stone used for grinding grain, from the top of the tower down upon Abimelech.[14] The millstone is described as "only" crushing his skull, although Abimelech is certain to die from the wound (Judg 9:43). Lest anyone say he met his death at the hands of a woman, Abimelech instructs his sword-bearer to kill him. The era of Abimelech ends when all his army returns home (9:55). The details of the narrative paint a picture of Abimelech as dividing the geographical area against itself when those outside of Shechem fight him. An editorial conclusion inserted by later revisionists interprets these events as the punishment Abimelech and the lords of Shechem justly deserved for the deaths they unjustly caused to the seventy sons of Jerubbaal, and as the fulfillment of Jotham's curse upon them (9:56-57).

Despite the lack of certain geographical data within the text, that is, the exact location of Arumah and Thebez, the dynamics of the events fall into place. Verse 22 reports that Abimelech's reign over Israel lasted for three years; while we have no reason to doubt the length of his reign, Abimelech's authority was not over all Israel, but rather was localized in the area surrounding Shechem. The events described in Judges 9 pertain to a very limited geographical area.

---

14. Gale A. Yee, in "By the Hand of a Woman: The Metaphor of the Woman Warrior in Judges 4," *Semeia* 61 (1993): 111–12, argues that the lack of distinction between the domestic and public spheres in premonarchical Israel meant that war was not strictly considered men's work. The connection between the military and the domestic worlds is illustrated by the fact that Abimelech's murderer uses a millstone, that is, a domestic

Abimelech attempted to establish his leadership through the kinship system. He assumes his right to leadership as one based in inheritance, from his father Jerubbaal to him as son, despite the existence of seventy half-brothers (Judg 9:2a) whose claim to rulership is based on their mother's status as a primary wife of Jerubbaal, while in contrast Abimelech's mother was a secondary wife. On the other hand, his greatest base of support comes not from his paternal kinsmen but from his maternal kinsmen. Abimelech tries to establish leadership through maternal kinship, emphasizing his mother's lineage (9:2b). Initially, his maternal kin at Shechem, which appears to be a non-Israelite city, support him in his efforts and supply him with funds to hire an army. However, despite the backing of the Shechemite lords, Abimelech uses another city southeast of Shechem as his base of operation. Abimelech's decision to take up residence elsewhere suggests that Shechem may not have been the center of his power operation and may not have been as important to him as his kinsmen had hoped. Ultimately, the Shechemites refuse to consider Abimelech their supreme leader. Abimelech strikes out against the Shechemites, burns their city to the ground, and attempts to extend his authority to other cities in the area. His so-called reign ends only when he is killed attempting to seize the tower at Thebez.

Abimelech's story raises many questions. How are we to interpret the events of this chapter? The later editing of the story and throughout the book of Judges leads the reader to believe that the problem caused by Abimelech was a theological one: at this time in history, the ideology of Yahweh as divine king was in place, and temporary human leadership came in the form of individuals singled out by God to provide military intervention. These human leaders functioned solely because God chose them. Of course, in the case of Abimelech, human initiative results in the selection of Abimelech as "king."

The events in the story of Abimelech presuppose that his father, Gideon — called only Jerubbaal in Judges 9 — saved the Shechemites from the Midianites, and that for this reason the Shechemites owe loyalty to Gideon's son(s). In Judges 9:16-17, Jotham, son of Jerubbaal, says to the Shechemites, " . . . if you have dealt well with Jerubbaal and his house, and have done to him as his actions deserved — for my father fought for you, and risked his life, and rescued you from the hand of Midian. . . ." In other words, the text introduces loyalty based on kinship issues — loyalty to the patrilineage of Gideon.

How does knowledge of the general workings of the kinship system in ancient Israel illumine our understanding of Judges 9? What specific social structures support Abimelech in his expectation of receiving the backing of his

---

item, to kill him. Yee concludes that women's involvement in military actions was acceptable, though not normative, at this time in Israel.

mother's kin at Shechem? To answer these questions and to understand the details of Abimelech's actions, we must refer to the discussion outlined above of social organization in ancient Israel. Despite the ambiguity in the Hebrew terms themselves, social structure in Judges appears to be based on kinship grounded in the *bêt 'āb,* or father's house.[15] Larger groupings of these houses are called lineages, which are grouped together into a *mishpāḥâ,* or clan. These clans are grouped together into the *shēbeṭ,* or tribe, although the biblical texts suggest that the reality of twelve tribes operating together — the organization referred to as "Israel" — did not exist until the development of a centralized monarchy, that is, until after the time period under consideration in Judges.[16] Each of the above Hebrew words appears to have more than one possible translation, but all appear to refer to socioeconomic organization.

Scholars argue that Abimelech's error is his attempt to assume leadership based on human initiative; this is an affront to God's ability to rule the people. Reasoning from the perspective of social organization based on kinship structure, I maintain that the central problem plaguing Abimelech lies less in the realm of divine versus human leadership and more in his attempt to undermine the legitimate ancient Israelite societal norm of patrilineal kinship.

In the United States, kinship is traced through both parents of an individual. Each of us is related equally to both our mother and our father's side of the family. By contrast, the Hebrew Bible recounts a system of kinship organization traced exclusively through the father's line. Once we recognize that the author of Judges 9 assumes the system of patrilineal descent, we can immediately recognize that Abimelech acted without legitimate authority when he attempted

15. Mieke Bal argues that the anthropological interest of the stories in Judges lies in the understanding of "house" at this time in Israelite history. She understands the violence against women in Judges to relate to a change from living with the bride's father to living with the groom's father. In the context of Judges, which Bal believes to convey information earlier than that provided in the narratives of Genesis, *pilegesh* refers to a particular type of wife, that is, one who lives with her father instead of with the groom's father rather than to a concubine or secondary wife, as it does in Genesis. Bal believes that the conflict in Judges 9 lies between Gideon's seventy sons, who live with their father's family, and Abimelech, who lives with his mother's kin. In Judges 8:31 Abimelech's mother is labelled a *pilegesh;* the term does not actually appear in Judges 9. For a full discussion of her position on these issues as well as an analysis of the texts in Judges describing violence against women, see Mieke Bal, *Death and Dissymmetry: The Politics of Coherence in the Book of Judges* (Chicago: University of Chicago Press, 1988).

16. Scholars note that before the time of the monarchy, "Israel" was a term that referred to individuals of marginalized sociopolitical status, whereas after the inception of the monarchy, that is, in the tenth century, the term refers to citizenship in a particular geographical area; Robert G. Boling, *The Early Biblical Community in Transjordan,* Social World of Biblical Antiquity series (Sheffield, Eng.: Almond Press, 1988), 57.

to base his leadership on kinship traced through bilateral descent, the form of social organization in which descent is traced through both the mother and the father's lineage. The problem can be stated thus: "The Shechemites make Abimelech king because he is their kin through his mother's line. However, the legitimate societal norm is kinship traced solely through the father's relations." Interestingly, in Judges 8:19, Gideon acts on behalf of his half-brothers (his brothers through his mother's lineage). The texts do support the perspective that there is a tension between descent traced through the father and descent traced through the mother. All the same, in the case of Abimelech, the situation becomes more complex. Gideon had numerous wives. Thus all his sons had the "appropriate" father, but not all his sons—in particular, Abimelech—had the correct mothers, that is, primary wives of Gideon. Abimelech's mother is on a lower rung of the socioeconomic hierarchy than Gideon's other wives, and the story is about the legitimate kinship structure for the organization of society. Abimelech dies as punishment for his attempt to rule based on bilateral kinship assumptions rather than the legitimate societal norm of kinship traced through only the father's line.

Studying only the Hebrew terms used to designate Abimelech's mother's status in isolation from their social context provides limited information on how kinship affects social structure. We need a social context in which to locate words referring to the status of women. The problem of interpreting the text of Judges 9 exists because after so many thousands of years modern scholars are unable to be certain of the range of meaning intended in any one word, and must recognize that this range may have changed over time. In particular, the word *pilegesh,* used to characterize the relationship of Abimelech's mother to his father Gideon, traditionally means secondary wife. Whether this term has sociological significance beyond that of the secondary legal and social status of a concubine, or secondary wife, remains open to debate. As is often the case in polygamous marriages, the secondary wife or wives may live separately from the primary wife and the husband (8:31). One scholar argues that the key to understanding Judges 9, as well as other texts in Judges, lies at the domestic, rather than the political, level, and that it has to do with the place of residence of women after marriage.

In society nowadays, newlyweds need not reside with either the bride or the groom's family of origin. Most newlyweds prefer to set up residence apart from both sets of parents, a pattern of living known as neolocal residence. In ancient Israel, because of the interest in retaining land within one family so that it could be passed down from one generation to the next, newlyweds typically lived with the groom's father. This pattern of residence after marriage reinforced the patrilineal system of descent. Mieke Bal believes that the topic of residence for women after marriage is relevant for understanding Judges 9. She argues that

Judges points to a time in Israelite history when residence patterns were shifting from the bride's living with her father to the bride's moving away to live with the groom's family. Bal contends that at an early stage in Israelite history *pilegesh* referred to a woman who continued to live with her father after her marriage, but that later on *pilegesh* meant a woman who lived with her husband's family. To argue that the word refers to residence patterns after marriage rather than to sociolegal status[17] is to ignore cross-cultural data on polygyny that indicates that no one residence pattern is normative in this type of marriage.

In the situation of polygyny, different patterns of residence for a man's wives may be understood in economic terms. A wealthier man can support wives in separate homes, while a less wealthy individual often takes a secondary wife who lives under the same roof as his primary wife, in order that he may benefit from their combined economic contribution to his income. The distinction between a woman living with her father after marriage and living with her husband's father is less a function of historical change or feminist ideology on autonomy for women, and more closely related to economic matters. Moreover, even in the case of polygamous wives dwelling in the same household, occasions such as arguments between the women or between the husband and the wife may result in a woman's returning to her father's home as a strategy for obtaining her wishes. She disrupts her husband's household in order to get his attention and to convince him of the validity of her request. Again, the basis for the entire marriage and residence arrangement is economic.

One cannot generalize about residence patterns in Judges 9 based solely on historical periods. In any historical time frame there will always be a variety of living arrangements that can be explained through economic circumstances. In contemporary Western society, there are cases where newlyweds move in with either the bride's or the groom's family owing to lack of financial resources or a housing shortage, even though we may consider it more typical, and more desirable, for the couple to start their life together in their own apartment or home.

Repeated usage of kinship terms serves to emphasize that issues of social organization through kinship structure hold the key to the problems plaguing Abimelech's attempt to govern. Abimelech uses these kinship ties to gain something from the Shechemites, something which they later do not want him to have. Abimelech retaliates for this disloyalty by killing them. Kinship through his mother originally provides him with the power base needed to assume control, yet ultimately his actions are understood as an abuse of the kinship system, that is, he acts with power but without legitimate authority. This is not the case in Judges 8:19, where Gideon avenges the death of his brothers through his

17. Bal, *Death and Dissymmetry*, 89.

mother—his maternal kinship line—by the hands of Zebah and Zalmunna, Midianite kings.

In the case of Abimelech, the killing of his seventy half-brothers compensates for Abimelech's biological origin through a secondary wife of Gideon, and establishes him as the social descendant of his father, that is, as one entitled—in his own mind, anyway—to assume leadership upon the death of his father. If such an interpretation is correct, Abimelech bases his power on kinship through both his mother's descendants and his father's kinship line. He murders his paternal brothers because they are the only ones who could legitimately oppose his right to rule; if they were no threat to him, their murder would be impossible to understand. Thus, although connected to each other, these men are distinguished from each other. Moreover, Abimelech says to the Shechemites, it is better for me than for the seventy sons of Gideon to rule over you. Thus one explanation for the events in the text rests upon the sociological distinction between power and authority. Power depends on might, while authority is determined by legitimate rights. Abimelech demonstrates his power and subsequently the Shechemites give him the authority to rule.

What rewards does this loyalty to Abimelech and his kin bring to the Shechemites? A shift in perspective to economic matters may help us understand what is going on here and will allow us to answer questions such as the following: What social realities lie behind Gaal's comment that the Shechemites no longer look with favor upon Abimelech? What are the Shechemite men doing to the passersby in the hill country that is detrimental to Abimelech, and how does their behavior help explain Abimelech's initial motives for demanding authority in the area? What is Zebul receiving from Abimelech as head of the city—and what is he giving back in return—that explains why he does not join the rebel forces of Gaal? Why are other cities in the area surrounding Shechem uninterested in the leadership provided by Abimelech—that is, what is the cost to them of such leadership?

To answer these questions, let us consider the following reconstruction of events. The Shechemites were in league with and conducted caravaning trade with the Midianites, who were exploiting them. Possibly the Midianites were also exploiting Gideon with the aid of the Shechemites. Thus the hierarchy from the top down would be Midianites, Shechemites, and Gideonites. Gideon succeeds in ridding the people of the Midianites, leaving the Shechemites to ambush people and caravans again as they travel through the hill country. The return of Shechemite dominance would bring on the enmity of Abimelech, who may have been attempting to place himself in the role formerly held by the Midianites. Abimelech may have expected a share of this caravan booty as a result of being proclaimed leader of the Shechemites, and failure on the part of the Shechemites to pay up could have brought retaliation against them. Zebul may have been Abimelech's paid informant or official, placed over the Shechemites to see that they paid their share of booty to Abimelech. As Abimelech's paid official, Zebul's loyalty would be to him, and so Zebul reported the Shechemite's planned insurrection.

We may even speculate that individuals travelling in the hill country were killed by Gaal and his men. Notice the patriotic tone of Gaal's speech explaining why the Shechemites should not follow Abimelech: "We are strong men who have a long history and are superior to him" (9:28). So earlier, while Gideon was alive, the Midianites were the foes against which the allies Shechem and Israel united; in the time of Abimelech, with the Midianites out of the picture, the former allies became enemies. What the Midianites had earlier attempted to do—control, tax, raid, and kill hill country travellers or traders—Israel now attempts to do. Since the Shechemites initially agreed to take Abimelech's side against his seventy half-brothers, it is reasonable to assume that more lies behind this choice than simple kinship loyalties and that the decision must have been sweetened with the promise of economic gain.

It appears that Gideon's seventy sons exercised some power within the region of Shechem, based on heredity through their father. However, Abimelech's right to rule stems not from his place in his father's lineage. Abimelech ultimately seizes the throne in Shechem as a result of the intervention on his behalf by his mother's kinsmen with the notables of the area. It appears that the latter, who should probably be considered the equivalent of the local ruling assembly, have the authority to designate Abimelech as their leader.[18] Thus, Abimelech manipulates the norm regarding legitimate kinship, resulting in an impact upon social organization.

We may understand Gaal as the leader of a group of mercenaries hired by the Shechemite assembly to organize resistance to Abimelech.[19] Once these rebels are defeated, Abimelech moves on to murder other resisters. Even if Abimelech had survived the attack against Thebez, for all intents and purposes his attempt to establish himself as king through an illegitimate manipulation of the kinship system fails. Leadership could no longer remain in his hands. Events would come to no good for him. He could only continue to murder all those who opposed him and wanted to overthrow him.

Yet another dimension of social organization that social scientific study may shed light on concerns types of leadership. The situation is the same as that of

18. J. Alberto Soggin, *Judges,* Old Testament Library series (Philadelphia: Westminster Press, 1979), 169–70.

19. Soggin, *Judges,* 185.

kinship: study of words alone cannot tell us enough about the social location of these words in ancient Israel. We must guide our analysis with the theoretical perspectives provided by cross-cultural study. The text reports that Abimelech ruled for three years as *sar.* In addition to this word for leadership, one must remember that other words for leadership are included in the text: *mālak, māshal.* Although these words may be synonyms for each other, scholars believe that each of these words represents a different concept of rulership from different historical times.

The interconnection between leadership and kinship guarantees that "stability of the social system depends on the lineage's being able to curb its natural tendency toward disunity."[20] In other words, lineage support brings stability to the social structure, while a breakdown in lineage support leads to disorder and even chaos in social organization. Kinship is a means of organizing social structure based on the emphasis of a particular relationship between individuals, especially in contexts where there is economic gain, or property, involved.

The final editing of the text within the Deuteronomistic History, which is designed to explain that the Babylonian exile was inevitable given Israel's disobedience to Yahweh's will from the beginning of its existence, places the blame for the events in Judges 9 on Abimelech's attempt to seize what should be divine initiative. Scholars believe that Jotham's parable derives from this late editing and that it reflects this theological perspective. The parable has been inserted as a means to assist the reader in interpreting the events surrounding Abimelech as reflecting the abuse of the monarchy and human leadership. The parable speaks of the bramble's offering something that sounds attractive and advantageous to the other trees, but which the bramble is actually unprepared to give.[21] Once we move beyond this editing framework, which explains events as being caused by an evil spirit sent from Yahweh (9:23), and consider the events from the perspectives provided by the social sciences, the dynamics of the text can be explained based on the kinship system which appears to be the basis for social organization in ancient Israel. As we have seen, the text illustrates not the ideal on kinship but serves as an example—a warning—of what can happen when an individual wrongfully manipulates the social structure to his personal advantage.

In conclusion, the events recounted in Judges 9 provide a sociology of culture; they inform us about how the breakdown in legitimate kinship organization ultimately results in the abolition of leadership at Shechem. This information is embedded within a narrative that was revised to conform to a new

20. Wilson, *Sociological Approaches to the Old Testament,* 42.
21. Soggin, *Judges,* 173–79.

historical context which understands that leadership is grounded in God, and that any violation of this pattern leads to disaster.[22]

Further Reading

BIRD, Phyllis A. "Israelite Religion and the Faith of Israel's Daughters: Reflections on Gender and Religious Definition." *The Bible and the Politics of Exegesis.* Edited by David Jobling, Peggy L. Day, and Gerald T. Sheppard, 97–108. Cleveland: Pilgrim Press, 1991. Addresses questions about how we may come to understand the religious faith of women in ancient Israel.

CLEMENTS, Ronald, ed. *The World of Ancient Israel: Sociological, Anthropological, and Political Perspectives.* Cambridge: Cambridge University Press, 1989. Contributors investigate diverse aspects of life in ancient Israel.

FLANAGAN, James W. *David's Social Drama: A Hologram of Israel's Iron Age.* Social World of Biblical Antiquity Series, no. 7. Sheffield, Eng.: Almond Press, 1988. Based on comparative sociological data, this study reconstructs the time of David and his emergence as king.

FRICK, Frank S. *The City in Ancient Israel.* Society of Biblical Literature Dissertation Series, no. 36. Missoula, Mont.: Scholars Press, 1977. A study of the role of the city in the social world of ancient Israel.

GOTTWALD, Norman K. *The Hebrew Bible: A Socio-Literary Introduction.* Philadelphia: Fortress Press, 1985. An introductory textbook aimed at explaining both literary and social scientific perspectives on the biblical text.

———. *The Anchor Bible Dictionary,* vol. 6, s. v. "Sociology (Ancient Israel)," 79–89. A survey of the results of using social scientific approaches to study the history of ancient Israel.

HACKETT, Jo Ann. "In the Days of Jael: Reclaiming the History of Women in Ancient Israel." *Immaculate and Powerful: The Female in Sacred Image and Social Reality.* Edited by Clarissa W. Atkinson, Constance H. Buchanan, and Margaret R. Miles, 15–38. Boston: Beacon Press, 1985. Contains a discussion of women's social and religious history in the time of the Judges and how the decentralization of political power at the time worked to give women more power than they previously had held.

LEMCHE, Niels Peter. *Early Israel: Anthropological and Historical Studies on the Israelite Society before the Monarchy.* Vetus Testamentum Supplements 37. Leiden: E. J. Brill, 1985. A highly detailed investigation of ancient Israel before the time of King David.

22. It is possible that the kinship link between Gideon and Abimelech is an editing device used by the Deutronomist to connect what were originally separate stories.

MEYERS, Carol. *Discovering Eve: Ancient Israelite Women in Context.* New York: Oxford University Press, 1988. Recovers data on the lives of women in early Israel after demonstrating that the biblical texts and their interpretations are male-centered and cannot be taken at face value.

OVERHOLT, Thomas. *Channels of Prophecy: The Social Dynamics of Prophetic Activity.* Minneapolis: Fortress Press, 1989. Examines the social processes that enabled biblical prophets to carry on their work.

PETERSEN, David L. "The Social World of the Old Testament." *The Oxford Study Edition of the Revised English Bible.* Edited by J. Suggs et al., 68–78. New York: Oxford University Press, 1992. An introduction to social structure in ancient Israel and to the place of religion within this structure.

SMITH, Daniel L. *The Religion of the Landless: The Social Context of the Babylonian Exile.* Bloomington, Ind.: Meyer-Stone Books, 1989. Based on social analysis of oppressed groups removed from their land in the contemporary world, this work provides models of how Jews adapted to life after they were removed from Israel by the Babylonians in 587 B.C.E.

STAGER, Lawrence. "The Archaeology of the Family in Ancient Israel." *Bulletin of the American Schools of Oriental Research* 260 (1985), 1–35. Uses archaeological data to reconstruct family life in premonarchical Israel.

STEINBERG, Naomi. *Kinship and Marriage in Genesis: A Household Economics Perspective.* Minneapolis: Fortress Press, 1993. An analysis of Genesis 12–50 from the perspective of cross-cultural patterns of kinship and marriage.

WILSON, Robert R. *Sociological Approaches to the Old Testament.* Philadelphia: Fortress Press, 1984. A critical introduction to how the social sciences can inform contemporary study of the Hebrew Bible.

4

FEMINIST CRITICISM: WHOSE INTERESTS ARE BEING SERVED?

J. Cheryl Exum

Feminist criticism takes many forms. By nature, it tends to be interdisciplinary, for it regards disciplinary boundaries as artificial and confining, and it resists the limitations that the use of any single methodology imposes on interpretation. The starting point of feminist criticism of the Bible is not the biblical texts in their own right but the concerns of feminism as a worldview and as a political enterprise. Recognizing that in the history of civilization women have been marginalized by men and denied access to positions of authority and influence, feminist criticism seeks to expose the strategies by which men have justified their control over women. And because women's cooperation in this state of affairs is necessary, to varying degrees, feminist criticism also seeks to understand women's complicity in their own subordination: What factors have encouraged women to accept a subordinate position, and how have women both adapted to and resisted the constraints of a world where men are in charge?

Some feminist critics have taken a historical approach to these issues. As Gerda Lerner observes, to understand women's subordination as the result of historical processes and not as something "natural" is to recognize that it can be ended by historical process.[1] She points out that in the building of civilization and in the preservation and transmission of culture from one generation to the next, women have shared equally with men. Yet women's contributions and concerns do not receive equal treatment in the historical record, for, until recently, the writers of history have been men, and men have recorded only

Throughout this essay, translations from the Hebrew are mine; in most cases, they are close to the NRSV.

1. Gerda Lerner, *The Creation of Patriarchy* (New York: Oxford University Press, 1986), 6.

those events they considered important and have interpreted them from their point of view. Moreover, women have been excluded not only from the historical record but also from the vital process of interpreting that record, the process of assigning meaning to the past. History, so the saying goes, is told by the winners, and increasingly in modern times groups whose experiences have been suppressed are laying claim to their own version of the story; in the United States, the African-American experience is a prime example. But whereas class or race or ethnicity has been responsible for the exclusion of various groups from the historical record, men have never been excluded simply because they were men. Only women have been excluded because of their sex.[2]

Lerner responds to this situation by attempting to document the creation of patriarchy and its subordination of women from earliest times, treating the biblical period as a stage in this complex process. She defines "patriarchy" as the institutionalization of male dominance over women and children in the family and, by extension, in society in general. In this chapter, I will be using the term "patriarchy" to refer both to a social system and to an ideology in which women are subordinated to men.

Though only one stage in the process by which men have established hegemony over women, the biblical period represents an important stage, for perhaps no other document has been so instrumental as the Bible in shaping Western culture and in influencing ideas about the place of women and about the relationship of the sexes. Indeed, because its influence has been so extensive and because it continues to play an important role for many people, women and men, the Bible needs to be approached from a critical feminist perspective.

It is fairly obvious that the Bible is about men, and that the biblical writers are not particularly interested in women and their experiences. When they appear in the biblical material, women almost always are in a subordinate role, usually as someone's wife or mother or daughter—for socially women were under the authority of their fathers before marriage and of their husbands after marriage. Their "stories," such as they are, are recounted in fragments, as snatches of the larger stories of men. Even the books that bear women's names are not necessarily concerned with women's experiences. There are, of course, exceptions, as there have always been exceptions: the extraordinary woman whose achievements receive recognition in a man's world (usually those achievements are in male-identified, and thus positively valued roles). Deborah, in the book of Judges, is an example of the exceptional famous woman— prophet, judge, and military leader—and we shall look at her "story" below.

If the Bible is so obviously about men, what about its authors and its in-

2. Lerner, *Creation of Patriarchy*, 4–5.

tended audience? It is reasonable to assume that the Bible was produced by and for men. Perhaps women were responsible for some of the traditions that found their way into the biblical story; possibly they sang some of the songs recorded in the Bible, or told some of the stories to their sons, who later wrote them down.[3] But even if the Bible's authors were not all male, it is the male worldview that finds expression in the biblical literature, for, as the dominant worldview of the time, it was shared by men and women alike.

It is also the case that, in the long history of biblical interpretation, men have traditionally set the agenda for interpreting the Bible. They pursued formal study of the Bible, and they decided what sorts of questions should be addressed to the text and what sort of answers were "legitimate."[4] This is not to deny women's engagement with the Bible; I am speaking here not of individual use of the Bible but about public use and the institutions — such as the academy, the synagogue, or the church — that "authorize" interpretation. Only recently have women been in positions to challenge established doctrines and to influence the course of biblical interpretation.

Given this state of affairs, it is easy to see why feminist criticism of the Bible does not take the biblical text itself as its starting point. If the Bible presents us with men's views of women — what men thought women were like, or what they wished them to be — the feminist critic must ask how, if at all, a woman's perspective can be discovered in, or read into, this androcentric literature. As long as we remain within the androcentric ideology of the biblical text — that is, as long as we accept the male-centered worldview that is inscribed in the biblical literature — we can do no more than describe ancient men's views of women. Many feminist critics thus find it necessary to step outside the ideology of the biblical texts and raise questions not simply about what the text says about women but also about what it does not say — questions about its underlying assumptions about gender roles (the roles society assigns to men and

3. On the issue of female authorship, see S. D. Goiten, "Women as Creators of Biblical Genres," *Prooftexts* 8 (1988), 1–33; Athalya Brenner and Fokkelien van Dijk-Hemmes, *On Gendering Texts: Female and Male Voices in the Hebrew Bible,* Biblical Interpretation Series 1 (Leiden: E. J. Brill, 1993).

4. The question of legitimacy in interpretation could be considered androcentric. As Jonathan Culler notes, in the literary criticism of a patriarchal culture one might expect to find "that there would be a great concern about which meanings were legitimate and which illegitimate (since the paternal author's role in the generation of meanings can only be inferred); and that criticism would expend great efforts to develop principles for, on the one hand, determining which meanings were truly the author's own progeny, and on the other hand, controlling intercourse with texts so as to prevent the proliferation of illegitimate interpretations." See Jonathan Culler, *On Deconstruction: Theory and Criticism after Structuralism* (London: Routledge & Kegan Paul, 1982), 61.

women on the basis of their sex),[5] about its motivation for portraying women in a particular way, about what it conceals and unintentionally reveals about the fact of women's suppression.

In approaching the Bible on their terms rather than on its terms, feminist biblical scholars have tended to look either to anthropology and sociology or to literary criticism for their methodological point of departure. Some use anthropological and sociological models to reconstruct the lives of ordinary women in ancient times,[6] or to investigate sources of power available to women and factors that influenced the status of women in Israelite society, such as class or urbanization.[7] Much can be learned about women's lives in biblical times by examining kinship patterns and the role played by women in the family,[8] or by inquiring into the particularities of women's religious experience.[9] Other feminist biblical critics employ a literary approach to expose strategies by which women's subordination is inscribed in and justified by texts.[10] One often hears of reading against the grain or reading for difference. Subversive readings or counterreadings can be produced by using the clues most authors provide (even if unconsciously) to alternative ways of reading the stories they narrate.

5. "Gender" refers to the cultural definition of behavior considered to be appropriate to the sexes in a given society at a given time (Lerner, *Creation of Patriarchy*, 238). In contrast to sex, which is a biological given, gender is culturally created.

6. Carol Meyers, *Discovering Eve: Ancient Israelite Women in Context* (New York: Oxford University Press, 1988).

7. Jo Ann Hackett, "In the Days of Jael: Reclaiming the History of Women in Ancient Israel," *Immaculate and Powerful: The Female in Sacred Image and Social Reality,* ed. Clarissa W. Atkinson, Constance H. Buchanan, and Margaret R. Miles (Boston: Beacon Press, 1985), 15–38; idem, "1 and 2 Samuel," *The Women's Bible Commentary,* ed. Carol A. Newsom and Sharon H. Ringe (Louisville, Ky.: Westminster/John Knox Press, 1992), 85–95.

8. Naomi Steinberg, *Kinship and Marriage in Genesis: A Household Economics Approach* (Minneapolis: Fortress Press, 1993).

9. Phyllis Bird, "The Place of Women in the Israelite Cultus," *Ancient Israelite Religion: Essays in Honor of Frank Moore Cross,* ed. Patrick D. Miller, Jr., Paul D. Hanson, and S. Dean McBride (Philadelphia: Fortress Press, 1987), 397–419; idem, "Israelite Religion and the Faith of Israel's Daughters: Reflections on Gender and Religious Definition," *The Bible and the Politics of Exegesis: Essays in Honor of Norman K. Gottwald on His Sixty-fifth Birthday,* ed. David Jobling, Peggy L. Day, and Gerald T. Sheppard (Cleveland: Pilgrim Press, 1991), 97–108, 311–17.

10. See, for example, Mieke Bal, *Death and Dissymmetry: The Politics of Coherence in the Book of Judges* (Chicago: University of Chicago Press, 1988); Carol A. Newsom, "Woman and the Discourse of Patriarchal Wisdom: A Study of Proverbs 1–9," *Gender and Difference in Ancient Israel,* ed. Peggy L. Day (Minneapolis: Fortress Press, 1989), 142–60; Alice Bach, "Breaking Free of the Biblical Frame-up: Uncovering the Woman in Genesis 39," in *A Feminist Companion to Genesis,* ed. Athalya Brenner (Sheffield, Eng.: JSOT Press, 1993), 318–42.

A feminist literary critic may choose to focus on women as characters, on women as readers, or on gender bias in interpretation (that is, how commentators read sexual stereotypes and their own gender biases into the biblical literature). By exposing male control of the production and interpretation of literature, feminist literary criticism attempts to subvert the hierarchy that has dominated not only readers but also culture itself. Since my own interest is primarily literary, I will be pursuing a literary approach here. It needs to be stressed, however, that these two major directions in feminist biblical criticism are interdependent, for texts construct social reality even as they are shaped by it. Thus anthropological and sociological approaches and literary critical approaches should be seen as complementary rather than as alternative ways of dealing with the biblical evidence.

Some Features of Feminist Literary Criticism

Feminist literary criticism is remarkably pluralistic and diverse. It not only recognizes the gains to be had from a variety of approaches; because it is suspicious of the notion that there is a "proper way" to read a text as an expression of male control of texts and male control of reading, it also encourages multiple, even contradictory, readings of the same text. Reading is not disinterested. Our interpretation of a text is the result of the kinds of questions we ask, and those questions are determined by our interests (acknowledged or not). It is a good idea, therefore, to ask of any interpretation: what reading strategy is being adopted and what kind of conclusions does it allow the interpreter to reach?

Among the questions feminist literary criticism might raise are:

- Is there a woman or a woman's point of view in this text? (The places where women do not appear in the text can be as significant as the places they do appear.)
- How are women portrayed in this text? Do they speak? Are we given access to their point of view?
- Who has the power in this text? How is power distributed? How do women get what they want (if they do)? And (Freud's famous question), what do women want?
- How does the text represent uniquely female experiences, such as childbearing, or traditionally female experiences, such as child rearing?
- How have women's lives and voices been suppressed by this text? Are women made to speak and act against their own interests?
- What hidden gender assumptions lie behind this text (for example, that women lead men astray, or that women cannot be trusted)?

One of the questions I have found most useful in my own work is: Whose interests are being served? I view women in the biblical literature as male constructs — that is to say, they are the creations of androcentric (probably male) narrators, they reflect androcentric ideas about women, and they serve androcentric interests. Since in androcentric texts like the Bible women often speak and act against their own interests, a strategic question to ask is: What androcentric agenda does this text promote? Does it, for example, function to keep women in their place, under the control of men? Does it show male control of women as something necessary for society to function smoothly, or as something women desire? What buried and encoded messages does this text give to women? Consider an example from the realm of fairy tales: the story of Sleeping Beauty. This tale does not encourage women to take control of their own lives. It recommends passivity — waiting patiently for the day your Prince Charming will come and bring happiness into your life. Marrying a socially superior man is a means to attain a higher social status. He will fulfill your dreams and provide for all your needs. For generations, women internalized the buried and encoded gender message of this tale and made their life choices in anticipation of marrying their hero and living happily ever after. Men, too, are given a subtextual message: they are expected (and the expectations are projected onto women) to fill the shoes of the hero who can offer his passive dream girl a new and better life. And, of course, she should be beautiful and he should be rich.

A Feminist Approach to Judges

It is generally agreed that Judges is a collection of stories that are only loosely connected to one another (see chapter 1). For the main part, the book presents a series of self-contained stories about individual deliverers (Othniel, Ehud, Deborah, Gideon, Jephthah, Samson) as well as about a few unsavory characters (Abimelech, Micah, the unnamed Levite of chaps. 19–21). Taking our cue from the structure of the Book of Judges itself, we can focus on the individual stories in which women play a role and consider in each case what androcentric interests these stories promote. As in the case of Sleeping Beauty, we shall look for the implicit messages these stories convey about gender roles and expectations. Since in what follows I will be more concerned with the messages given to women than with those given to men, I will focus on the stories in which women figure prominently: Deborah and Jael (Judg 4, 5); Jephthah's daughter (11); Samson's mother, his Timnite wife, and Delilah (13–16); and the nameless woman of Judges 19.

Deborah/Jael (Judges 4–5)

This story, in which a male warrior is eclipsed by a woman (warrior), provides a good opportunity both to explore constructions of masculinity and to observe the way male ideology co-opts a woman's voice. Interpretations of this text influenced by its political ideology approve the "heroes," those on the "right" side—Deborah, Barak, the Israelite troops, and Jael (even though they have difficulty condoning Jael's way of contributing to Israelite victory)—and criticize those on the "wrong" side—the Canaanites, Sisera, and Sisera's mother. Since the gender code operates independently of the question of who is on which side or which side is the "right" side, we shall read this story not in terms of the Israelites-versus-Canaanites dichotomy but rather with a view toward clarifying the gender positions occupied by the characters. In terms of the roles they play in this story, what do the men have in common and what do the women have in common?

What is expected of a man? Not just in these chapters but in Judges as a whole, men are warriors; they are expected to fight and to be brave. We find this ideology succinctly presented at the beginning of Judges in the paradigm story of the model judge, Othniel (Judg 3:7-11), and in one way or another it informs the way the other judges are presented. Othniel is inspired by God, he judges Israel, he goes to war, he is victorious, and he brings security to the land. Like Othniel, Barak and Sisera are leaders of men, generals who rally their troops to battle. Sisera commands "nine hundred chariots of iron, and all the men who were with him, from Harosheth-ha-goiim to the river Kishon" (4:13), and Barak has ten thousand men (4:14) "at his heels" (5:15). In the male ideology of war, the winner destroys his enemies until none are left (as 4:16 has it), or he leads away captives humiliated in defeat (so 5:12). For all their military might, however, both Sisera and Barak fall short of what is expected of a hero-warrior. Barak is hesitant; he refuses to go to war unless Deborah goes with him. His reluctance is implicitly reprimanded when Deborah replies that she will go but he will not get the glory. Men fight for glory, for acclaim, and to have their valor praised in victory song (like the *Iliad,* or the Song of Deborah, for instance). But (so this song implies) because Barak behaved in a womanly way, showing uncertainty (cowardice?), he will suffer an insult to his male pride: a woman will snatch his glory from him (4:9).[11] Similarly, Sisera fails to

---

11. Compare Meir Sternberg's comment (*The Poetics of Biblical Narrative: Ideological Literature and the Drama of Reading* [Bloomington, Ind.: Indiana University Press, 1985], 274): "Of the two leaders, it is he who plays the woman; and having been summoned to do a man's job, he refuses to act unless the woman who delegated it to him

be genuinely heroic, for surely fleeing the battle scene on foot rather than fighting to the end with his army is an unmanly way to behave.

Who is Barak? What image stands behind his portrayal? In his dependence on Deborah, he seems almost childlike. He is the little boy who still needs his mother—Deborah, the "mother in Israel" (5:7). Without her, he won't fight: "If you will go with me, I will go, but if you will not go with me, I will not go" (4:8). Sisera, too, resembles a frightened little boy, seeking the security his mother provides. He won't fight either, once the odds are against him, so he runs away. He finds refuge with a woman who, for all appearances, is a nurturing mother, but who turns out to be a cunning assassin.

If the men in this story are in the symbolic position of little boys, the women are their mothers. Deborah is the good mother. Before she "arose as a mother in Israel" (5:7), conditions were wretched. Deborah delivers her children from danger and makes their lives secure. She is the life-giving mother. Jael, on the other hand, is the death-dealing mother. Her behavior is maternal: she offers Sisera security ("turn aside to me") and assurance ("have no fear," 4:18). The picture of Jael covering Sisera and giving him milk to drink suggests a mother putting her son to bed. She even watches over him while he sleeps to protect him from harm ("Stand at the door of the tent, and if any man comes and asks you, 'Is anyone here?' say, 'No,'" 4:20). But the nurturing, protective mother can suddenly, unexpectedly, turn deadly. The bad mother is cold and bloodthirsty. She may attack her son in his sleep, when he is utterly defenseless (4:21). Or she may turn on him in the essential motherly act of feeding him (5:25-27). The differing descriptions of Jael's assassination of the unsuspecting Sisera in Judges 4 and 5 are different expressions of anxiety about the mother's threatening side.

According to much psychoanalytic theory, the mother's body is the source of desire and fear, of love and hate. The nurturing mother offers security and protection. But the mother is also a source of anxiety and frustration, because she may deny her body to the infant. Or the child may feel smothered by her. Her presence may be perceived as overwhelming, threatening the child's identity and making the child's differentiation from the mother difficult. Anxiety over this duality in the mother gives rise to a fundamental ambivalence toward her. The text projects its anxieties onto the women, who are all mother figures.

The dangerous mother and the nurturing mother are one and the same (thus my title "Deborah/Jael" for this section, not "Deborah and Jael"). Although at first glance it may seem that the text separates the two aspects of the mother, making Deborah the good mother and Jael the sinister one, actually it demon-

---

comes along to give him moral courage." The same ideology is found in the story of Abimelech, who dies dishonorably because he is felled by a woman's hand (Judg 9:54).

strates that it is not possible to experience only one side of the mother and not the other. Jael is both nurturing and deadly. Deborah not only gives life to Israel but also sends her "sons" off to war, where many of them will die. Moreover, as Sisera shows, you can never be sure when the good mother may turn into the bad mother.

The infant's desire for the mother's body has a sexual aspect, which explains the mixture of erotic imagery and maternal imagery in the account of Sisera's encounter with Jael. Jael invites Sisera into her tent, much as the "strange" woman of Proverbs invites the young man to "turn aside" to her. While he sleeps there, she "comes to him," an expression often used of sexual intercourse. He bends over between her legs, falls and lies there. The verb "to lie" can also refer to sexual intercourse. Mieke Bal observes that the entire scene can be read as a reversed rape.[12] Danna Fewell and David Gunn's reading of Judges 5:6 produces the even more graphic image of the woman approaching the man and thrusting a phallic tent peg into his mouth:

> She reached out her hand to the tent peg,
>   her right hand to the workman's hammer;
> She hammered Sisera,
>   she smashed his head,
>   she pierced and struck through his mouth.[13]

That the erotic imagery does not extend to Deborah may reflect patriarchy's attempt to deny the mother's sexuality, especially in the case of the good mother. The good mother is not a sexual mother, as we shall see in the case of Samson's mother.

There is another mother in the story, Sisera's mother (Judg 5:28-30). She is anxious about her son's well-being, but she cannot protect him. She so desperately desires his success that she tries to convince herself of it by imagining that his delay is caused by taking and dividing the spoils of battle.

> Are they not finding and dividing the spoil?
> A female, two females for every hero;

---

12. Mieke Bal, *Murder and Difference: Gender, Genre, and Scholarship on Sisera's Death* (Bloomington, Ind.: Indiana University Press, 1988), 134; similarly, Robert Alter, *The Art of Biblical Poetry* (New York: Basic Books, 1985), 49; Danna Nolan Fewell and David M. Gunn, "Controlling Perspectives: Women, Men, and the Authority of Violence in Judges 4 and 5," *Journal of the American Academy of Religion* 58 (1990): 394.

13. Fewell and Gunn, "Controlling Perspectives," 403; for their argument, see pp. 393–94 and n. 11.

> spoil of dyed stuff for Sisera,
> spoil of dyed stuff,
> dyed embroidery, two embroideries for my neck
>   as spoil?

(Judg 5:30)

This mother serves as the mouthpiece for the male ideology of war, in which pillage and rape go together. To the victor belong the spoils: the victorious men get to rape the defeated enemy's women, and the victorious men's women get the defeated enemy's finery. The androcentric narrator who places these words in the mouths of Sisera's mother and her female attendants thus suggests that men go to war to plunder for the sake of their women, and that this is something women want ("two embroideries for my neck as spoil").[14] He also has a mother endorse the rampant rape of other women and their daughters—the Hebrew reads, "a womb or two for every hero."

As Fewell and Gunn recognize, placing these words in the Canaanite women's mouths puts them in the position of approving their own imminent rape.[15] (According to Judges 4:16, all the men in Sisera's army are killed, so the captives led away in 5:12 are women and children.) The narrator who puts words in the Canaanite women's mouths puts their words in Deborah's mouth. The result is a victory song in which Deborah, a woman, a mother in Israel, sings about another woman, Sisera's mother, who sings (this is a poetic text) about women being raped in war. By means of this song within a song, not only Sisera's mother's voice but also that of the good mother, Deborah, is appropriated to advocate the male ideology of war in which rape is taken for granted as a weapon of terror and revenge. This is not Canaanite ideology; it is male ideology.

If one wished to argue that the narrator is using Sisera's mother's speech to condemn rape, one would have to say he is also condemning plunder, and thus condemning war. Israel's mission, however, is to dispossess and despoil the Canaanites, and this is what the Song of Deborah and the Book of Judges are about. There is no reason to expect the Israelite victors to treat the defeated men's women any better than their Canaanite counterparts are pictured as doing. Indeed, Israelite men took women prisoners for their sexual use, as we

---

14. The obscurity of Judges 5:30 limits our ability to interpret it precisely. If translated "for the necks of the spoiler," then the victorious men get the finery and the women. It is a moot point, however, since the women on the winner's side will share the booty.

15. Fewell and Gunn, "Controlling Perspectives," 408.

know from the law in Deuteronomy 21:10-14. This law attempts to place restrictions on male behavior toward female captives, but does not deal with women who were raped on the spot and abandoned or killed.

It is true, I think, as Fewell and Gunn observe, that we lose sympathy with the Canaanite women when they callously imagine the rape of innocent women. Should we not also lose sympathy with Deborah, who imagines Sisera's mother and her attendants imagining the rape of innocent women? And should we not hold the narrator accountable, who, in the interests of his ideology, exploits women's voices to accept rapists who exploit women's bodies?

Bat-jiftah (Judges 11)

Jephthah's daughter is one of many anonymous female characters in Judges. One way to restore her to the subject position she is denied in the story is to give her a name. Mieke Bal calls her "Bath," which in Hebrew means "daughter," to remind us of the role that defines her: she is bath-Jephthah, "the daughter of Jephthah."[16] Following Bal's lead, but using the fuller form of the name, I call her Bat-jiftah (Bat-jiftah is a closer approximation to the Hebrew than Bath-Jephthah and is easier to pronounce).

Bat-jiftah's story is shocking. She is offered by her father as a human sacrifice to God in fulfillment of a vow. Incredibly, she makes no protest; she accepts the fate to which her father's vow consigns her with alarming composure. What is more, God does nothing to stop the sacrifice. There is no divine staying of the father's hand and provision of a ram as a substitute for the child, as was the case when Abraham was prepared to sacrifice his son Isaac (Gen 22). There is no narratorial condemnation of the sacrifice either, no "Now the thing that Jephthah had done was evil in the sight of the LORD," such as we find in the framework of Judges.[17] All these features make for a strange and disturbing story.

We do not know who or what Jephthah has in mind when, in return for victory, he vows to sacrifice to God "the one coming forth who comes forth from the doors of my house to meet me, when I return in peace from the Ammonites" (Judg 11:31). But his reaction (v. 35) indicates that he did not expect to be met by his daughter. First he rends his garments in an act of mourning. Then he speaks, displacing the blame onto the victim in an effort to express his sense of not being solely responsible for this horrible outcome: "Ah, my daugh-

16. Bal, *Death and Dissymmetry*, 43.

17. This kind of narrative judgment occurs elsewhere within the individual stories in Judges; for example, Gideon (8:27), Abimelech (9:56–57). Compare 2 Sam. 11:27.

ter, *you* have brought me very low and *you* have become the source of my trouble."[18]

The narrator does not tell us how Bat-jiftah knows or surmises the terms of her father's vow. She simply responds to Jephthah's speech with a speech of her own, in which she surrenders her volition, submitting to the authority of the father: "My father, you have opened your mouth to the LORD; do to me according to what has gone forth from your mouth, now that the LORD has granted you vindication against your enemies, the Ammonites" (v. 36). Notice how the narrator has the young woman speak against her own interests here. She neither questions the man who has consigned her to death nor blames him for her misfortune. Like her father, she accepts the vow as irrevocable and unalterable.[19] In encouraging her father to fulfill his vow, she subordinates her life to her community importance, accepting her role as sacrificial victim so that the sacrifice might be performed. The seriousness of the vow is thus upheld, the sacrifice promised to the deity is performed, and paternal authority goes unchallenged.

The paternal word is not to be countermanded but simply postponed: Bat-jiftah asks only for a two-month reprieve before the vow is carried out—a period of time that she will spend in the mountains with her companions. According to most translations of v. 37, the young woman goes away to "bewail my virginity," but the meaning of the phrase is far from clear. The word translated "virginity" does not indicate a physical state but rather the point of transition from child to marriageable young woman. It may refer to some type of puberty rite that signifies her physical maturity and readiness for marriage—some experience she wants to have before she dies. In other words, the issue for Bat-jiftah may be participation in this rite with her friends and not regret over never having experienced sexual intercourse.[20]

Virginity is, however, an issue for the androcentric narrator, who emphasizes Bat-jiftah's tragic plight in dying so young by adding that she died a virgin ("she had not known a man," v. 39). In the androcentric economy, bearing

18. I see this as the narrator's way of displacing the blame from God onto the woman. Jephthah's vow was, after all, made under ambiguous circumstances (is he not under the influence of the spirit of the Lord when he makes it?) and in ignorance of its outcome. For fuller discussion of this problematic aspect of the story, see J. Cheryl Exum, *Tragedy and Biblical Narrative: Arrows of the Almighty* (Cambridge: Cambridge University Press, 1992), 45–69.

19. The story assumes the inviolability of Jephthah's vow, whereas Leviticus 27:1–8 stipulates monetary payment by which a person vowed to God could be released.

20. This is Bal's argument; see Mieke Bal, *Death and Dissymmetry,* chaps. 2, 4, and 5; see also Peggy L. Day, "From the Child Is Born the Woman: The Story of Jephthah's Daughter," in *Gender and Difference in Ancient Israel,* 58–74.

children was a woman's most important function and the thing for which she was most valued. To die without offspring meant to die unfulfilled and incomplete. But the unnamed daughter who leaves behind no children as a legacy is not forgotten. Her memory is kept alive by the ritual remembrance of women. Because she does not protest her fate, Bat-jiftah poses no threat to patriarchal authority. And because she voluntarily performs a daughter's duty, her memory may be preserved. The narrator rewards her for her submission to the paternal word by memorializing her in a yearly ritual: "It became a custom in Israel that the daughters of Israel went year by year to commemorate Jephthah the Gileadite's daughter, four days each year" (Judg 11:39-40). Patriarchal ideology here co-opts a woman's ceremony in order to glorify the victim. The encoded message this story gives to women is: submit to paternal authority. You may have to sacrifice your autonomy; you may lose your life, and even your name, but your sacrifice will be remembered, even celebrated, for generations to come. In my opinion, we find here the main reason Jephthah's daughter's name is not preserved: because she is memorialized not for herself but *as a daughter.* The phrase translated above, "it became a custom in Israel," could also be translated, "she became an example in Israel" — a rendering that would further underscore Bat-jiftah's value to the patriarchal system as a model for proper, submissive female behavior.

The precise nature of the ritual held by the women of Israel in honor of Bat-jiftah is not clear. The rare word that the NRSV translates "to lament" in v. 40 occurs only one other time in the Bible. In Judges 5:11 it refers to recounting the victories of YHWH. This usage suggests that the women recite Bat-jiftah's story, and for this reason I translated it above as "to commemorate." Significantly, however, these other women are not actually permitted to speak in the narrative. They are there to remember, and their yearly ritual is used by the narrator to keep alive the memory of the victim.

If we allow the women's ceremonial remembrance to encourage glorification of the victim, we perpetuate the crime against Bat-jiftah. How, then, do we reject the concept of honoring the victim without also sacrificing the woman? Recognizing that the narrator uses the women of Israel to elevate the willing victim to honored status allows us to expose the text's valorization of submission and glorification of the victim as serving androcentric interests. Acknowledging the victim's complicity in the crime enables us to move beyond a simplistic view that sees Bat-jiftah as an innocent victim. She does not resist (which is to say, the narrator does not allow her to resist). She speaks on behalf of the sacrificial system and patriarchal authority, absolving it of responsibility.

Even as the narrator controls Bat-jiftah's words, however, imprisoning her within the confines of the patriarchal word, her speech bears traces of her attempts to assert herself.

She said to him, "My father, you have opened your mouth to the LORD; do to me according to what has gone forth from your mouth, now that the LORD has vindicated you against your enemies, the Ammonites." And she said to her father, "Let this thing be done for me, let me alone two months that I may go and wander upon the hills and bewail my nubility, I and my companions."

Whereas Jephthah shifts the blame to his daughter when he calls her the source of his trouble (v. 35), Bat-jiftah reminds him — and us — of his responsibility: "*You* have opened *your* mouth to the LORD; do to me according to what has gone forth from *your* mouth" (v. 36). More importantly, though she surrenders her volition in the first part of her speech, in the second part, her speech transports her to a point of solidarity with her female friends. Unlike her father, who faces this ordeal alone, she has companions with whom to share her distress (where are the Israelites who returned victorious from battle with Jephthah?). *Ra'yotay,* "my companions," is her last spoken word in the narrative; *'abi,* "my father," was her first. Symbolically, through speech, she journeys from the domain of the father who will quench her life to that of the female companions who will preserve her memory. This image is too powerful to be fully controlled by the narrator's androcentric interests. The androcentric text segregates women: the daughter spends two months with female companions, away from her father and the company of men; the ritual of remembrance is conducted by women alone. But the rite of passage, which Bat-jiftah observes with her friends, and the women's ceremony, in which Bat-jiftah is commemorated, transform female segregation into female solidarity.[21] By resisting the androcentric agenda that motivates this story, and by engaging in some feminist symbol-making of our own, we can redefine its images as images of female solidarity.

Samson's Women (Judges 13–16)

There are two kinds of women according to this story: the good (safe) woman and the bad (threatening) woman. The good woman is usually placed on a pedestal, as a mother or a virgin. She is idealized in her nonsexual role. The bad woman is defined by her sexuality: she is the sexually available, "wanton" (from the perspective of male ideology) woman, who arouses in men both desire and animosity (men blame *her* for *their* lust). This stereotype is still with us today. The distinction, like the double standard in which it finds expression, applies only to women; men are not judged respectable or disreputable on the

---

21. As Gerda Lerner (*Creation of Patriarchy,* 242) points out, when women "are confined by patriarchal restraint or segregation into separateness (which always has subordination as its purpose), they transform this restraint into complementarity and redefine it."

basis of their sexual behavior. Delilah is often referred to as a "loose woman" but no one calls Samson a "loose man."

Samson's mother belongs to the category of "good woman." The story highlights her role and underscores her virtues. For example, she receives more information from the divine messenger about the child's destiny than her husband: she alone is told that the boy's hair may not be cut, and she alone learns that he will be the first to deliver Israel from the Philistines (compare vv. 3-5 with v. 7 and vv. 13-14). In addition, she is more perceptive than Manoah: she senses something otherworldly about the visitor from the start (v. 6), whereas it takes a miracle for Manoah to recognize him (vv. 16, 21). Finally, she understands the divine intention better than Manoah (vv. 22-23).

But if she is more favorably portrayed than her husband, it is because she poses no threat. She does nothing on her own, which is a trait that patriarchy finds desirable in a woman. Unlike the Timnite and Delilah, who pry into Samson's secrets, she does not ask questions of the mysterious visitor: "I did not ask him from where he came, and he did not tell me his name" (13:6). In spite of the fact that the messenger appears to her on two different occasions when she is alone, she makes no attempt to engage him in conversation. Rather, both times she runs off to tell her husband, who will ask all the questions in this family. She may be more perceptive than her husband, but she does not challenge Manoah's position of authority. Significantly, we are not told the woman's view of her situation (does she long for a child?) or her circumstances (is her sterility a source of misery?) or even her name. (We don't even know if the news makes her happy, though some commentators are convinced that she is overjoyed.) By suppressing information about her, the narrator focuses our attention on her role as a mother. I suggested above that Jephthah's daughter's name is not preserved because she is remembered as a *daughter.* Similarly, this woman's name is not preserved because she is remembered as a *mother.* She, too, needs to be given a name in order to restore her to her full subject position. A rabbinic text calls her Hazzelelponi, and I shall borrow this name.[22]

To see how the positive portrayal of Hazzelelponi serves male interests, we need to interrogate the ideology that motivates it. Texts like this served as a means of social control. Thus we need to ask: What is it about this woman that would make women in ancient Israel want to be like her? What is it about the image of the *mother* that makes those responsible for maintaining the social and symbolic order want to manipulate it?

Patriarchy could not exist without women's cooperation. Force and fear are often relied upon to keep women in their place. But rewarding women for their

22. Midrash Rabbah to Numbers 10:5 identifies her with the Hazzelelponi of 1 Chronicles 4:3.

complicity is one of patriarchy's most successful strategies, because it can often achieve a level of cooperation that force or threat cannot guarantee. Motherhood is patriarchy's highest reward for women; it offers women one of the few roles in which they can achieve status in patriarchal society. It is also in the interests of patriarchy that women should want to be mothers, and thus motherhood is presented as something women themselves most desire (witness the many biblical accounts of barren women who desperately desire and finally give birth to a long-awaited son).[23]

If motherhood confers honor and status, what areas of women's experience does it fail to address? Patriarchal literature, with its underlying attitude toward woman's sexuality as something to be feared and therefore to be carefully regulated, severs the relationship between eroticism and procreation. It affirms motherhood but denies the mother's sexual pleasure. Judges 13 not only denies the mother's sexual pleasure; it goes so far as to dissociate her pregnancy from the sex act, not even acknowledging, in typical biblical fashion, "Manoah knew his wife and she conceived." Instead it begins with the (male) emissary telling the woman she is pregnant. Indeed, the miraculous birth of a child to a sterile woman demonstrates that the deity controls her reproductive ability. The absence of sex from this chapter is particularly remarkable when viewed against Samson's sexual liaisons in chaps. 14–16. The erotic is associated not with the mother but rather with another kind of woman — the disreputable woman, the bad woman, the foreign ("other") woman.

None of the three women with whom Samson becomes amorously involved ever becomes a mother. (Motherhood redeems women and these women are irredeemable.) Although the text specifically identifies only one of these women as Philistine (Samson's wife from Timnah), most readers assume all three are Philistines. Is the harlot whom Samson visits in Gaza a Philistine simply because she lives in a Philistine city? She could be a "foreign woman" who happens to live in Philistia — an Israelite woman, for example. Few commentators raise the possibility that Delilah, who has a Hebrew name and lives on the boundary between Israelite and Philistine territory, might be Israelite. Most take her for a Philistine, just as they assume the other women are Philistine, for surely an Israelite woman would not betray Samson to his enemies!

Though the text does not identify Delilah as a harlot, it is often assumed that she is one (perhaps because Samson visits a harlot in 16:1-3?). Because she is not identified in terms of her familial relationship to a male — she seems to have her own house, and Samson is apparently her lover though she is not his

23. See Esther Fuchs, "The Literary Characterization of Mothers and Sexual Politics in the Hebrew Bible," *Feminist Perspectives on Biblical Scholarship,* ed. Adela Yarbro Collins (Chico, Calif.: Scholars Press, 1985), 130.

wife — other possibilities for understanding her position in society are rarely entertained. Another assumption one frequently encounters not only about Delilah but also about the Timnite woman is that the women use sexual wiles to discover Samson's secrets. Are readers who make such assumptions and draw such conclusions about these women simply reading in accordance with the ideology of the text, picking up on the latent message about the danger of women's sexuality? Or do they create this association from their own biases, which they project onto the text?

I would argue that both these processes are at work, and that the story encourages us to read in accordance with an ideology that classifies women according to negative and positive images: the foreign woman and the mother. Both the negative image of the foreign woman and the positive image of the mother (legitimate wife) are well established in the Bible, and our narrator therefore does not need to set up this contrast. He simply assumes it and builds upon it, and he counts on us to accept it and apply it when we read. We are led to assume that Israelite women behave respectably, while foreign women are disreputable and treacherous.

Why does Samson reveal his secrets to a woman? His riddle offers the key. The answer to it (14:14) is another riddle (14:18), whose answer is "love," whatever other sexual meanings can be found in it. Love is Samson's weak point, his Achilles' heel. The story expresses the male's fear of surrendering to a woman. It also recognizes the temptation a woman offers, the male's attraction to her. Samson sees women as desirable but chooses to ignore their danger, even with three chances to learn. Delilah does not betray Samson so much as he betrays himself by telling her the secret of his strength. She does not disguise her intentions. By the fourth time she inquires about Samson's strength, it is clear what she will do with this information. In psychoanalytic terms, if Samson tells her anyway, it can only be because he has a subconscious need to tell her — that is, a subconscious need to give in to woman's sexual power. He needs to prove his love by surrendering something uniquely his, a part of himself — the answer to his riddle (Judg 14), the source of his strength (16) — something that gives the woman power over him. Surrender is both attractive and dangerous — too dangerous, according to our story, since it threatens a man's distinctness as male and thus his superior status (women are supposed to surrender to men, not the other way around). The text's message to the Israelite male is, "Don't do it!" Women rob men of their strength. The man who surrenders is emasculated; he loses his potency. At another level, this is the male fear of losing the penis to the woman, an anxiety that finds representation in Samson's symbolic castration, which takes place when his hair is cut and he is blinded.

Like the book of Proverbs, this text teaches the Israelite male a lesson about the dangers of foreign women. Nationalism reinforces its gender ideology. Philistines are by definition bad. The reader identifying with the ideology of the text is predisposed to think the worst of women who are allied with them. The women do not have to be specifically identified as foreign women but only to *behave* like foreign women to *be* foreign women and therefore dangerous, capable of robbing a man of his vitality. The text complicates the nature of the male–female relationship by casting it in terms of Israel's relation to foreigners. The only good woman is an Israelite woman, but the text is uneasy about the Israelite woman, for she is good only to the extent that her sexuality is controlled. Thus the only Israelite woman in the story appears in the role of mother. Beneath the apparent, surface distinction between Israelite and foreigner lies the gender issue of nonsexual (and thereby nonthreatening) woman versus sexual (and threatening) woman.

The threat posed by women's sexuality can be reduced by regulating women's behavior. In popular notions of the tale, women are blamed for Samson's downfall, although in the biblical story both the Timnite woman and Delilah act as they do because they are manipulated by the Philistines. Their power over Samson is appropriated by men, in the interests of an androcentric agenda. In teaching its lesson about the danger of women, the text uses the strategies patriarchy has historically relied upon to control women. One is reliance on female fear of male aggression; in other words, by intimidation, as in the case of the Timnite, who tells her countrymen the answer to Samson's riddle because they threaten to set fire to her and her father's house (14:15). The threat of physical harm has traditionally been an effective means by which men control women. But it is not always the most desirable. Often a better way is by reward, as Delilah's example indicates. There are more subtle forms of reward than outright bribery, of course, as Samson's mother illustrates: patriarchy rewards women with honor and status in return for their assent to their subordination and cooperation in it.

The division of women into respectable women and disreputable women also works to regulate female behavior by making gender solidarity impossible. (What might have happened if Samson had brought his wife from Timnah to his parents' house and she had met his mother?) We can now see why Samson is not endangered by the harlot at Gaza (16:1–3) as he is by his wife and by Delilah. The harlot is no threat to the patriarchal system; she already appears in an inferior, subordinate, and carefully regulated role in society. The women to whom men are inclined to make a commitment are the ones they must beware of; Samson gave in because he loved.

The notion that women are not to be trusted enables patriarchy to justify their subjugation. Women, as the account of the Timnite shows, are easily intimidated and manipulated, and, as Delilah shows, morally deficient. Even Hazzelelponi is not above suspicion. She, after all, does not tell Manoah the whole message concerning Samson's future. Nor does Manoah really trust her, since he is not content with her account of the visitation but prays for the messenger to come "to us" to "teach us" about the boy. Even though Manoah never gets as much information as Hazzelelponi about their son's future, he does receive confirmation of Hazzelelponi's story from the (male) messenger. If the text teaches men a lesson about the dangers of women and justifies patriarchy's control of women's sexuality, its lesson to women depends upon women's accepting its distinction between respectable and disreputable women. The story encourages women to become lawful and loyal mothers. This is the only role in which they can achieve status. The only alternative this text offers to the image of mother is that of the disreputable woman.

In Judges 13–16, the Philistine oppressors are represented by women, and the oppressed Israelites by Samson. Whereas the narrator wants to see Israel's situation of oppression reversed, the oppression of women is taken for granted. Women's subordination to men is, after all, considered to be the natural state of things. But the recognition in the story that something is wrong with the structure of power relations opens the possibility that other relations may be imbalanced. In order to deny that this is the case with the position of women and to justify patriarchy, the narrator portrays women as either esteemed in (Hazzelelponi) or deserving of (the three "foreign women") their inferior status. But the fact that Samson loses his life in the process of establishing his superior position over the threat posed by woman's sexuality shows how costly the struggle to maintain supremacy is.

Bat-shever (*Judges 19*)

In Judges 19, we meet another unnamed woman, a victim of gang rape whose anonymity distances the reader by making it harder to view her as a person in her own right. On the analogy of the name Bat-jiftah, I call her Bat-shever (daughter of breaking) — a name that recalls her treatment by the men of Gibeah and her subsequent dismemberment by her husband. In addition to meaning "breaking" or "fracture," the Hebrew word *shever* also refers to interpretation in the phrase, "breaking of a dream" (Judg 7:15). Thus the name also signifies the role feminist interpretation plays in breaking open the text's androcentric ideology and exposing the buried and encoded messages it gives to women.

The English translation, "concubine," gives the impression that this woman is not legally married, whereas the Hebrew word *pilegesh* refers to a legal wife of secondary rank. According to the Hebrew text of v. 2, the Levite's wife "played the harlot against him." Because the text provides no evidence of sexual misconduct on the woman's part, most translations follow the versions in translating v. 2 as she "became angry with him." This reading also makes more sense in light of what follows in vv. 2-3, for it seems unlikely that she would become a prostitute and go to her father's house. It is even more unlikely that the Levite would go after her to bring her back if she had become a prostitute.

But what if the Hebrew phrase means something else altogether? Bat-shever leaves her husband and returns to her father's house. That sounds more like divorce than adultery, but Israelite law did not recognize divorce on the part of a wife. Let us assume, therefore, that Bat-shever's assertion of autonomy is tantamount in the narrator's eyes to an act of harlotry.[24] The concept of "harlot" or "whore" has meaning only within an ideology according to which women's bodies are the property of men. Only women are harlots or whores; if the terms are applied to males it is only in an extended or figurative sense.[25] At issue in Judges 19, then, is male ownership of women's bodies, control over women's sexuality. A woman who asserts her sexual autonomy by leaving her husband — and whether or not she remains with him is a sexual issue — is guilty of sexual misconduct. This is the ideology that determines the way gender relations are understood and evaluated in this story. In the end, the woman is raped by a mob and dismembered by her own husband. As narrative punishment for her sexual "misconduct," her sexual "freedom," she is sexually abused, after which her sexuality is symbolically mutilated.

It is not clear at what point the woman died or even that she is dead when the Levite dismembers her. Why is the dismemberment, a superfluous act of violence, necessary? It conveys to women an implicit message about sexual behavior. By leaving her husband the woman makes a gesture of sexual autonomy so threatening to patriarchal ideology that it requires her to be punished sexually in the most extreme form. But it is not enough that the woman who has offended sexually, by acting as if she and not the man owned her body, is abused sexually, by having her body possessed by many men. Because it has offended, the woman's sexuality must be destroyed and its threat diffused by scattering. Cutting up the woman can be viewed on a psychological level both as an expression of male fear of women's sexuality, which must therefore be destroyed, and as an attempt to discover the secret of woman's sexuality. Because woman is the seductive and dangerous other, her mystery must be opened up by force.[26]

---

24. Robert G. Boling, *Judges,* Anchor Bible 6A (Garden City, N.Y.: Doubleday, 1975), 274; Yair Zakovitch, "The Woman's Rights in the Biblical Law of Divorce," *The Jewish Law Annual* 4 (1981), 39, Bal, *Death and Dissymmetry,* 88.

25. This is true in Hebrew as well as English; see Phyllis Bird, "'To Play the Harlot': An Inquiry into an Old Testament Metaphor," *Gender and Difference in Ancient Israel,* 76–79; see also Bal, *Death and Dissymmetry,* 86; Andrea Dworkin, *Pornography: Men Possessing Women* (New York: Plume, 1981), 203–9.

26. I borrow this notion from Elaine Showalter, *Sexual Anarchy: Gender and Culture at the Fin de Siècle* (New York: Penguin Books, 1990), 110.

If one man, her husband, cannot possess her, then many men will. But in the end, no one can possess her. What is the husband to do with his damaged goods? He destroys the evidence of the rape in a manner that symbolically repeats it, by sharing the woman's body among men, but that at the same time desexualizes the female body, by dismembering it and scattering the parts. He also destroys the evidence of the crime against the woman by giving a different account of what happened when he offers his testimony to the Israelite assembly.

In this story, the men of Gibeah are portrayed as intending to rape the Levite: "Bring out the man who came into your house, that we may know him" (v. 22). Rape is a crime of violence, not of passion, and the men of Gibeah want to humiliate the Levite in the most degrading way, by forcing him into a passive role, into the woman's position. But instead of the man, they get a woman. Moreover, they are offered two women, and get only one. Since they could easily overpower the host and his guests, why do they settle for only Bat-shever? I believe two impulses are at work here: homosexual rape is too threatening to narrate, and, in terms of the gender-motivated subtext, it would leave the woman unpunished. The narrative possibility of the Levite's rape by the mob is therefore abandoned. How are we to explain the fact that, although both Bat-shever and the host's daughter are offered to the mob, only Bat-shever is thrown out? If we understand Bat-shever's abuse as her narrative punishment, then the sparing of the virgin daughter makes sense: she is not mistreated because, unlike Bat-shever, she has not committed a sexual offense against male authority. Decoded, the message the story of Bat-shever gives to women is that any claim to sexual autonomy (presented as unfaithfulness or misconduct) has horrendous consequences. Male violence is something every woman fears. The best defense is, stay out of the way; maybe you won't be noticed. The survival of the host's daughter illustrates that sometimes this stratagem works.

In cases of rape, the issue of the woman's responsibility is often raised. Why was she dressed like that? What was she doing alone at night in that neighborhood? Had Bat-shever stayed in her place, under her husband's authority where she belonged, she would not have ended up at the wrong place—Gibeah of Benjamin—at the wrong time. By insinuating that women, by the way they behave, are responsible for male sexual aggression, the narrator relies on a fundamental patriarchal strategy for exercising social control over women. Using women's fear of male violence as a means of regulating female behavior is one of patriarchy's most powerful weapons. And it remains effective. If the message to women encoded in the story of Jephthah's daughter was: yield to the paternal word and you will be remembered and celebrated for generations to come; and that of the Samson story was: there are only two kinds of women, and you don't want to be the wrong kind; the message in Judges 19 is a cautionary one: if you do anything that even remotely suggests improper sexual behavior, you invite male aggression.

Do the crimes against Bat-shever go unpunished? The other Israelite tribes go to war against Benjamin (the tribe to which Gibeah belongs) to avenge crimes against a man and his property. Notice that they do not know what we know; they have only the Levite's account of events in Gibeah (Judg 20:4-7), and his version is different from the earlier account of the horrible crimes against the woman, both the gang rape and the dismemberment. The Benjaminites are punished for siding with the rapists and would-be murderers. The mutilation of the woman's body by the Levite, in contrast, is neither redressed nor explicitly censured. The fate of her dismembered body seems to be forgotten as intertribal warfare breaks out. This does not mean that the mutilation is unproblematic, however. After the Levite dismembers Bat-shever and sends the parts of her body throughout Israelite territory, we read: "All who saw it said, 'Such a thing has never happened or been seen from the day that the people of Israel came up out of the land of Egypt until this day; consider it, take counsel, and speak'" (Judg 19:30). What is meant by "such a thing" that has never happened or been seen before? Since only later does the Levite tell the tribes what happened at Gibeah, "such a thing" can only refer to the dismemberment and parceling out of the woman's body. When the tribes assemble at Mizpah, they ask the Levite: "Tell us, how did this evil come to pass?" (20:3). Here, too, the only obvious referent for "this evil" is the dismemberment. These oblique references hint at some lingering guilt on the narrator's part about the dismemberment, and we may view these signs of his dis-ease as evidence of a guilty narrative conscience.

In three days of fighting, the Israelites kill all but six hundred Benjaminite men. They also kill noncombatants, including all the Benjaminite women, when they destroy the Benjaminite towns. When they realize that they have almost wiped out an entire Israelite tribe, they have a change of heart. To rebuild the tribe of Benjamin, wives are needed for the surviving Benjaminite men, but because the other Israelites have sworn not to give their daughters in marriage to the Benjaminites, they procure wives for these men by destroying the town of Jabesh-Gilead, killing all the men and all the women except for four hundred young women who are virgins. These adolescents, spoils of war like the rape victims mentioned in Deborah's Song (Judg 5:30), are "awarded" to the Benjaminite men and forced to become their wives. The sexual violence does not end here. Because still more wives are needed for the Benjaminite men, the Israelites commission them to capture wives from the dancers in the yearly festival at Shiloh. As the Book of Judges draws to a close, male violence reinscribes the story of female violation, with Israelite men repeating on a mass scale the crimes of the men of Gibeah.

Fear of and Violence against Women

What do the stories we have examined have in common? In one way or another, they all betray a fear of women and of women's sexuality, and they are all aimed at circumscribing and controlling women's behavior. Women in biblical times were under the control of men — fathers, husbands, brothers — and these stories justify and inscribe women's subordination to male authority. One of the few roles in which women could achieve status was that of mother. Much as patriarchy might like to represent itself as natural and necessary, it cannot conceal the traces of its anxieties and inherent contradictions. The story of Deborah/Jael unsettles the patriarchal ideal of the mother as nurturing and self-sacrificing by recognizing the mother's threatening side. The mother cannot be controlled. The power of the mother is patriarchy's Achilles' heel.

Something else our stories have in common is violence. Fear of women's sexuality leads to violence against women as a means of control. According to Andrea Dworkin, men become advocates of violence in order to master their fear of violence. They *do* violence in order not to be victimized by it, in order not to be weak and powerless like women.[27] One of the ways men deny their responsibility for violence is by scapegoating women, blaming women for violence of which they are the victims. We can see this tactic at work in the texts we have examined. But the violence unleashed against Bat-shever is not her fault, any more than it was Bat-jiftah's fault (as Jephthah implies) that she became the sacrificial victim, or the Timnite woman's fault that the Philistines retaliated against her when Samson burned their fields, or Delilah's fault that Samson was captured by the Philistines (he didn't *have* to tell her his secret). Attention to the gender politics of Judges enables us to expose the phenomenon of scapegoating women for what it is: a strategy patriarchy uses to avoid facing and having to deal with its own violent legacy.

In the Book of Judges, violence against women is part of the larger problem of social and moral decay in Israel. The breakdown of social and moral order is presented as if the gender of the victims of violence were irrelevant. Yet the fact that the final illustration of Israel's descent into lawlessness is the gang rape and dismemberment of a woman calls attention to the role gender plays, on a deeper level, in the presentation. And the book ends with women, again, the objects of male violence. Only recently have we begun to distinguish ethnically or racially motivated violence from other kinds of violence. That violence is also gender-motivated may soon become not just something we know but a legal issue. Exposing gender-motivated violence in a biblical text is, of course, far removed from the real-life issue. But recognizing gender-motivated vio-

27. Dworkin, *Pornography*, 51–53.

lence, even in a biblical text — and perhaps especially in a biblical text, because of the Bible's continuing influence on our society — is a contribution feminist biblical literary criticism can make to the work of feminism as a political enterprise.

Further Reading

General

BACH, Alice. "Reading Allowed: Feminist Biblical Criticism Approaching the Millennium," *Currents in Research: Biblical Studies* 1 (1993): 215–35. A lively discussion of the current state of feminist biblical criticism; the bibliography includes important works in feminist criticism in general as well as feminist biblical scholarship.

BRENNER, Athalya, and Fokkelien van Dijk-Hemmes. *On Gendering Texts: Female and Male Voices in the Hebrew Bible.* Biblical Interpretation Series 1. Leiden: E. J. Brill, 1993. Presents an important challenge to traditional ideas about the authorship of biblical texts by looking for female and male voices or gender-positions (as distinct from female and male authorship) in a range of biblical material. Various texts are creatively analyzed.

CAMP, Claudia V., and Carole R. Fontaine, eds. *Women, War, and Metaphor: Language and Society in the Study of the Hebrew Bible. Semeia* 61 (1993). Articles in this collection treat the relationships of images of women and war, a topic particularly relevant to the study of Judges in view of its representation of warfare and violence against women. An essay by Gale A. Yee deals with Judges 4; Alice A. Keefe deals with Judges 19; and there are scattered references to Judges throughout the volume.

DAY, Peggy L., ed. *Gender and Difference in Ancient Israel.* Minneapolis: Fortress Press, 1989. A collection of essays on diverse texts dealing with women; from the Book of Judges, Jael and Jephthah's daughters are represented.

FUCHS, Esther. "The Literary Characterization of Mothers and Sexual Politics in the Hebrew Bible," *Feminist Perspectives on Biblical Scholarship,* edited by Adela Yarbro Collins (Chico, Calif.: Scholars Press, 1985): 117–36. An early, important critique of how patriarchal ideology shapes the picture of motherhood we find in the Hebrew Bible. Includes discussion of Samson's mother.

LERNER, Gerda. *The Creation of Patriarchy.* Oxford: Oxford University Press, 1986. Investigates the origins of patriarchy and women's complicity in it. Impressive in its scope and breadth, it begins with the origins of civilization and traces the development of patriarchy (as social system and ideology) through the biblical and classical Greek periods. Contains a helpful section of definitions that distinguishes between such concepts as suppression and subordination, patriarchy and paternalism, gender and sex, etc. There is also a second volume, *The Creation of Feminist Consciousness from the Middle Ages to Eighteen-Seventy* (Oxford: Oxford University Press, 1993).

WARHOL, Robyn R. and Diane Price Herndl. *Feminisms: An Anthology of Literary Theory and Criticism.* New Brunswick, N.J.: Rutgers University Press, 1991. A useful anthology containing many well-known essays on feminist criticism, including classics by Shoshana Felman, Annette Kolodny, Elaine Showalter, Hélène Cixous, Luce Irigaray, Jane Gallop, Patrocinio Schweickart, and Mary Jacobus, among others.

Feminist Criticism of Judges

BAL, Mieke. *Death and Dissymmetry: The Politics of Coherence in the Book of Judges.* Bloomington, Ind.: Indiana University Press, 1988. A brilliant counterreading of Judges in terms of its gender-bound violence and the social revolution that gives rise to it. Daughters who are the victims of male violence (Jephthah's daughter, Samson's wife, and the Levite's wife — called Bath, Kallah, and Beth) are avenged by Jael, the Woman-with-the-Millstone, and Delilah, symbolizing the displaced mother. Not readily accessible to beginners, but worth the effort.

———. *Lethal Love: Feminist Literary Readings of Biblical Love Stories.* Bloomington, Ind.: Indiana University Press, 1987. Contains a provocative psychoanalytic reading of the story of Samson and Delilah; also treated are Bathsheba, Ruth, Tamar, and Eve. A good point of entry into Bal's work.

———. *Murder and Difference: Gender, Genre, and Scholarship of Sisera's Death.* Trans. by Matthew Gumpert. Bloomington, Ind.: Indiana University Press, 1988. Discusses the Deborah/Jael story in terms of differences between the "masculine" prose account in Judges 4 and the "feminine" song in Judges 5, and criticizes the way commentators read sexual stereotypes and their own gender biases into the biblical literature.

BRENNER, Athalya, ed. *A Feminist Companion to Judges.* The Feminist Companion to the Bible 4. Sheffield, Eng.: JSOT, 1993. An extremely valuable collection of articles, some previously published, dealing with Judges from feminist and womanist perspectives.

EXUM, J. Cheryl. *Fragmented Women: Feminist (Sub)versions of Biblical Narratives.* JSOTSup 163. Sheffield, Eng.: JSOT Press; Valley Forge, Pa.: Trinity Press International, 1993. Asking what androcentric interests these stories promote, one chapter deals with the women in the Samson story; another reads the story of Jephthah's daughter against that of David's wife, Michal; another reads the Levite's wife against Bathsheba. Other chapters discuss Sarah, Rebekah, Rachel, and Leah.

FEWELL, Danna Nolan. "Judges." *The Women's Bible Commentary*, 67–77. Edited by Carol A. Newsom and Sharon H. Ringe. Louisville, Ky.: Westminster/John Knox Press, 1992. A survey of the Book of Judges concentrating on the women characters.

NIDITCH, Susan. "Samson as Trickster, Culture Hero, and Bandit." *Catholic Biblical Quarterly* 52 (1990): 608–24. A folkloristic analysis that offers important insight into the feminization of Samson.

O'CONNOR, M. "The Women in the Book of Judges." *Hebrew Annual Review* 10 (1986): 277–93. Surveys women's roles as represented in Judges, with emphasis on the issue of marginalization.

TRIBLE, Phyllis. *Texts of Terror: Literary-Feminist Readings of Biblical Narratives.* Philadelphia: Fortress Press, 1984. Contains chapters on Jephthah's daughter and the Levite's wife that highlight male violence and the victimization of the women. A classic study with valuable observations; it is limited, however, by a methodological approach that requires the reader to remain within the ideology of the text, thus leaving women powerless.

5

STRUCTURALIST CRITICISM: THE TEXT'S WORLD OF MEANING

David Jobling

"**S**tructuralism is a philosophical view according to which the reality of the objects of the human or social sciences is relational rather than substantial."[1] This definition indicates the wide scope of structuralism's claim — to offer the most appropriate orientation to all the fields of study having to do with human individuals and societies. But it is also very open-ended, suggesting that the many efforts to define structuralism more precisely are unhelpful or even wrong.

According to this view, we do not come to terms with the world of experience as a set of isolated items, but as a set of relationships among items. It is the recognition of these relationships that makes the world intelligible. Our minds develop through the awareness of these relationships (so that it is not possible to say whether the relationships are "in" the world or "in" our minds — they are at once the condition and the developing product of our mental activity).[2] All the products of human minds, including literary texts, express meaning through the structured patterning of the elements of which they are made. Structural analysis of texts is the process of moving from their perceived patterning to the "messages" they carry. The patterning need not represent the conscious intention of the producer of the text; indeed, the linguistic analogy to which I shall turn in a moment suggests that it probably does not. And the patterning *I* find in a text is at the same time something my individual mind has *achieved,* and it will not be identical to what anyone else finds.

1. Peter Caws, *Structuralism: The Art of the Intelligible* (Atlantic Highlands, N.J.: Humanities Press International, 1988), 1.
2. According to Caws, we seek intelligibility in "the matching of structured systems," which "is experienced by us as primordially meaningful" (ibid., 112). Our minds simply do not develop in a way that lets us experience things in isolation; it is only as systems

I shall return to the implications of these critical issues, and to the question of where structuralism is located on the map of biblical methods (see below, "Structuralism and Criticism"). First, I shall review the development of literary and biblical structuralism, with illustrative examples taken, when possible, from work on Judges. I shall not offer a comprehensive proposal for how to do structural analysis — how to get from text to message — although I shall make reference to some such proposals and try to put them into a framework that will enable the reader to understand and use them critically.

The Analogy of Language

We sometimes ask of a text, "What is it trying to say?" This seems an odd question — presumably, what it is trying to say is what it says. Yet we do ask the question, which suggests that we perceive a "message" in the text different from the words themselves, a message for which the text is, perhaps, only one possible vehicle. We may even, paradoxically, sense a "message" in the text that the text does not clearly or fully convey; we think we know what it's "getting at," even when this isn't identical to what it says! What is the nature of this peculiar relationship of text to meaning?

Structuralism deals with these questions by analogy with ordinary language as it is studied in the science of linguistics. It is with linguistics that structuralism began, and this is where we must begin in trying to understand it. We must put aside for the moment issues having to do with an extended *text* like Judges, for linguistics works primarily with language on a much smaller scale — from the smallest units of sound (phonemes) up to the level of the sentence.

Suppose, in a conversation, I speak an English sentence to another person, and she accepts it, and responds. By "accepts," I do not mean she agrees with what I say, simply that she recognizes my sentence as a properly formed English sentence. What has happened here? Something very complex and, on both our parts, mostly unconscious. It is not on the basis of experience or memory that I speak or that she understands. In all likelihood, neither of us ever spoke or heard that identical sentence; indeed, it may never before have been spoken or written by anyone. Yet my interlocutor dealt with it as easily as I produced it.

We were both, quite unconsciously, drawing on our knowledge of English. But what exactly is "English"? It consists of a vast *system* of relationships among English words, some relationships having to do with differences of meaning,

---

of relationships that we are capable of coming to terms with what we experience; hence, "structure is fundamental to intelligibility, not merely one aspect of it" (ibid., 114).

other relationships having to do with correct word order.[3] It is by reference to this system that both I and my hearer measure the correctness of my sentence. But there are some odd facts about this system. First, I need no *conscious* awareness of it in order to speak or understand English. For instance, English speakers who couldn't say what a noun or an adjective is still put adjectives in front of nouns, as English syntax requires, rather than behind them. Second, the system has no existence separate from the real sentences that people produce. Books may attempt to describe the system; academies may exist (as in France) to try to preserve its "purity." But the books and the academies have no independent measuring-rod of what is acceptable — they simply distill into abstract terms what the speakers of the language *deem* acceptable.

Structural linguistics began in the early part of this century with the work of the Swiss linguist Ferdinand de Saussure,[4] and the issue just raised was expressed by him as an opposition between *parole,* the actual utterance, and *langue,* the mysterious underlying system.[5] A second key opposition in Saussure is that between two kinds of linguistics, two ways of studying language. *Synchronic* linguistics imagines *langue* as frozen at a particular moment in time, and consisting of all the relationships existing between elements of the language at that moment; *diachronic* linguistics studies the change in language over time. Saussure demanded that linguistics be basically synchronic; the development of language over time he regarded as unimportant compared with its systemic character at a given moment.

A third fundamental aspect of Saussure's linguistics requires lengthier presentation, namely, that language is a system of *relationships* rather than of fixed terms. Words have a relationship to objective reality, but that does not mean that there is anything in objective reality which guarantees *the* meaning of any given word. Rather, the whole vocabulary of a language is available to come to terms with reality in complex and shifting ways. A given word is defined by what *differentiates* it from related words. The word "house" has a nice objective sound to it; but someone seeking specificity as to size or location might prefer, for the same object, "mansion" or "cottage," while someone thinking of function might prefer "home." The introduction into the language of some new word, like "condominium," may signal less a new reality than a reorganization

---

3. Even "word" is a simplification — a linguist would speak of word-elements, or "morphemes," such as the "-ation" at the end of a class of English nouns.

4. For the following, see Ferdinand de Saussure, *Course in General Linguistics,* ed. Charles Bally et al., trans. Wade Baskin (New York: McGraw-Hill, 1959).

5. The French terms are usually retained in English discussion, but another pair of terms, "performance" and "competence," have virtually the same meanings.

of the words used for existing things. The most obvious way of making the point is to note that when we go to the dictionary to find the meaning of a word all we find are other words (whose meanings can be expressed only in yet other words). Meaning lies entirely in relationship, in the unstable system of differences between related words. This does not deter us from consulting dictionaries, or from being satisfied, for practical purposes, with the "meanings" we find there. For we are used to working with language as a system of differences, rather than of fixed terms, even if we are not aware that this is what we are doing. But if we ask ourselves what the "meaning" of a word really is, we cannot do better than to say that it is "that for which the majority of the linguistic community does not prefer some other word"!

With this summary of structural linguistics, we return to our main concern, which is literary texts. Literary structuralism depends on the possibility of drawing an analogy between the text and the linguistic sentence. The analogy has to cover the three Saussurean emphases we have identified. First, by analogy with *parole/langue,* the text will have to be seen as a particular "utterance" generated out of a system of *possible* utterances that its producer, as a member of her group, has unconsciously internalized. Second, in terms of the synchronic/diachronic opposition, the text will have to be studied primarily not as the result of a process of development (which is how the historical critical methods mostly look at biblical texts), but as part of a *system* which links it to other texts, and which links its own different parts to each other. Third, the text will have to be examined as having meaning not in itself, but in relation to other texts, in the structured *differences* between it and them.

The Main Tradition of Biblical Structuralism

After Saussure, the figures whose theories have most shaped biblical structuralism are Vladimir Propp, Claude Lévi-Strauss, and A. J. Greimas. In presenting the main features of their work, my intention is not to offer a history of great structuralists. These three names are merely foci for larger discussions of which they were a part. What is important is to identify the questions that, as a result of these discussions, we have learned to put to biblical texts.

Vladimir Propp and the Russian Fairy Tale

Propp was a Russian folklorist whose major work was *Morphology of the Folktale* (1928).[6] In it he examined a hundred Russian fairy tales to discover what they

---

6. Vladimir Propp, *Morphology of the Folktale,* 2d ed., trans. Laurence Scott (Austin, Tex.: University of Texas Press, 1968). For what follows, see pp. 19–65.

had in common at the levels of character and plot. His most productive suggestion had to do with plot structure; he claimed that all the stories could be
reduced to thirty-one story elements, which he called "functions." The first of
these are:

I. One of the members of a family absents himself from home.
II. An interdiction is addressed to the hero.
III. The interdiction is violated.
IV. The villain makes an attempt at reconnaissance.

And so on through:

XXIX. The hero is given a new appearance.
XXX. The villain is punished.
XXXI. The hero is married and ascends the throne.

These functions can be grouped in a way that indicates the broad structure of
the tale:

Setting the stage for the main action (I–VII)
The "villainy" or lack that disturbs the status quo (VIII)
The finding, equipping, and journey of the hero (IX–XV)
The "combat" in which the hero overcomes the villain or the lack (XVI–XIX)
Events of the hero's return journey (XX–XXII)
The recognition and glorification of the hero (XXIII–XXXI)

Propp's major discovery was that although no one fairy tale contains (or could
contain) all thirty-one functions, *the ones that a given tale does include are always
in the given order.* This finding supports the analogy between the literary text
and the linguistic sentence. At least in the case of Russian fairy tales, there seem
to be rules of "syntax" for acceptable stories, analogous to rules for word order
in English. The storytellers and hearers are applying these rules, unconsciously
internalized, in their telling and hearing. The analyst can discover things about
the underlying "system," the *langue* of Russian fairy tales; but this, like the
system of language itself, has no other existence than in the individual stories,
the *paroles.*

Propp implies that a large group of tales all tell, in different ways, the "same"
story. For example, in the very common type of the "seeker" hero, the normal
working of a society is in some way disrupted. To deal with the disruption, the
hero must be separated from the society, part of whose resources must be di-

verted to equip him for what he must do.[7] The hero overcomes the villainy or lack, but this does not end the story. In order for the society to resume its normal working, the hero must be reintegrated into it, and this proves far from easy (for example, the returning hero often has difficulty being *recognized* by his own society). But reintegrated he eventually is, usually by his marriage. The social importance of this message is not hard to appreciate, and the society repeats it over and over in all its stories of this type.

The Book of Judges provides a case unique in the Bible of a series of stories that have a common structure. This structure appears most concisely in 3:7-11, the account of the judge Othniel:

1. "The Israelites did what was evil in the sight of Yahweh" (3:7).
2. Yahweh in anger gave them into the power of an enemy (3:8).
3. "The Israelites cried out to Yahweh" (3:9a).
4. "Yahweh raised up a deliverer for the Israelites" (3:9b).
5. The deliverer with Yahweh's aid defeated the enemy (3:10).
6. "The land had rest" during the rest of the deliverer's life (3:11).

Immediately upon the death of Othniel, a new cycle begins, and the same pattern can be traced through the longer story of Ehud (3:12-30). Indeed, nearly all the material through Judges 16 can be fitted into the same pattern, and scholars refer to the "judge-cycles" of Othniel, Ehud, Deborah, Gideon, Jephthah, and Samson.[8] Is the point of the series to instill a single message by repetition, as Propp perceived his fairy tales to do?

An application to Judges of a method related to Propp's is found in Robert Culley's *Themes and Variations*.[9] Culley identifies in biblical narrative nine "action sequences" (having to do with rescue, prohibition, etc.) which could just as well be thought of as pairs of "functions" in Propp's sense.[10] In his section on Judges,[11] Culley shows how each cycle is based on two obligatory action sequences; a WRONG → PUNISHED sequence, dealing with Israel's apostasy against God and the punishment, and a DIFFICULTY → RESCUED sequence, dealing with Israel's servitude to a foreign oppressor and the deliverance.

---

7. The hero may be female, but in that case she is a "victim" rather than a "seeker" hero (ibid., 36). I am discussing in this paragraph the message of the seeker hero type of tale.

8. The material that does *not* fit the pattern consists of 3:31, 8:33 — 10:5, and 12:8-15.

9. *Themes and Variations: A Study of Action in Biblical Narratives* (Atlanta: Scholars Press, 1992). For Culley's own comment on the relationship of his work to Propp's, see p. 11.

10. Ibid., 47–76.

11. Ibid., 97–109.

Within this necessary framework, the different stories make use of other sequences in various combinations, but only sequences of one of two types: TASK → ACCOMPLISHED (e.g., in Judges 4, Barak's commission to muster Israel's army) and ANNOUNCEMENT → HAPPENED (e.g., Deborah's prediction that a woman will get the glory from this campaign). Culley makes the further observation that, from the Gideon cycle onward, *all* of these elements get more and more incorporated into a quite different and more complex kind of sequence, which he calls the "life story."

As his title suggests, Culley wants to strike a balance between what is common to the judge-cycles and how they differ. The differences are considerable; in particular, there is much tension between the "life-story" pattern and the action sequences. But in his desire to give adequate attention to the common pattern, Culley works in the spirit of Propp. The best analogy to Propp is to be found, however, in the work of the biblical narrator (often called the Deuteronomist), for this narrator has provided, as a prelude to the judge-cycles, a "theoretical" statement of the meaning that all the stories will share! This statement is found in Judges 2:11-19, and refers not to *particular* events but to what would happen *repeatedly* in a series of situations involving different judges. The Deuteronomist thought of the stories of the judges, as Propp thought of his fairy tales, as repetitions of the "same" story.

From Propp we have learned to ask, What constant patterns can we find in different stories, and what is the significance of these patterns?

Claude Lévi-Strauss and the Structural Analysis of Myth

The individual most responsible for the emergence of an interdisciplinary structuralist movement in this century is the French anthropologist Claude Lévi-Strauss, whose major work belongs to the period after World War II. He argues that each of the various activities of a society can be understood as a sort of language, and analyzed by techniques analogous to Saussure's linguistics. For example, kinship rules (which attain a fantastic complexity in societies termed "primitive") form a system in which permissible marriages are analogous to "proper" sentences in language, and forbidden marriages are like wrongly formed sentences.[12]

Much of Lévi-Strauss's anthropological work has no direct relation to our main concern, *literary* structuralism.[13] But his most important accomplishment

12. See Claude Lévi-Strauss, *The Elementary Structures of Kinship,* rev. ed., trans. James Harle Bell, John Richard von Sturmer, and Rodney Needham (Boston: Beacon Press, 1969).

13. This does not mean that his other work has been neglected in biblical studies. See, for example, Mara E. Donaldson, "Kinship Theory in the Patriarchal Narratives,"

does consist in reading texts, albeit texts of a very special kind, namely, transcriptions of Amerindian mythology. This work can perhaps best be introduced by referring to Lévi-Strauss's critique of Propp. When Propp's work was translated into French in the 1950s, Lévi-Strauss wrote one of the first reviews, in which (as well as expressing great admiration) he complained that Propp locates the meaning of his tales in what they have *in common* rather than in their differences.[14] He considers a group of story-fragments adduced by Propp (here slightly simplified):

1. A king gives the hero an eagle, which carries him away to another kingdom.
2. An old man gives the hero a horse, which carries him away to another kingdom.
3. A sorcerer gives the hero a little boat, which carries him away to another kingdom.[15]

The latter part of each sentence is the same, but the first parts differ. Propp's suggestion is that the roles played by the king/old man/sorcerer, on the one hand, or by the eagle/horse/boat, on the other, are empty categories ("donor," "magic agent") into which anything plausible can be put, so as to tell the "same" story over and over. Based on his work on myth, Lévi-Strauss suggests, on the contrary, that what a culture produces is *sets* of parallel stories in which the differences are as important as the parallels, since it is through these stories that the society comes to terms with its experience of similarity and difference in the world. He notes how, in the myths of the Americas, different birds — for example, eagle, owl, raven — appear in parallel stories. Propp would see these myths as equivalent, but Lévi-Strauss wants to probe the differences. Using a method based on Saussure's, he analyzes the differences into *binary oppositions* — eagle versus owl constitutes the opposition between the categories of "day" and "night," for example, while eagle/owl versus raven constitutes the opposition between "hunting" and "scavenging."[16] Applying this method to Propp's group

---

Journal of the American Academy of Religion 49 (1981): 77–87; Mary Douglas, *Purity and Danger: An Analysis of Concepts of Pollution and Taboo* (London: Routledge & Kegan Paul, 1966); Terry J. Prewitt, *The Elusive Covenant: A Structural-Semiotic Reading of Genesis* (Bloomington, Ind.: Indiana University Press, 1990).

    14. Claude Lévi-Strauss, "Structure and Form: Reflections on a Work by Vladimir Propp," in *Structural Anthropology Volume II,* trans. Monique Layton (London: Allen Lane, 1977), 115–45.

    15. Ibid., 118–19; cf. 129–38. See Propp, *Morphology of the Folktale,* 19–20.

    16. Analysis into binary (two-term) oppositions is fundamental to Lévi-Strauss and to all structuralism in the Saussurean tradition.

of magic agents, eagle, horse, and boat, suggests the oppositions animate versus inanimate, and, within the animate, earth versus air. The critical question would then be whether there is any linkage between the particular magic agent in a given tale and the corresponding "donor" (king, old man, sorcerer). Lévi-Strauss would claim that there are indeed such linkages, that within the mythic or folktale stock of a given culture, a change in one variable will be linked to changes in others (which are therefore covariable).

But to work out the system one needs a very large sample of stories. In his own major work on myth, Lévi-Strauss studies over eight hundred Amerindian myths as they appear in around two thousand known transcriptions.[17] The extreme complexity of the oppositions that he finds operating in this vast corpus admits of no summary, but a small example, from near the beginning of the analysis, may be given.[18] Certain South American Indians have two theories about the origin of fire — that it was stolen from the jaguar, or that it was learned from the monkey. The first theory stresses the *difference* between the human and the nonhuman: the gaining of fire is part of a human conquest of the nonhuman world. The second theory stresses the *similarity* of the human to the nonhuman: the gaining of fire depends on human likeness to one kind of animal, monkeys. These theories generate (in Lévi-Strauss's analysis) two parallel sets of myths in which the protagonists are, respectively, jaguars and monkeys, and jaguars and humans. In these sets, "jaguars" is a constant, while "monkeys" or "humans" is a variable, and the choice of monkeys or humans entails a number of other choices between other pairs of variables (for example, in one myth a jaguar opens its mouth to swallow a monkey, while in a parallel myth a jaguar closes its mouth to avoid swallowing a human). One achievement of the parallel myths is to set monkeys and humans in extreme contrast, to counteract the uncomfortable sense of their closeness.

Some of the most stimulating biblical readings based on Lévi-Strauss's methods are those of the British anthropologist Edmund Leach. None of his

17. Claude Lévi-Strauss, *The Raw and the Cooked,* trans. John and Doreen Weightman (New York: Harper & Row, 1970); *From Honey to Ashes,* trans. John and Doreen Weightman (New York: Harper & Row, 1973); *The Origin of Table Manners,* trans. John and Doreen Weightman (New York: Harper & Row, 1978); *The Naked Man,* trans. John and Doreen Weightman (New York: Harper & Row, 1981). These four volumes constitute *Introduction to a Science of Mythology,* but are always known by their individual titles. The best brief statement of Lévi-Strauss's approach is his essay "The Structural Study of Myth," in *Structural Anthropology,* trans. Claire Jacobson and Brooke Grundfest Schoepf (New York: Basic Books, 1963), 206–31.

18. In what follows, I summarize the diagram on p. 133 of *The Raw and the Cooked,* and the discussion that precedes it.

major readings concentrates on Judges, but he does devote a few pages of a general theoretical lecture to Judges 19–21.[19] These chapters, according to Leach, function as a way to deal with an opposition between Gibeah and Bethlehem, the hometowns of Saul and David, Israel's first two kings, and by extension with the opposition between the two kings themselves. Judges 19, the story of the Levite's "concubine,"[20] moves from Bethlehem (the woman's home) to Gibeah (the scene of the outrage). This incident, notes Leach, leads to the rise of Saul: in Judges 21, all the men of Jabesh-Gilead are exterminated so that their virgin women can become wives to the male Benjaminite survivors of the war that followed the outrage, and it is presumably from one of these unions that Saul, a Benjaminite from Gibeah, emerges. Saul's first major act is to rescue the people of Jabesh-Gilead (who have somehow recovered from their extermination; 1 Sam 11). When Saul is killed (opening the way for David), it is the men of Jabesh-Gilead who rescue his body from Philistine outrage (1 Sam 31), and David commends them for this act (2 Sam 2:4-7). As soon as the remnants of Saul's house have been killed, David takes Saul's bones from Jabesh-Gilead and restores them to Gibeah (2 Sam 21:1-14), and this final incident in the saga is followed immediately by a reference to a Bethlehemite slayer of Goliath (21:19). Leach summarizes:

> Overall, the men of Jabesh-Gilead play a complementary role to the Levite's concubine. The latter takes the story away from Bethlehem in a context of fragmentation; the former brings [*sic*] it back again in a context of reunification.[21]

This analysis is, as Leach notes, much too brief and sketchy. Yet it is hard to doubt, however one feels about the particulars of the analysis, that he is on to something. The complex interplay in a series of passages in Judges and Samuel around the locations of Bethlehem, Gibeah, and Jabesh-Gilead demands some sort of explanation, and Leach has been able to pull the elements together. But his general attitude to the Bible is controversial, for he considers all biblical stories to be *myth,* and believes that they should be analyzed "without consid-

---

19. Edmund Leach, "Anthropological Approaches to the Study of the Bible During the Twentieth Century," in Edmund Leach and D. Alan Aycock, *Structuralist Interpretations of Biblical Myth* (Cambridge: Cambridge University Press, 1983), 7–32 (I deal here with pp. 26–28). In addition to Leach's essays in this book, see also Edmund Leach, *Genesis as Myth and Other Essays* (London: Jonathan Cape, 1969), which contains the most successful of his biblical essays, "The Legitimacy of Solomon."

20. Many scholars believe that this traditional translation of the Hebrew *pilegesh* is unsatisfactory, and that "secondary wife" or "matrilocal wife" would be better. See, for example, Mieke Bal, *Death and Dissymmetry: The Politics of Coherence in the Book of Judges* (Chicago: University of Chicago Press, 1988), 80–86.

21. Leach, "Anthropological Approaches," 28.

eration of the order in which they appear," that is, like a jumble of mythic fragments.[22]

From Lévi-Strauss we have learned to ask, What is the significance of differences within similarities? Why are similar stories told with different protagonists? What are the fundamental (binary) oppositions with which the set of stories is working, and why are these oppositions so critical?

A. J. Greimas and Structural Narratology

Perhaps even more influential than Lévi-Strauss on the structural analysis of biblical narrative has been another French thinker, A. J. Greimas. Greimas continues and deepens Propp's impulse to formulate rules for how texts are structured. But he goes far beyond Propp's concentration on a particular class of texts, seeking to posit models that apply to narrative in general. Finding Propp very imprecise methodologically, he turns to Saussure, Lévi-Strauss, and others for rigor of method, and his approach is based on the linguistic paradigm. Here, I concentrate on two well-known models proposed by Greimas, to indicate their flexibility and breadth of application.

The first is the *actantial model*.[23] Anything that happens in a story, from the action of the story as a whole to some very tiny piece of action within it (even action that is contemplated or intended, without actually occurring) can be mapped onto the following grid:

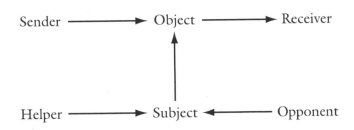

The *sender* is the one who initiates the action, with the purpose of transferring some *object* to a *receiver*. The action is to be carried out by the *subject*, who is aided and/or opposed in this by *helpers* and *opponents* respectively. Thus, for "Little Red Riding Hood," we have the following pattern:

22. Ibid., 29.
23. A. J. Greimas, *Structural Semantics: An Attempt at a Method* (Lincoln, Nebr.: University of Nebraska Press, 1983), 207.

However, it is unusual for the characters in a story to line up so conveniently, one to each category. Sometimes more than one character can occupy the same slot, and a character can even occupy more than one slot. The roles of "helper" and "opponent" are not always filled. The pattern for "The Three Billy Goats Gruff," for example, is:

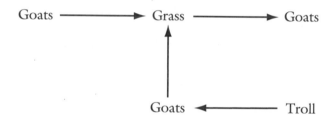

Such a model is of enormous generality, and may seem no more than a matter of common sense. Yet the roles in a story may be far from obvious to a superficial view, and deep insight can develop from trying to work out what they really are. I do not know of any creative application of the actantial model to a Judges text, but it has had an impact on study of the book of Genesis. In one of the earliest of all structural analyses of the Bible, the French critic Roland Barthes applies the model to Jacob's wrestling with the angel in Genesis 32.[24] He concludes that a single actor, God, occupies in this story the roles of both sender and opponent. Barthes regards this situation as very rare, and suggests that the only type of story for which it is characteristic is stories about *blackmail!*[25] For biblical theology, this is a startling possibility, especially since the same pattern of divine activity has been posited in another major Genesis story, the account of the Garden in Genesis 2–3.[26]

24. Roland Barthes, "Wrestling with the Angel: Textual Analysis of Genesis 32:23-33," in *The Semiotic Challenge,* trans. Richard Howard (New York: Hill and Wang, 1988), 246–60.

25. Ibid., 257.

26. David Jobling, *The Sense of Biblical Narrative: Structural Analyses in the Hebrew Bible,* vol. 2 (Sheffield, Eng.: JSOT Press, 1986), 24–26.

Though it continues to be a handy tool, the actantial model grows stale with overuse, and it should be noted that some fundamental problems caused Greimas to drop it from his mature system. More important is another of his contributions, the *semiotic square:*[27]

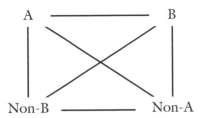

A and B are any two items felt to be opposites, for example, "hot" and "cold." Their relationship is called *contrary*. Non-A is "whatever is not hot," and its relation to A is called *contradictory* (likewise B and non-B). The vertical relations of non-A to B and of non-B to A are called relations of *implication*. That something is cold implies at least that it belongs to the class of things that are not hot. Hence B implies non-A (though the opposite is not necessarily the case), and likewise A implies non-B.

If the categories A and B cover all possibilities, then the square is trivial. For example, if we have a two-way switch and call "on" A and "off" B, then B and non-A, "off" and "not on," are exactly the same thing. But the example of hot and cold, trivial as it is, shows that things are not always so simple. The very existence of a term like "lukewarm" implies that when we talk of things being hot or cold, there are some things which are *both* not hot *and* not cold. If we knew exactly what we meant by "hot"—for example, "hot enough to burn skin"—everything would be hot or cold. But, as I have already indicated in discussing language, we *do* and *must* use words without knowing exactly what we mean by them!

Some of the binary oppositions identified by Lévi-Strauss in myths provide useful illustrations. For example, let A and B be "life" and "death." What would non-A, "non-life," be? It seems a very broad category, which might include both inanimate things and things that once were living but now are dead. But there are entirely different ways of thinking of the "non-life" category that lead to new possibilities of meaning. One possibility is to include in this cate-

27. A. J. Greimas, *On Meaning: Selected Writings in Semiotic Theory,* trans. Paul J. Perron and Frank H. Collins (Minneapolis: University of Minnesota Press, 1987), 49. Arrows are often included at the ends of some of the lines in the diagram. This is done inconsistently, and I shall omit them.

gory whatever is not *conducive* to life, and this is what seems to happen in certain mythic transformations in which "war" stands for non-life, and "agriculture" for non-death.[28]

The square becomes even more fruitful when we begin to define complex terms that combine more than one of the corner positions.[29] Combining the two right corners, for example, we ask, "What is both B and non-A?"; combining the bottom two, "What is both non-A and non-B?" Greimas offers an example concerning how we respond to propositions ("God is omniscient," or "It's a nice day").[30] A is "affirm"—we agree that the proposition is true; B is "refuse"—we deny its truth. Non-A is "doubt," which takes in the whole realm of things we do not specifically affirm, while non-B, similarly, is "admit," covering all the things we do not specifically refuse. The combination of A and B (affirm and refuse) implies a *legalistic* society, one that wants to be definite about everything, while the combination of non-A and non-B (doubt and admit) is *libertarian,* both skeptical and open. The combinations on the left and right axes suggest *optimism* (affirm and admit) and *pessimism* (refuse and doubt). This would open the possibility of analyzing real human societies as libertarian/pessimistic, or whatever. Greimas's square may be expanded to include the complex terms, as follows:

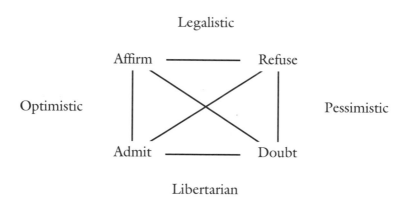

Greimas's influence on biblical studies is largely due to the work of Daniel Patte, who is both a member of Greimas's circle and an American New Testament scholar. Patte has provided the most pedagogically helpful model, based on Greimas, for the structural analysis of biblical texts.[31]

28. Lévi-Strauss, *Structural Anthropology,* 224–25.
29. Greimas, *On Meaning,* 49–53.
30. Ibid., 168–70. My discussion expands considerably on Greimas.
31. Daniel Patte, *Structural Exegesis for New Testament Critics* (Minneapolis: Fortress Press, 1990). Students of the Jewish Bible need not worry about the title; the method

From Greimas we have learned to ask, What general models are useful in analyzing the great variety of existing or possible literary texts? How general can we make the models before we encounter diminishing returns in the understanding of particular texts?

Structuralism and Criticism

Structuralism has ceased to be a fashionable current in biblical or in general literary criticism. It is held by many to be passé, to have been overtaken by new currents, those of "poststructuralism." According to this account, some of the major figures who were active during the time that structuralism was in fashion have been able to move in profitable new directions, while others, notably Greimas, have continued to try to mine a spent deposit.[32]

Structuralism is criticized on many counts. Some of the criticisms are valid and necessary, but others are based on a stereotypical view of structuralism that needs to be challenged. My account will be based on that of Peter Caws, whose definition of structuralism I quoted at the outset.[33] Caws argues that structuralism is well able to defend itself against its critics, but only on condition that it become much more *self*-critical. If it does so, it will resume its place as an essential element in the current discussions out of which the other chapters of this book emerge.

One complaint against structuralism is that it tries to imitate the methods of the *natural sciences,* seeing its models for the analysis of texts as "natural laws," objectively valid for all texts, or at least all texts of a certain kind;[34] also that, in pursuit of this quest, it generates a mass of unnecessary quasi-scientific jargon. In this kind of structuralism, the text becomes just an example of general laws, leaving no place for subjectivity and the active role of the reader.[35] Another complaint is that, in its insistence on a synchronic view of the text, structuralism is *ahistorical and antimaterialist,* positing timeless structures that

---

is adaptable. This book does not make clear how the model is based on the semiotic square; readers wishing to understand the theory more deeply should consult Patte's *The Religious Dimensions of Biblical Texts* (Atlanta: Scholars Press, 1990).

32. See Richard Harland, *Superstructuralism: The Philosophy of Structuralism and Post-Structuralism* (New York: Methuen, 1987), 77–91 (on Greimas and others in his tradition), 52–64, 167–69 (on Roland Barthes and Julia Kristeva), 101–20, 155–66 (on Michel Foucault). See also The Bible and Culture Collective, *The Postmodern Bible* (New Haven: Yale University Press, 1995), especially chap. 2, "Structuralist and Narratological Criticism," 70–118.

33. Caws, *Structuralism.*

34. See Christine Brooke-Rose, "Whatever Happened to Narratology?" *Poetics Today* 11 (1990): 287–89.

35. Ibid., 285–86.

take no account of the text's belonging to a particular set of historical circumstances, and seeking to abstract from the text's material context patterns that have no material existence. Finally, structuralism is seen as *positivistic,* suggesting that there is a single "right" answer to the problems of the text, and as claiming that its view is *the* comprehensive one, able to account for all rival views and go beyond them.[36]

This is indeed a formidable catalogue of alleged errors! Caws does not minimize the problems of structuralism, but claims nonetheless that it offers a major new option for understanding the human and social sciences, and that it has not been given anything like an adequate chance to show its potential. He sees the rejection of it as due more to the vagaries of academic fashion than to careful consideration of its claim to provide a new explanation of the fundamental fact that human beings find the world intelligible.

But structuralism must stop indulging in "megalomaniac pretensions" of being able to create models that are universally valid.[37] The mind's work of discovering patterns in experienced reality begins with what is immediately presented to it, with what is close at hand, and structuralism too should therefore concern itself first with small-scale and local intelligibility. Similarly, structuralism's concern is with the *material,* for the mind must begin with what is materially present to it. To understand this point, recall the difference between Propp and Lévi-Strauss. Where Propp wanted to turn things like eagles, horses, and boats into mere instances of general categories, Lévi-Strauss insists on their material differences, differences that exist in the mind's perception of the material world — in this case connections with air, earth, and water. It is true that abstract models are part of the mind's — and of structuralism's — way of working, but they have no reality in separation from the material world. For example, Greimas's actantial model consists of very general categories, but it should not be thought of as having any existence aside from particular cases where particular entities occupy the slots.[38]

Structuralism is likewise untrue to its basic impulse when it tries to bracket out subjectivity and the role of the *individual* mind in sense-making. The human subject cannot be treated objectively, as if it were merely a part of the intelligible world, since it itself *makes* the world intelligible.[39] The only place where the world's intelligibility can reside is in *individual* minds. Again, the analogy of language is helpful. Where is the "system" of English, English as a *langue,* to be found? It exists in a huge number of individual minds (Caws's

36. Harland, *Superstructuralism,* 59–64.

37. Caws, *Structuralism,* 153.

38. Similar considerations should lay to rest any claim that structuralism, in its basic philosophical position, is ahistorical; ibid., 256–57.

39. Ibid., 237–41.

word is "distributively"), and in no two identically. Its existence continues and changes through the endless interaction of all of these minds. One reason the claims of structuralism cannot be objectively true is that structuralism itself (like anything else) has only this kind of distributive existence. What it is for you will not be exactly the same as what it is for me, even if you accept my account of it. Even if you read the books I recommend, they will not say to you what they say to me. The reasons structuralism appeals, or not, to one person or another have to do with the individual characteristics of the people, not with the "truth" of structuralism.

Finally, to insist on this kind of critical view of structuralism is to break down the distinction between it and "poststructuralism." The latter is not a very satisfactory term. Along with "postmodernism," it is used to refer to the current intellectual climate, in which everything that has been regarded as stable, certain, and "natural"—from the nuclear family to the superiority of certain "classics" over other literature—is shown to be the result of historical developments that favor the political interests of specific human groups at the expense of others. Deconstruction, one of the main movements within post-structuralism (see chapter 6 of this volume), is for Caws simply structuralism in a critical mode. Structuralism implies a hermeneutic of suspicion: "The need for deconstruction arises when the externalization of knowledge [makes people] acquire ready-made structures . . . uncritically."[40]

The modes of literary structuralism—based on Propp, Lévi-Strauss, and Greimas—that I considered in the previous section lay themselves open to the kinds of criticisms I have enumerated. But they also have potential for being put at the service of a radically critical structuralism. Consider, for example, the appropriation of Greimas by Fredric Jameson, an American Marxist critic who is at the center of current postmodern debate and has provided a major impulse toward the "ideological" reading of texts, including biblical ones.[41] Jameson wrote the foreword to the English translation of one of Greimas's major works.[42] Though Jameson has no use for any "orthodox" Greimasian system, he asserts the incomparable political value of Greimas's approach, provided it is used in a critical and flexible manner.

His main enthusiasm is reserved for the semiotic square. He insists that the square is *not symmetrical*, for example, that "white versus black" is not the same as "black versus white."[43] The square's greatest potential emerges at the non-B

40. Ibid., 214; cf. 159–64.

41. See chapter 7 of this book, and also David Jobling and Tina Pippin, eds. *Ideological Criticism of Biblical Texts* (*Semeia* 59; Atlanta: Scholars Press, 1992).

42. Fredric Jameson, foreword to Greimas, *On Meaning*, vi–xxii.

43. Ibid., xv. Greimas and his group are aware of this—see especially Patte's use of the terms "positive" and "negative" for the A and B points of the square (e.g. *Religious Dimensions*, 94–95).

corner, which is generally the last to be occupied in analysis.[44] The white versus black example suggests why this is so. If we begin with A = white and B = black, then non-A will be a category that is familiar to us — the term "non-white" is common in our discourse. But no one ever says "non-black," which shows that the two initial terms are not symmetrical. "White" connotes "sharing in European culture," and non-white connotes not doing so. The white-black opposition is revealed as a shorthand, Eurocentric way of saying "us versus the rest." The square forces those of us of European background to ask what "non-black" might mean, and the fact that we are not able to answer this question shows that even when using the category "black," we never considered what might be specific to and valuable in black culture.

The person who has most insisted on a critical structuralism in biblical studies is Mieke Bal, and it happens that the Book of Judges has been the focus of her work on the Bible. Bal comes from a structuralist tradition different from the one described above, associated especially with the work of the French literary critic Gérard Genette. Genette's approach is more pragmatic and less philosophical, and more bound to the particular discipline of literary (especially narrative) studies. But it shares the structuralist impulse of trying to describe and organize the characteristics of narrative writing as such.[45]

Bal proposes "a model for narratological analysis,"[46] based on the functions in the text of speaking, seeing, and doing. How are these distributed, among the characters, and between the characters and the narrator? Are there characters who are only the objects, never the subjects, of these functions? Mere quantity is not the only issue; some characters may speak a lot, but may use only questions, while others use commands. What Bal means by speaking and doing is obvious; it is in seeing, or "focalization," that her special contribution lies. She shows the subtlety with which the point of view of the narrative shifts between characters and narrator, and the critical significance of these shifts. (The one who sees at a given moment can be a character whom the text does not even name! For example, the birth scene in Genesis 25:25-26 is seen from the point of view of a midwife, though none is mentioned; a character in the story is here *created* by critical analysis.)

Bal applies the categories of action and focalization to the following speech

44. Jameson, foreword to Greimas, *On Meaning,* xvi.

45. Gérard Genette, *Narrative Discourse: An Essay in Method,* trans. Jane E. Lewin (Ithaca, N.Y.: Cornell University Press, 1980). Bal rarely uses the word structuralism, preferring "critical narratology." For an account of her relationship to structuralism, see Mieke Bal, *On Story-Telling: Essays in Narratology,* ed. David Jobling (Sonoma, Calif.: Polebridge Press, 1991), 1–24.

46. For a tabular summary of the model, see Bal, *Death and Dissymmetry,* 248–49, and *On Story-Telling,* 166–67. The theoretical discussion of the model in *On Story-Telling*

in Judges 19. The old man who offered hospitality to the Levite is responding to the mob's demand that the Levite be handed over to them for sexual abuse:

> No, my brothers, do not act wickedly. Since this man has come to my house, do not do this wantonness. Behold my nubile daughter and his concubine; let me bring them out. Rape them and do to them what is good in your eyes; but against this man do not do this wanton thing.[47]

The man focalizes the actions (actual and intended) of the other characters, and tries to get the mob to share his point of view, to "see it his way" (he fails; cf. 19:25). He presents the Levite as an *acting subject* — "this man has come to my house" (the NRSV's "is my guest" misses this) — in contrast to his *objectification* of the women. He also focalizes the potential actions of the mob in a way that sharpens the contrast of male and female. Bal seizes on the difference between "act wickedly" and "do what is good" (a structuralist eye fixes automatically on this kind of opposition). For the mob's intended action toward the male Levite, the man uses only the language of wickedness; when referring to what they may do to the women, he uses the term "good." Bal is well aware that "do what is good in one's own eyes" is a conventional expression which usually refers to something *bad,* but this does not lessen the force of the verbal contrast. In order to get the mob to focalize outrages committed against a *man* as bad, the host invites them to focalize ("in your eyes") outrages committed against *women* as good.

In another book devoted to the accounts of Jael's killing of Sisera in Judges 4:17-22 and 5:24-27, Bal makes critical use of the semiotic square.[48] For example, she looks at how modern commentators treat the theological opposition between Yahweh and the gods of Canaan, and uses the square to work out the links by which these commentators arrive at ethical value judgments. As Bal analyzes the procedure, the commentators first transform the opposition "Yahweh versus the gods of Canaan" into two others oppositions, "high versus low" and "monotheism versus polytheism" (i.e., "singular versus plural"), resulting in the following squares (reduced to the four main terms):

(159–68) is superior to that in *Death and Dissymmetry* (32–39). In her treatment of Judges texts, Bal does not always show *how* she is using the model, but she always *is* using it.

47. Judges 19:23b–24; my translation based on Bal's argumentation, *Death and Dissymmetry,* 122.

48. Mieke Bal, *Murder and Difference: Gender, Genre, and Scholarship on Sisera's Death,* trans. Matthew Gumpert (Bloomington, Ind.: Indiana University Press, 1988). I am here summarizing Bal's discussion of the two semiotic squares on pp. 41 and 44.

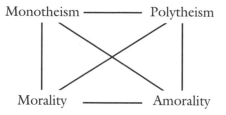

The high-low distinction has, first of all, a quite literal sense; Yahweh is a god of heaven, in contrast to the earth (agriculture) gods of the Canaanites. But this is transferred to "high" and "low" morality. The singular-plural distinction starts with monotheism and polytheism, but is transformed into the realm of sexual ethics via monogamy and polygamy, the latter being made to tie up with Canaanite sacred prostitution. These are semiotic processes going on not (at least not mainly) in the text, but in the guise of sophisticated "objective" scholarship.

To conclude this section, I ask the reader to observe how the discussion has touched on the subject area of every chapter in this book. Narrative and social scientific criticism belong to the foundations of structuralism and all its subsequent development, feminism comes to the fore in Bal, deconstruction in Caws, ideological criticism in Jameson. I do not intend to imply by this that structuralism has the most comprehensive view of the current scene in biblical studies — it is for this sort of claim that it has been rightly criticized. But the discussion has shown that structuralism fully belongs to the interplay and conflict of methods that mark the current scene, and that the critical methods we use always impinge upon each other.

A Reading of "Fords of the Jordan" Incidents

Three times in the judge-cycles (3:27-29, 7:24 — 8:3, 12:1-6), there is recorded an incident in which the judge-deliverer's group occupies the crossing points of the River Jordan against another group, and inflicts great slaughter upon them as they try to cross. So similar are these incidents that one is at first tempted to count them among the elements that different judge-cycles have in common (compare my earlier discussion of Culley). However, on closer examination, one finds that the differences are even more compelling. Perhaps the most obvious difference is that, while the defeated enemy in the first two instances are foreigners, in the last case (12:1-6) they are fellow Israelites! The following reading will consist first of an analysis along the lines of Lévi-Strauss, whose method is well adapted to the treatment of such difference within similarity. Later, I shall employ Mieke Bal's model and the semiotic square to suggest how formal analysis may lead to broad-ranging critical conclusions.

The following presentation of the three incidents highlights both similarities and differences.

3:27-29   The judge (Ehud) summons the tribe of Ephraim to the war
at the beginning of the war.
Together they hold the fords of the Jordan,
thus defeating the whole enemy (Moab).
There is no tension between Ehud and Ephraim.

7:24 — 8:3   The judge (Gideon) summons Ephraim to the war
after the decisive battle.
Ephraim alone holds "the waters . . . and also the Jordan,"[49]
thus defeating a small part of the enemy (Midian).
A quarrel ensues between Gideon and Ephraim; it is resolved.

12:1-6   The judge (Jephthah) fails to summon Ephraim to the war
and defeats the enemy (the Ammonites) without them;
Ephraim arrives after the war is over.
An irresoluble quarrel ensues between Jephthah and
Ephraim.
Jephthah hold the fords of the Jordan,
thus defeating Ephraim (who has become the enemy).

The common framework is the defeat by the judge of a foreign enemy. Also common to all three incidents is the theme of calling on Ephraim (the major tribe of the Israelite confederacy) to join the war. But this Ephraim theme is treated in very different ways, and represents the most obvious *variable*. The first and last passages present a complete contrast. In the first, Ephraim is summoned at the outset and takes a full part in the victory; in the last, Ephraim is not summoned and takes no part in the victory. In the first, the judge is in alliance with Ephraim; in the last, he is totally antagonistic to them. The two outer passages set up, therefore, two major oppositions:

1. Summon Ephraim (at the outset) *versus* Not summon Ephraim
2. Judge in alliance with Ephraim *versus* Judge antagonistic to Ephraim

49. The geographical reference here is different from the other two stories, and rather obscure: "the waters as far as Beth-barah, and also the Jordan," instead of "the fords of the Jordan." I suspect that "the Jordan" has been tacked on as a result of the very process whereby the separate stories have developed into a set of structurally related stories.

The middle passage in the sequence seems, in an uncanny way, to occupy a middle position also in its meaning. In terms of the first opposition, Ephraim *is* summoned, but not at the outset, so that it takes only a small part in the victory. In terms of the second, antagonism *does* arise between the judge and Ephraim, but it gets resolved. In summary, something between a summons and no summons leads to something between full and nonparticipation in the war, and to something between alliance and antagonism! To use the language of Lévi-Strauss, the middle passage *mediates* the opposition between the other two.[50]

Our analysis cannot proceed any further along this line, because we have identified only one variable, the relationship of the judge to Ephraim (the other differences are simply consequences of this). We need to identify a *covariable,* something quite different that changes as the relationship of the judge to Ephraim changes. I suggest that the tribal geography of the judge provides such a covariable. Ehud belongs to Benjamin, a tribe located (like Ephraim) *west* of the Jordan. At the other extreme, Jephthah belongs to Gilead, a tribe located *east* of the Jordan. Again, the outer stories offer a simple opposition, east versus west. The middle story mediates this opposition too, for Gideon belongs to Manasseh, the only tribe whose territory spans *both* sides of the Jordan. These stories carry, it seems, a message about antagonism between the parts of Israel lying on the two sides of the Jordan, a message that can be carried only by a *group* of stories in their organized differences from one another and not by any one of the stories alone.[51]

Bal's model allows us to carry the discussion further. If I am right that the passages give insight into a deep-seated conflict, does the narrative remain neutral or take sides? One's first guess would be that stories of judges are told with a bias in favor of the judge. But does the treatment of action, speech, and focalization in the three stories support this?

In 3:27-29, everything is harmonious. Only Ehud speaks, and the Ephraimites obey him. He and they act in unison. The two parties focalize the events in complete reciprocity; the Ephraimites see Ehud "at their head," while he sees them "following after" him.

Judges 7:24 — 8:3 begins in a way that is superficially similar to 3:27-29, with a summons to the Ephraimites and their successful seizing of the waters. But,

---

50. For example, see Lévi-Strauss, *Structural Anthropology,* 224–27. For a much more elaborate example of the creation of a "middle semantics" to mediate between extremes, see my treatment of Genesis 2–3 (Jobling, *The Sense of Biblical Narrative,* vol. 2, 27–39).

51. My essay "The Jordan a Boundary" (ibid., 88–134), from which the foregoing analysis is taken (125–27), contains verification of this suggestion from elsewhere in the Bible.

aside from the fact that the decisive battle has already occurred before Gideon summons the Ephraimites, it may be significant that he does not summon them *personally.* The use of "messengers" seems to create distance, so that we are less surprised by the subsequent disharmony. In the conflict scene, 8:1-3, the Ephraimite view of the situation is given first (8:1), before Gideon's (8:2-3). And the reader who has been following the story carefully will agree with the Ephraimite version, for Ephraim is missing from the list of tribes summoned at the outset of the campaign (6:35). We may also see a contrast between the *speech* qualities of the two parties—the Ephraimites forceful, Gideon conciliatory and even wheedling. Thus this narrative seems to take the Ephraimites' side.

Most interesting is the final story in 12:1-6. Jephthah and the Gileadites dominate the *action,* initiating the battle (12:4) and setting the Ephraimites a test, which they fail (12:5-6). The same dominance extends to a lesser extent to *speech.* Though the Ephraimites begin the dialogue with a strong speech (12:1, cf. 8:1), Jephthah responds with one just as strong (12:2-3; contrast Gideon's words in 8:2-3). And the test the Ephraimites fail is a speech test! Thus analysis of action and speech suggests a pro-judge bias. *Focalization,* however, yields a different picture. As in the case of Gideon, the reader agrees with the Ephraimite view, since the rest of the story confirms that Jephthah never summoned them. More important, v. 4 seems to give the Ephraimite view not only of this campaign, but of the fundamental relationship between Ephraimites and Gileadites. This verse is obscure, but taken literally (as in the NRSV) it suggests that the Gileadites formerly lived with the Ephraimites *west* of the Jordan, and that their migration to the east was blameworthy.

In all the passages, then, the Ephraimites seem to have the "right" view (that is, the narrator's view) of what is going on. It is jarring to read of the fall of forty-two thousand Ephraimites (12:6), but perhaps even this is to be seen as part of a powerful critique of Jephthah, a critique that begins with the tragic story of his daughter (11:30-31, 34-40) and ends with the note that he judged Israel only six years rather than the usual forty (12:7). The analysis suggests, then, that the message of the set of passages is pro-Ephraim, rather than pro-judge; or perhaps one had better say that there is tension in the Book of Judges between these two perspectives. Bal's analytic approach is well adapted for identifying such tensions.

The semiotic square may take us even deeper. I suggest that the most profound opposition that emerges from this set of stories is between "inside" and "outside." The Ephraimites, who stand for those living in the land of Canaan, west of the Jordan, see themselves (and the narrator likely shares their perspective) as "insiders"—definitely members of Yahweh's community. Non-Israelites they see equally clearly as outsiders. The status of people calling themselves

Israelites but living outside the land of Canaan, east of the Jordan, is anoma-
lous—are they inside or outside?[52] This suggests the following square:

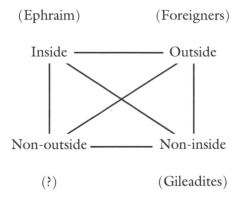

The Gileadites, who are geographically outside but who belong to Israel and
ought to be inside, appropriately occupy the position of "Non-inside" in the
workings of the semiotic square. But who, in that case, fit the "Non-outside"
position? Presumably those who are geographically inside but ought to be outside, that is, foreigners who live *in* the land.

   This suggestion may help explain an odd feature of the structure of the Book
of Judges as a whole. I have referred to the "theoretical" statement about how
judgeship works, which the Deuteronomist includes near the beginning of the
book (2:11-19). Instead of moving directly from this statement into the judge-
cycles (which begin at 3:7), the editor interposes the section 2:20—3:6, which
deals with the issue of why Canaanites were left in the land after Joshua. Given
that this is not an issue that will receive particular attention in the judge-cycles,
why is it included in the programmatic introduction to them? Perhaps, a structuralist would say, because, although it is not part of the surface agenda, it is
part of the deep-structural problematic of the whole book. The possibility of
Israelites outside the land, which I have argued to be an issue in the "fords of
the Jordan" passages, implies, at the level of the mind's semiotic activity, the

---

52. There are other indications of this problematic. The Ehud story seems to equate
"Israelites" with Ephraimites (3:27). In both the Gideon and the Jephthah stories, the
Ephraimites turn quarrelsome when they cross the Jordan (7:25; 12:1)—perhaps merely
doing so makes them ill at ease. The Jephthah story even posits a linguistic difference
between the groups east and west of the river (12:5–6). It also suggests that Israelites
living east of Jordan are "fugitives" from their proper place. This may explain the curious double use of "fugitives of Ephraim"; in 12:4 it refers to the Gileadites, but in
12:5 to the Ephraimites themselves. Perhaps by the very act of crossing the Jordan, the
Ephraimites have made themselves "fugitives."

possibility of *non-Israelites inside* the land, and hence focuses attention on the problem of the Canaanites. The odd presence of 2:20 — 3:6 betrays an aware- ness (conscious or unconscious) of the importance of this problem.

Conclusion

Structuralists suggest that meaning comes to us only in patterns. Patterns are what the mind can perceive; indeed, minds create themselves through their perception of the patternedness in reality. In reading a text, the patterning activ- ity of *my* mind responds to the patterning activity of other minds that produced the text. But there is every reason to expect that the structures will be im- mensely complex, and also, since so many minds have been at work, *unstable;* particularly so with an ancient text like the Bible, where these minds have worked in many languages (both in the normal sense of language and in the extended sense of cultural "languages," or sets of expectations). The mind's patterning activity is also an unpatterning activity — of seeing old patterning from a new perspective as problematic, of trying to unravel the bits of meaning and put them back together in more usable ways.

The most enduring and satisfying image of such activity is one suggested by Lévi-Strauss, that of the *bricoleur,* the "odd-job man."[53] The *bricoleur* uses what- ever odds and ends he can find to fix things up, inventing tools if they are not available, always improvising to produce a workable world. This, according to Lévi-Strauss, is what primitive peoples do in creating myths — they take what- ever bits the world offers and put them together in ways that seem to help to make sense, to make the world workable. But "advanced" minds do not do anything different in principle. Lévi-Strauss himself, in his myth-analyses, pro- vides an excellent example. He does not take to his myth-analysis a set of struc- tural techniques that he expects will clarify all the data. Rather, like the *bricoleur,* as he goes along he invents structural models that seem adequate to some of the data, and extends, modifies, or rejects them as further data demand. Jame- son jokingly borrows this image of the *bricoleur* to describe his own approach to Greimas's system; he takes only what he finds useful for building his own models.[54]

It is as a *bricoleur* that you should approach this chapter and the analytical models that have been mentioned in it. These models are based on large num- bers of texts, and have been found *satisfying,* in that they give at least to some minds a sense of seeing what is going on in texts, including biblical texts. They

53. Claude Lévi-Strauss, *The Savage Mind* (Chicago: University of Chicago Press, 1966), 16–33.
54. Jameson, foreword to Greimas, *On Meaning,* viii.

and other available models should be used for what they prove to be worth, for their ability to satisfy us as we bring to the text our endless varieties of questions. But all models (whether their proponents admit it or not) have limits to their helpfulness. If your structural readings are limited to the wooden employment of other people's models, they will be impoverished and even boring. You have to make the work *your own*. If the structuralist account of the mind is correct, "structural analysis" is what you do all the time, as you look for significant patterning in the data you perceive, and create models that make the data workable for you. Formal structural analysis simply brings this process to greater self-consciousness. In fact, the formal models that have been found most useful, especially the semiotic square in the hands of a Bal or a Jameson, are the ones that provide the barest framework, and leave nearly everything to the people who employ them.

Your work as a structuralist is this: Bringing your own questions as determined by your own setting, using other people's techniques only for help in devising your own, *to see what you can make* of the Book of Judges.

Further Reading

General

BARTHES, Roland. *The Semiotic Challenge*. Translated by Richard Howard. New York: Hill and Wang, 1988. See especially "Introduction to the Structural Analysis of Narratives" (95–135), a classic account of structuralist methodology, and "Wrestling with the Angel: Textual Analysis of Genesis 32:23-33" (246–60), one of the most influential structural readings of the Bible.

CAWS, Peter. *Structuralism: The Art of the Intelligible*. Atlantic Highlands, N.J.: Humanities Press International, 1988. A philosophical statement of the claims of structuralism; also a defense against its critics that takes the criticisms seriously. The last part is for the philosophically trained, but the rest is reasonably accessible and of great importance.

GREIMAS, A. J. *Structural Semantics: An Attempt at a Method*. Translated by Daniele McDowell and others. Lincoln, Nebr.: University of Nebraska Press, 1983. A translation of the foundational work of a theoretician highly influential in the formation of biblical structuralism.

GREIMAS, A. J., and J. Courtés. *Semiotics and Language: An Analytic Dictionary*. Translated by Larry Crist et al. Bloomington, Ind.: Indiana University Press, 1982. The standard reference work for all aspects of structuralism and its application to literary studies.

HARLAND, Richard. *Superstructuralism: The Philosophy of Structuralism and Post-*

Structuralism (New York: Methuen, 1987). A bold and readable book that critiques structuralism from a poststructuralist perspective.

LEVI-STRAUSS, Claude. "The Structural Study of Myth." *Structural Anthropology,* translated by Claire Jacobson and Brooke Grundfest Schoepf, 206–31. New York: Basic Books, 1963. Of enormous influence, and the best brief statement of Lévi-Strauss's approach to myth.

———. *The Raw and the Cooked.* Translated by John and Doreen Weightman. New York: Harper & Row, 1970. The first of a four-volume work on Amerindian mythology, this demonstrates (as the preceding article does not) the scope and resourcefulness of the author's myth analysis.

PROPP, Vladimir. *Morphology of the Folktale.* 2d ed. Translated by Laurence Scott. Austin, Tex.: University of Texas Press, 1968. This first attempt to apply a recognizably structural method to the analysis of narrative (Russian fairy tales) has been very influential in biblical studies.

SAUSSURE, Ferdinand de. *Course in General Linguistics.* Edited by Charles Bally et al. Translated by Wade Baskin. New York: McGraw-Hill, 1959. The founding document of structuralism, introducing the linguistic categories with which later structuralists — and also poststructuralists — have continued to work.

SCHOLES, Robert. *Structuralism in Literature: An Introduction.* New Haven: Yale University Press, 1974. An early work that continues to be one of the best general introductions.

Biblical

BAL, Mieke. *Death and Dissymmetry: The Politics of Coherence in the Book of Judges.* Chicago: University of Chicago Press, 1988. The most extended biblical work of an author who insistently brings biblical studies in touch with current critical theory. Bal's method, critical narratology, leads into a range of feminist, psychoanalytic, and ideological issues.

THE BIBLE AND CULTURE COLLECTIVE. *The Postmodern Bible.* New Haven: Yale University Press, 1995. An extended, critical account of achievements and prospects in the application of new methods to biblical studies. See especially "Structuralist and Narratological Criticism."

JOBLING, David. *The Sense of Biblical Narrative: Structural Analyses in the Hebrew Bible.* 2 vol. Sheffield, Eng.: JSOT Press, 1988. Six structural analyses that use a method loosely based on Greimas and, especially, Lévi-Strauss, and stress the potential of structuralism for practical biblical exegesis.

LEACH, Edmund. *Genesis as Myth and Other Essays.* London: Jonathan Cape, 1969. Brilliant and maddening structuralist interpretations of biblical themes by a leading anthropologist and an irreverent follower of Lévi-Strauss. Most successful is "The Legitimacy of Solomon."

PATTE, Daniel. *The Religious Dimensions of Biblical Texts: Greimas's Structural Semiotics and Biblical Exegesis.* Atlanta: Scholars Press, 1990. A thorough presentation of Greimas's mature method by the most influential advocate of structuralism in North American biblical studies.

———. *Structural Exegesis for New Testament Critics.* Minneapolis: Fortress Press, 1990. Part of the Guides to Biblical Scholarship series, this book offers a simple practical method for the analysis of biblical texts. It is theoretically thin, and many readers will want to augment it with Patte's *The Religious Dimensions of Biblical Texts.*

WHITE, Hugh. *Narration and Discourse in the Book of Genesis.* Cambridge: Cambridge University Press, 1991. In a difficult but very important book, White develops a semiotic method that moves beyond Saussure's linguistic model, and applies it to Genesis through a series of brilliant readings.

6

DECONSTRUCTIVE CRITICISM: ACHSAH AND THE (E)RAZED CITY OF WRITING*

Danna Nolan Fewell

What Is Deconstruction and Why Should Anybody Bother with It?

In the field of literary studies, deconstruction has received a lot of bad press.[1] Its theoreticians (most noted of whom in the West have been French philosopher Jacques Derrida and the late Belgian critic Paul de Man)[2]

*More and more I am coming to realize and take advantage of the communal aspect of scholarship. I would like to thank the following friends who have helped me formulate and sharpen this particular piece: my students John Havea and Elaine Robinson, who have been especially helpful (in ways they don't even know) to the exegetical enterprise; my colleague Jouette Bassler and my editor Gale Yee, who have devoted their attention to the chapter's accessibility; my reliable resource on theory, Gary Phillips, who has served as a gentle but diligent educator on the subject of deconstruction. I strongly encourage my readers to turn to Phillip's own work (cited below and in the further reading) to fill the theoretical gaps that I inevitably leave in this cursory treatment.

1. The following discussion focuses almost exclusively on deconstruction as a way of thinking about language and texts. This, of course, is merely a part of a broader philosophical discourse that has profound social and cultural ramifications (some of which will be discussed below). The notion of undecidability is the linguistic application of a larger understanding that questions anyone's ability to capture completely the nature of reality in any one theoretical description. Just as the world is more than anyone can possibly comprehend, so, too, a text is elusive to comprehensive interpretation. For a more detailed treatment, see Gary Phillips, "Exegesis as Critical Praxis: Reclaiming History and Text from a Postmodern Perspective," *Semeia* 51 (1990): 7–49; and "The Ethics of Reading Deconstructively, or Speaking Face-to-Face: The Samaritan Woman Meets Derrida at the Well," in Elizabeth Struthers Malbon and Edgar McKnight, eds., *The New Literary Criticism and the New Testament* (Sheffield, Eng.: Sheffield Academic Press, 1994), 283–325.

2. Other critics commonly associated with deconstruction are Roland Barthes, Jacques Lacan, Michel Foucault, and members of the "Yale School" J. Hillis Miller, Geoffrey Hartman, and Harold Bloom.

have been attacked as being linguistic acrobats, unnecessarily obscure and all but unreadable. As a reading process, deconstruction has been accused of being a nihilistic, apolitical, academic exercise which may have inspired some clever textual interpretations, even some radical theology (or atheology), but which has done little to change the ways in which most people read their texts and live their lives.

Deconstruction, with its radically different understandings of textuality and reading, has been particularly unwelcome to many in the field of biblical studies. Not only does deconstruction open biblical texts to nontraditional readings, thereby "decentering" the authority of traditional interpretations, but it also challenges the monopoly of what has come to be the authorized and acceptable methods of study, namely those falling under the rubric of historical criticism and the more "established" kinds of literary and social scientific criticisms.[3] Deconstruction threatens most where absolutism is dearest, whether the subject be "Truth," a firmly entrenched theory or method, or religious faith.

So, if you teach and write about the Bible, why should you promote deconstruction as a critical understanding if the end results are that you confuse your students, rankle your colleagues, and get yourself labeled a heretic by whatever religious constituency might be contributing to your salary? Or, if you are a student in biblical studies, either working on a liberal arts degree or preparing for some sort of leadership role in synagogue or church, why subject yourself to a view of language and culture that will only complicate the way you read, the way you write, the way you behave, and the way you view biblical authority and your own personal responsibility? Who needs the hassle?

Well, precisely those who thrive on hassle. Reading texts, after all, involves a lot of hassles. Any serious student of exegesis knows this. One passage can spawn a legion of interpretations. Sometimes an entire reading can stand or fall based on the translation of one little preposition. Simply identifying the beginning and end of the text to be studied can involve difficult and often arbitrary decisions. Even the most seemingly straightforward of texts have this uncanny habit of (to use the words of lyricist Paul Simon) "slip-sliding away" just when you think you have them all figured out.[4]

---

3. Historical critics tend to ignore the challenge of deconstruction, treating it as if it had nothing to do with their enterprises. Literary critics tend to be divided: some ignore it; others either make an effort to deal with it (see entries in the further reading) or eschew it outright (see Robert Alter and Frank Kermode's "General Introduction" in *The Literary Guide to the Bible* [Cambridge: Harvard University Press, 1987] and the more recent writings of Alter).

4. The metaphor taken from songwriter Paul Simon's lyric "The nearer your destination, the more you're slip-sliding away" seems particularly appropriate in this context because it implies (by analogy) the contribution of the reader and the reading process to the slipperiness of textual meaning.

Other Truths

For readers who recognize and who are not too bothered by how slippery texts are, deconstruction provides a helpful way of thinking and reading and writing. Deconstruction, as a theory of texts, allows that texts, like people, differ within themselves. No characterization, no matter how exhaustive, can completely capture the essence of who a person is. Our personality traits do not blend smoothly into one harmonious whole. If they did we would be stereotypes rather than real people. There is always something Other about us, something Else that differs from, something in excess of, the ways in which we are generally perceived. Likewise, a text does not manifest one uncontestable meaning.[5] There is always something Other, something Else, that falls through the cracks of any one interpretation. Moreover, just as we change through our encounters and relationships with other people, so textual meanings change as different readers read in different contexts with different goals in mind. The range of a text's possible meanings and functions (like our own various roles in life) are

---

Unfortunately, the metaphor of slipperiness has a negative connotation in a culture that overtly values such notions as steadiness, certainty, stability, and consistency. I would like to suggest that slipperiness is a positive image, which, unlike the conceptual repertoire of "steadfastness," slipperiness represents the "beyondness" of our comprehension, the challenge to reach past authorized limits, the radical freedom of the world to be more than we can name.

5. Barbara Johnson uses excerpts from Rousseau's *Confessions* to illustrate this notion of the divided self and its analogy to textuality:

Rousseau's opening statement about himself is precisely an affirmation of difference: "I am unlike anyone I have ever met; I will even venture to say that I am like no one in the whole world. I may be no better, but at least I am different" (Penguin edition, 1954, p. 17). Now, this can be read as an unequivocal assertion of uniqueness, of difference between Rousseau and the whole rest of the world. This is the boast on which the book is based. But in what does the uniqueness of this self consist? It is not long before we find out: "There are times when I am so unlike myself that I might be taken for someone else of an entirely opposite character" (p. 126). "In me are united two almost irreconcilable characteristics, though in what way I cannot imagine" (p. 112). In other words, this story of the self's difference from others inevitably becomes the story of its own unbridgeable difference from itself. Difference is not engendered in the space between identities; it is what makes all totalization of the identity of a self or the meaning of a text impossible.

"The Critical Difference: BarthesS/BalZac," *The Critical Difference: Essays in the Contemporary Rhetoric of Reading* (Baltimore: Johns Hopkins, 1980), 3–12; repr. in Robert Con Davis, ed., *Contemporary Literary Criticism: Modernism Through Post-Structuralism* (New York and London: Longman, 1986), 439–46, 440–41.

not even necessarily compatible. More often, they are in tension with one another, competing, conflicting, and unsettling one another.

Let's try another image.[6] Imagine a large blue painting at the far end of the room — an abstract painting, nothing but blue. As you approach the work you realize that the blue is not uniform. Various shades shift back and forth from background to foreground depending upon the angle of your perspective. You draw closer to examine the texture. You discover that the painting is not completely blue at all. There are red dots of various sizes, mostly around the margins, but a few scattered across the middle. You cannot tell if the red is emerging from beneath the blue or if the red has been applied on top of the blue. You first think that the red is an accidental spattering, perhaps not even intended by the artist. But then you begin to imagine that, if you scraped away the blue, you might find a whole field of red beneath. Then you wonder, What else might be beneath all that blue? What else is being eclipsed in order for blue to rule the canvas?

What does this painting mean? Is it a painting about blue? Or is it a painting about red? Is it a painting about dominance and submission, that is, the dominance of blue and the submission of red? Or is it a painting about subversion, that is, the subversion of blue by red? Or does the painting suggest that red lends blue its meaning? Or vice versa? How do you decide what this painting is about? The minute you settle on one interpretation, another claims your attention. What you discover is that the painting is not about *either* this *or* that. Rather, it is about *both* this *and* that. The meaning is undecidable, because, in fact, the meaning is unstable.

Texts are like this painting. There are obvious dominant subjects, subjects that both common and critical readings have recognized and accented. But even those subjects, accepted by consensus, do not elicit uniform interpretations. There are always various hues in the text, various dimensions of character, nuances of argument, ambiguities of imagery, vocabulary, and syntax that keep even the most commonly accepted subject from being decidable. And then there are elements that are often not considered to be subjects at all, seemingly incidental red dots scattered through the text that go unnoticed by many. Yet these supposedly incidental elements both define and are defined by whatever most readers consider to be of dominant concern. They may disturb, they may counter, they may discredit, they may dismantle, they may subvert, they may twist, they may draw attention away from the dominant meanings and subjects

---

6. David Gunn and I both have used the following image with great success with our own students and have incorporated a version of it into the introduction of Danna Nolan Fewell and David M. Gunn, *Gender, Power, and Promise: The Subject of the Bible's First Story* (Nashville: Abingdon Press, 1993), 9.

of the text. But whatever they do, they surely complicate and destabilize meaning.

Instability of meaning goes against the grain for most readers. Most readers want to know what a text says in order to categorize it, to file it away somewhere, and not to have to think about it again. We are trained to think in either/or categories and to regard learning as the accumulation of tidy facts and figures. We master texts. We decide what they are about. And once we have established the "truth" of the text, we move on to something else.

Our preoccupation with the "truth" of a text is grounded in a philosophical tradition (stemming from Plato) that posits that "reason can somehow dispense with language and arrive at a pure, self-authenticating truth or method."[7] The idea of an attainable, self-present truth compels most textual critics to look for *a* meaning, a "right" interpretation, and a method of reading that will allow us to reach that right (or at least "highly probable") interpretation. In biblical studies this usually takes the form of attempting to discover the original intention or the original situation or the original form of a text's inception. In other words, if we could just get back to the actual utterance, to that self-present truth, we could know what was meant.

Deconstruction, however, critiques this endeavor. As literary critic Christopher Norris writes,

> Language can fulfil the condition of self-present meaning only if it offers a *total and immediate* access to the thoughts that occasioned its utterance. But this is an impossible requirement. We simply cannot have what Derrida calls "a primordial intuition of the other's lived experience." In which case . . . it has to be admitted that language must always fail to achieve expressive self-presence, and must always partake of the indicative character which marks . . . the suspension of meaning.[8]

As with reading, so with writing: we cannot get beyond language. All systems of thought trying to arrive at truth are bound by their textuality. As texts they are subject to the disruptive effects of language, the suspension and the Otherness and the excess and the oscillation of meaning.[9] Despite every attempt to be direct, clear, and univocal, that is, singular in point and purpose, we cannot

---

7. Christopher Norris, *Deconstruction: Theory and Practice* (London and New York: Routledge, 1982; repr. 1991), 19.

8. Norris, *Deconstruction*, 46.

9. We are trained to be precise in our (scholarly) writing, to eschew irony and wordplay and humor. We are taught that the pursuit of knowledge and truth is serious business, and we constrain our writing to reflect that seriousness. Deconstructionists, on the other hand, following Derrida's lead, often employ wordplays in resistance to Western scholarly genres in order to accentuate excess of meaning.

eradicate the Other from our discourse. There is always an excess of meaning. Traces of something Other inevitably remain.[10]

Speaking of Writing

Deconstruction is a reading event and cannot be appropriately separated from textual work.[11] The most famous example of a text's deconstruction, often cited and alluded to in discussions of deconstructive criticism, is Derrida's own analysis of a passage from Plato's *Phaedrus*.[12] In the passage Socrates tells of an encounter in which the god Theuth divulges his "arts" to the Egyptian king Thamus, suggesting that these arts would be of benefit to human beings. Thamus, however, refuses the art of writing, remarking, "If men learn this, it will implant forgetfulness in their souls; they will cease to exercise memory because they rely on that which is written, calling things to remembrance no longer from within themselves, but by means of external marks. What you have discovered is a recipe not for memory, but for reminder." Agreeing with Thamus's negative pronouncement on writing, Socrates goes on to praise speech instead as the legitimate conveyor of meaning, of which writing is merely an inadequate copy.

Derrida deconstructs the text (or indicates how the text deconstructs itself) by pointing out the discrepancy between what the text says and what it does. What it says is that writing is to be condemned. What it does is to elevate writing by relying on writing as the medium to make the point that writing should be condemned. Hence the text is clearly at odds with itself.

Its language is slippery as well. The word translated "recipe" in Thamus's speech is the word *pharmakon,* which, as Derrida points out, can mean, among

10. As Timothy Beal writes, "In every text there are traces of that which has been excluded or repressed (Derrida has called them erasure marks), or even of that which is altogether absent. Indeed, a text's boundaries of meaning are always established through exclusion, repression, and marginalization. But traces remain. When attended to, these traces open beyond the narrow confines of the particular text and into relation with other texts. Traces lead readers to stray into the margins and off the page." "Glossary," in Danna Nolan Fewell, ed., *Reading Between Texts: Intertextuality and the Hebrew Bible* (Louisville, Ky.: Westminster/John Knox Press, 1992), 24.

11. Deconstruction is not a method per se. Method, of any stripe, strives toward systemization, universality, generalization. Method is not designed to appreciate the uniqueness of individual texts and consequently is not equipped to account for what is Other in a text. See Jacques Derrida, *Limited Inc.,* Gerald Graff, ed., Samuel Weber and Jeffrey Mehlman, trans. (Evanston, Ill.: Northwestern University, 1988), and the helpful discussion in Phillips, "Ethics of Reading."

12. Jacques Derrida, *Dissemination,* trans. Barbara Johnson (Chicago: University of Chicago Press, 1981).

other things, both "cure" and "poison." Is writing a cure or is it poison? What-ever Plato's intention, the word stands—as does the entire text—with all its traces, contradicting itself and simultaneously preserving and discrediting the general gist of the passage as whole.

(Ex)posing Power

So, what *is* deconstruction? Any specific definition would be reductionist and would fly in the face of what deconstruction is all about. Derrida himself claims that "There is no one single deconstruction"[13] and is more comfortable talking about what deconstruction is not than what it is.[14] Nevertheless, we must start somewhere. So, acknowledging the paradox of this endeavor, I offer Barbara Johnson's formulation (which is a distinctly literary one) as an accessible and helpful starting point:

> Deconstruction . . . is a careful teasing out of the conflicting forces of signification that are at work within the text itself. *If anything is destroyed in a deconstructive reading, it is not meaning per se but the claim to unequivocal domination of one mode of signifying over another.* This implies that a text signifies in more than one way, that it can signify something more, something less, or something other than it claims to, or that it signifies to different degrees of explicitness, effectiveness, or coher-ence. A deconstructive reading makes evident the ways in which a text works out its complex disagreements with itself.[15]

The presupposition here is that a text cannot be univocal. It has many voices, many meanings. What deconstructive reading does is to spell out these mean-ings and to disallow the "unequivocal domination" of one meaning over all the others. In the same vein, David Jobling writes, "What deconstruction decon-structs is the accumulation of power in discourse."[16]

Power? Domination? That's rather strong language to describe the rather simple process of communication, is it not? Do we not all speak and write in the interests of making plain sense, of conveying the truth as we understand it? What do power and domination have to do with it?

13. Derrida, *Limited Inc.*, 141.

14. Jacques Derrida, "Letter to a Japanese Friend," in *Derrida and Différance,* David Wood and Robert Bernasconi, eds. (Evanston, Ill.: Northwestern University Press, 1988).

15. Barbara Johnson, "Teaching Deconstructively," G. Douglas Atkins and Michael L. Johnson, eds., *Writing and Reading Differently: Deconstruction and the Teaching of Com-position and Literature* (Lawrence, Kans.: University of Kansas Press, 1985), 141. Italics mine.

16. David Jobling, "Writing the Wrongs of the World: The Deconstruction of the Biblical Text in the Context of Liberation Theologies." *Semeia* 51 (1990): 102.

This is precisely where our customary thinking in "either/or" categories enters the picture. We are trained to think in binary oppositions: truth/error, presence/absence, serious/nonserious, theory/practice, literal/figurative, male/female, light/dark, positive/negative. Our oppositions, however, are rarely equal. Rather, we operate with a fairly value-laden hierarchy: truth is superior to error, presence to absence, theory to practice, and so forth. When texts argue "this" and "not that," or when we argue that a text means "this" and "not that," hierarchy is at work, and thus power and domination. Any claim to truth, whether blatant or subtle, is an exercise of power over any notion or person or social construction that does not fit that claim's definition of truth. And yet claims to truth cannot escape their linguistic packaging. Hence, they are subject to the slip-sliding effect: oppositions breaking down, hierarchies losing their footing. As hard as texts want to promote the "either/or" nature of their message, the "both/and" continues to manifest itself. Traces of other "truths," some completely incompatible with the dominant assertion of truth, flicker across the surface of the text, creating enough of a disturbance to keep a perfectly unified image from stabilizing.

Deconstruction seeks to uncover these disturbances. But deconstruction is far from being simply an academic enterprise. Rather, its ramifications address issues of power and domination both in the academy and in society at large. In "The Conflict of Faculties," Derrida writes,

> What is somewhat hastily called deconstruction is not, if it is of any consequence, a specialized set of discursive procedures, still less the rules of a new hermeneutic method that works on texts or utterances in the shelter of a given and stable institution. It is also, at the very least, a way of taking a position, in its work of analysis, concerning the political and institutional structures that make possible and govern our practices, our competencies, our performances. Precisely because it is never concerned only with signified content, deconstruction should not be separable from this politico-institutional problematic and should seek a new investigation of responsibility, an investigation which questions the codes inherited from ethics and politics.[17]

What does this mean? It means (among other things — there are always other things!) that deconstruction is not simply an operation we perform on texts or something that texts do to themselves. Deconstruction is not just another method or theory of interpretation taking its place among other methods and theories in the Academy. Rather, deconstruction's attention to Otherness leads

---

17. Jacques Derrida, "The Conflict of Faculties," Michael Riffaterr, ed., *Languages of Knowledge and of Inquiry* (New York: Columbia University Press, 1982). Cited in Jonathan Culler, *On Deconstruction: Theory and Criticism after Structuralism* (Ithaca, N.Y.: Cornell University Press, 1982), 156.

readers "to stray into the margins and off the page"[18] into the surrounding culture and society. Attention to the Other leads to a critique of mainline scholarly traditions, canons, and institutions that have excluded the Other; it leads to a critique of social and political systems that marginalize the Other. In other words, how we read texts affects how we read the world. The opening of texts calls for the opening of politico-institutional structures. This is risky business in a world that encourages the status quo and rewards conformity.

Deconstruction does not, in and of itself, produce alternative (say, non-oppressive) structures. It is, after all, about opening up structures, not about bringing closure and security. Nevertheless, when coupled with ideological or political criticism, deconstruction can be used as an agent of change.[19] The moment we shift the question from "What truth is being claimed and what suppressed?" to "Whose truth is being claimed and whose suppressed?" we are in the business of politics. We are not only looking for traces, we are listening for marginal voices. We are discovering that the seldom-heard voices have truth to impart and that their truth is often at odds with a text's or an institution's "party line." To use Brenda Marshall's words, we are giving up "the luxury of absolute Truths, choosing instead to put to work local and provisional truths."[20]

Unsettling Judges

As a literary, religious, and political text, the Bible is certainly not immune to the kinds of conflicts, disturbances, and self-dismantling procedures we have been discussing. Nor is the field of biblical studies as a whole. As Jobling writes,

> The Bible needs to be read as a focus for fields of force—in the conditions both of its production and of its "reproduction" in historical and modern interpretation; as a battleground, over meaning, over interpretation, over the right of interpretation. "Biblical studies" is a discourse with no demilitarized boundaries in any direction.[21]

In recent years the Book of Judges has indeed become such a battleground. Historical and literary critics alike claim it as their territory, each camp insisting that their respective methods can recover "what the book is about." A deconstructionist might argue, however, that *re-cover* is indeed the operative word

18. See Beal's quotation in note 10.
19. See Jobling, "Writing the Wrongs of the World."
20. Brenda K. Marshall, *Teaching the Postmodern: Fiction and Theory* (New York and London: Routledge, 1992), 3.
21. Jobling, "Writing the Wrongs of the World," 100.

here, because in practice "uncovering" one meaning has resulted in "covering over" others.[22] The critical enterprise is one long exercise in re-covering.

All this re-covering does, nevertheless, point to the ways in which Judges deconstructs itself and can be deconstructed by readers. Ever since Martin Noth argued that the cyclical framework of Judges (sin, oppression, repentance, deliverance) domesticated the obviously older stories in the book to fit the Deuteronomistic Historian's agenda, there has been a spate of readers working either on individual stories or on the cycle as a whole who have shown that, alas, Noth's description (however brilliant) is far too simple.[23] Even traditional readings that have taken the thematic approach, assuming, for example, that the book is about the "settlement" or about holy war have now been challenged by Mieke Bal's call for a countercoherence: namely, that the book is about murder and, in particular, about the dissymmetry between the murder of men by women and the murder of women by men.[24]

What these newer readings have noticed are the incongruencies between the text's explicit assertions of meaning (which in and of themselves are not univocal) and the stories used to illustrate those assertions. For example, the Book of Judges asserts that it is about the settlement (2:6); the conquest (1:1-26); the reasons for the failure of the settlement and conquest (1:27-36; 2:20-23); Israel's repeated infidelity (2:11-19); and Israel's need for the monarchy (18:1; 19:1; 21:25). The stories supposedly illustrating those assertions, however, tend to be focused more on individuals (and, according to Bal, the scenario of murder) and less on the nation's exploits. To return to our painting metaphor: the blue,

---

22. Indeed this is often the tactic used in scholarly debate. Some scholars seem to think that, in order to elevate their own theories, they are obliged to "dump on" (to put it gently) the theories of others. Of course, the "covering over" takes place in other ways, too, for example, through censorship in academic publication. For years, the works of literary critics in biblical studies were not accepted in standard biblical studies journals. Even today, editors and editorial referees are not always above academic politics when it comes to making selections for publication.

23. The work on individual stories is far too extensive to be listed here. Some of the more intentionally deconstructive work on the cycle/book-as-whole include David M. Gunn, "Joshua and Judges," in Robert Alter and Frank Kermode, eds., *The Literary Guide to the Bible* (Cambridge: Harvard University Press; London: Collins, 1987), 102–21; Gabriel Josipovici, "The Rhythm Falters: The Book of Judges," *The Book of God: A Response to the Bible* (New Haven and London: Yale University Press, 1988), 108–31; J. Cheryl Exum, "The Centre Cannot Hold: Thematic and Textual Instabilities in Judges," *Catholic Biblical Quarterly* 52 (1990): 410–31; Danna Nolan Fewell, "Judges," in Carol A. Newsom and Sharon H. Ringe, eds., *The Women's Bible Commentary* (Louisville, Ky.: Westminster/John Knox Press, 1992), 67–77.

24. Mieke Bal, *Death and Dissymmetry: The Politics of Coherence in the Book of Judges* (Chicago: University of Chicago Press, 1988).

with its varying hues, shouts out the interests of the nation as a whole, while the red dots whisper unsettling questions about Other subjects — women, children, foreigners, murder, oppression, self-deception, divine and human self-interest, and so on.

This incompatibility between assertion and illustration is but one of the ways in which the text is at odds with itself. Other possible sites of conflicting meanings might include ambiguous words or syntax, incompatibilities between what a text says and what it does, incompatibilities between literal understandings and figurative ones, and obscurity.[25] Such sites of conflict become apparent only in the act of reading — deconstruction is, we must remember, a reading event and not a particular method or procedure. Thus, we turn now to a specific text, Judges 1:11-15.

Textual Incites: Achsah and the (E)razed City of Writing

Judges 1:11-15 offers a brief account of Caleb's offer of his daughter Achsah to the man who takes the Canaanite settlement Kiriath-sepher, and Achsah's subsequent request to her father for land and water. Though brief and seemingly straightforward, the story is not without its twists and turns and slips and excesses of meaning.

I offer four "authorized" translations of the text. By making concrete decisions concerning word choice and sentence structure, these translations have attempted to tame the text, to give a particular account of it. A quick comparision and contrast of the readings reveals how difficult a procedure this actually is. Different readers (in this case, readers who happen to be professional translators) find different meanings in the very same set of words. One might also note that, despite the differences, the translations are also quite similar. This is obviously due, in part, to the common text. But it is also due to the similarity of readers. Despite the current calls for diversity in scholarly pursuits, the vast

---

25. Barbara Johnson outlines these sites as well as what she calls fictional self-interpretation, that is, when texts "appear to comment upon themselves, to solve the enigmas they set up." One might interpret these comments as "allegories of reading." (See Johnson, "Teaching Deconstructively.")

Though this concept is less helpful for the following analysis of Judges 1:11–15, it can be illustrated in the broader text of Judges. For example, the narratorial comment that "in those days there was no king in Israel; every man [*sic*] did what was right in his own eyes" might be seen as an allegory about interpretation. That is, every reader reads what he or she thinks the text ought to say. Or, to be gender-specific (as the text is), men have the authority to read any way they want to, the implication being that women have no such freedom, that is, they read the way men tell them to.

NRSV	REB
From there they went against the inhabitants of Debir (the name of Debir was formerly Kiriath-sepher). Then Caleb said, "Whoever attacks Kiriath-sepher and takes it, I will give him my daughter Achsah as wife." And Othniel son of Kenaz, Caleb's younger brother, took it; and he gave him his daughter Achsah as wife. When she came to him, she urged him to ask her father for a field. As she dismounted from her donkey, Caleb said to her, "What do you wish?" She said to him, "Give me a present; since you have set me in the land of the Negeb, give me also Gulloth-mayim." So Caleb gave her Upper Gulloth and Lower Gulloth.	*From there they marched against the inhabitants of Debir, formerly called Kiriath-sepher. Caleb said, "I shall give my daughter Achsah in marriage to the man who attacks and captures Kiriath-sepher." Othniel, son of Caleb's younger brother Kenaz, captured it, and Caleb gave him his daughter Achsah. When she became his wife, Othniel induced her to ask her father for a piece of land. She dismounted from her donkey, and Caleb asked her, "What do you want?" She replied, "Grant me this favour: you have put me in this arid Negeb; you must give me pools of water as well." So Caleb gave her the upper pool and the lower pool.*

majority of Bible readers in the West are still at the mercy of scholars who, for the most part, are trained to read alike. Consequently, while the following discussion focuses on a particular biblical passage, we shouldn't forget, to use Derrida's words, "the political and institutional structures that make possible and govern our practices, our competencies, our performances." As we discuss this text, its readers, and some of its meanings, we might also remember that larger political issues are at stake, namely, how texts should be read and who should read them.

What's in a Name?

The first bits of slippery language that we notice are the place names. There is a tendency to transliterate rather than to translate the words. This produces a certain amount of obscurity for the non-Hebrew reader, since, as transliterations, the words merely designate place, providing the reader geographic information without contributing significantly to the meaning(s) of the story. The effect is misleading. The NRSV's use of Gulloth-mayim is a case in point. So Achsah wasn't happy with a place in the Negeb; she wanted a place called Gulloth-mayim. Some folks are never satisfied — always looking for a better neighborhood! If the meaning is limited to proper nouns, Achsah is portrayed as an ingrate. The words, as the other translations indicate, signify more: she's been settled on dry land; she needs a reliable water source to make the land arable. Within the names there are meanings, "traces," that constitute a reasonable request. But by obscuring the traces, translations such as the NRSV's keep

Tanakh	Boling, Anchor Bible[26]
From there they marched against the inhabitants of Debir (the name of Debir was formerly Kiriath-sepher). And Caleb announced, "I will give my daughter Achsah in marriage to the man who attacks and captures Kiriath-sepher." His younger kinsman, Othniel the Kenizzite, captured it; and Caleb gave him his daughter Achsah in marriage. When she came [to him], she induced him to ask her father for some property. She dismounted from her donkey, and Caleb asked her, "What is the matter?" She replied, "Give me a present, for you have given me away as Negeb-land; give me springs of water." And Caleb gave her Upper and Lower Gulloth.	*From there they attacked the inhabitants of Debir. Debir used to be called Qiriath-sepher. Caleb had said, "Whoever devastates Qiriath-sepher and cap-tures it, to him I'll give my daughter Achsah as wife." Othniel ben Qenaz, Caleb's "brother"—who was younger than he —captured it; and so he gave him his daughter Achsah as wife. When she arrived, he nagged her to ask tilled land from her father. But when she alighted from the donkey and Caleb said to her: "What's wrong?" she said to him: "Give me a blessing! The Negeb-land you have given me and you shall give me basins of water?" So Caleb gave her her heart's desire, The upper basins and the lower basins.*

the control of meaning in the hands of elite scholars who happen to know Hebrew.

A second case is that of the city itself. The Israelites—more specifically, the men of Judah—are to go up against the inhabitants of Debir. But, we are told, Debir was not always Debir, but was once known as Kiriath-sepher. Caleb even refers to it by its old name, thus indicating that the Israelites themselves change the city's name to Debir. All this information is, of course, to provide a bit of historical and geographical orientation. It also functions, less benignly, to illustrate that words and s/words are both means of control. To the victors belong the power to rename.

The power to rename is not absolute, however. Traces of meaning remain in these names so casually bandied about. Kiriath-sepher is, literally, "the city of writing" or "the city of books." But it is in the interests of the Israelites (and apologetic translators as well) to suppress that meaning. To spell out that the

26. Robert G. Boling, *Judges: A New Translation with Introduction and Commentary* (New York: Doubleday, 1975), 51, actually prints vv. 14–15 in poetic verse. In order to lay the translations side by side, however, I have printed this material as prose. The question of whether these verses are prose or poetry can also affect the meaning of the passage. It not only raises the question of whether we are dealing with literal or more figurative language, but it also questions which words are actually to be included in the text itself. For example, it seems to encourage Boling to follow the LXX in including the phrase "her heart's desire"; he argues that the postulated Hebrew original, *kᵉlibbah,* plays upon the name Caleb. Once "heart" is incorporated into the passage, Boling then notes that the heart was the seat of the mind and will (57). This observation could then, in turn, a/ effect one's understanding of the character of Achsah as someone whose mind is made up and who is firmly stating her will.

city to be destroyed is the city of books casts this conquest in a rather different light for any reader who respects learning and culture. Though the predominant tone in Joshua and Judges 1:1-18 foregrounds triumphalism, remnants of meaning undermine that attitude, suggesting that the place to be destroyed is a center of learning: a place where records are kept, where history and order are valued, a place where texts are produced. Information from outside this text further substantiates the city's pre-Israelite reputation: Joshua 15:49 identifies Debir as Kiriath-sannah, the city of instruction.[27] Even when one's allegiances lie with the Israelites, the loss of such culture may give the reader pause.[28] A city of writing is simply erased.

The Israelites erase and write over the city by word as well as sword. The new version of the city is called Debir. And what might "Debir" mean? An "inner sanctuary" (say the commentators). The root letters (*dbr*) support other traces, however: the verb "speak" and the nouns "speech" and "matter" and "plague." And so the new name stands struggling to contain its nuances. Religiosity, exclusion, privileged divine knowledge and presence, speech (as opposed to writing),[29] death, and just plain "stuff." The name Debir covers a culture with an ambiguous lot of stuff.[30]

The traces in Kiriath-sepher glimpse the loss of human life; for there to be a city of books, there must be a city of scribes. For there to be a center of learning, there must be a city of learners. But the text focuses its rhetoric elsewhere. The citizens of Kiriath-sepher are granted but one sign.[31] Only once are "inhabitants" mentioned. Then they are simply erased.[32] For these inhabitants,

27. H. Freedman's translation, "Joshua: Introduction and Commentary," A. Cohen, ed., *Joshua and Judges* (London: Soncino, 1959), 89.

28. Indeed, the notion has been known to spawn sharp resistance. Notice, for example, the discomfort in H. Wheeler Robinson's explanation: "No inference can be drawn from such an etymology as to the literary life of Canaan. It is quite likely that some (unknown) Canaanite word, resembling *sepher* in sound, has been reproduced in a form familiar to Hebrew ears." *Joshua* (Century Bible); quoted by Freedman, 89.

29. In light of Derrida's argument that writing precedes speech, the actions of the Israelites are shown to be doubly arrogant. They not only think they can erase a city's history and identity by renaming it, their action suggests that their speech (which is present and immediate) should take priority over Canaanite writing (which represents what is past and absent). Ironically, Israelite speech (and victory) must be captured in writing in order to be remembered and is thus vulnerable to the same procedures of erasure.

30. I am indebted to John Havea for suggesting the wording "stuff," which has, of course, its own provocative "traces" in current American usage.

31. "A sign," writes Umberto Eco, "is everything which can be taken as significantly substituting for something else." *A Theory of Semiotics* (Bloomington, Ind.: Indiana University Press, 1976), 7.

32. Of course, even the method of "erasure" can be debated. The mission is to "strike" (*nkh*) and "capture" (*lkd*) the city. Is the strike a fatal or nonfatal blow? Is the

this is no longer a place of words. Nor is this a place where bodies are allowed to be their own signs.[33] No bodies in this story. Only the city and the land stand as subjects of value.

The Subject of Achsah

The national warfare is quickly reduced to personal matters: marriage and property. But even this keen observation of the obvious does not stand uncontested. Many commentators argue (or rather assume) that this story is not about individuals at all, but about whole clans or tribes and their settlement history. John Gray's description is a prime example of such thinking: "The tribal history here takes the form of popular saga, with charming personal touches. . . ." Achsah should be understood not as a woman, but as "a local or tribal dependent of the powerful Caleb clan of Hebron, which was affiliated with the kindred clan of Othniel after the occupation of Debir."[34] Such a figurative understanding turns the text into a quaint story, a folk-etiology whose sole, or at least main, function is to explain (though "with charming personal touches") how particular groups of people came to settle particular areas.

Displace "tribes" and "history" as the center of focus, however, and rather different meanings emerge. A father sets up his daughter as a military prize. Whoever takes the city can have his daughter. *Whoever,* he says. Luckily for her (we assume) that the whoever turns out to be an Othniel and not an Attila or, reading closer to home, an unnamed Levite from the hill country of Ephraim (see Judg 19). The "whoever" does raise questions about how we are to assess this kind of bargain. On the one hand, this is the stuff fairy tales and folk tales are made of: princesses being married off to heroes. No doubt sexist, but consider the era. Besides, she could have done a lot worse.

On the other hand, what of Achsah herself? How is she perceived? Perhaps a clue is Achsah's name: "bangle" or "anklet." Is she a person? Or is she a trinket? Is she a subject in her own right? Or is she simply an ornament in the story, a "charming personal touch"? The name Achsah has other traces as well, as is borne out by its Arabic cognate, which means "to tether," or more specifi-

---

capture total destruction or is it a peaceful capture, like David's capture of Jerusalem? The rhetoric of the conquest would lead one to conclude total devastation (cf. Boling's translation), but the text is never explicit.

33. Unlike the story of the Levite's wife in Judges 19–21, where bodies become the most deafening signs. On this story, see Gale A. Yee, "Ideological Criticism: Judges 17–21 and the Dismembered Body," chapter 7 in this volume.

34. John Gray, *Joshua, Judges, Ruth* (New Century Bible Commentary; Grand Rapids: William B. Eerdmans and Basingstoke, Eng.: Marshall, Morgan & Scott, 1986), 137.

cally, "to hobble." This is something done to an animal or a captive. Suddenly we are invited to consider that ornaments and hobbles may indeed have something in common. Is Achsah another spoil of war? To her father, she is bait. To her future husband, she is his due reward. She is hobbled by her name and her ornamental role. Who needs to consider seriously a girl named Trinket? Like the land, Achsah is there to be taken. (And this won't be the last time we see the taking of a city associated with the taking of a woman, as we well know from the stories of David and Bathsheba [2 Sam 11] and Absalom and his father's concubines [2 Sam 16].) Does the text condone her use as a bargaining chip? Or does the fact that the bargaining chip turns bargainer render the original bargain somewhat ironic?

How does Achsah perceive herself and her circumstances? The text limits and renders ambiguous her subjectivity.[35] On the one hand, we see her obediently submitting to her father's arrangement; on the other, we hear the anklet rattling—we see her making demands that indicate she is less than satisfied with her lot. In the end, however, specific feelings are not voiced. Or are they? The Tanakh's reading grants her a self-awareness usually denied her. While other translations read her speech (in 1:15) as something like, "Give me a blessing, for you have given me Negeb (or desert) land" the Tanakh has her insist, "Give me a present, for you have given *me* away as Negeb-land; give me springs of water." In the first instance she is the recipient of the gift of the land; in the second she is the gift, a gift equated with the land, and a cheap gift at that. These readings slip back and forth, both allowing her a critical sense of her circumstances and yet unable to agree on the precise nature of her self-understanding. Is she aware that she, like the land, is to be taken and owned by a victorious soldier? Or does she see herself as the landowner, attempting to improve her property? And in the end, we must recognize that Achsah's subjectivity, however it emerges, is at odds with how the text has told her story. For all her talk of gifts and giving, language that she has co-opted from her father (cf. 1:12), we know that "gifts" and "giving" merely dress up the fact that she has been bought and the land has been taken by warfare. She has been used as the incentive for heroism and territorial expansion; she is the collateral for a piece of Canaanite real estate. Of course, the question remains, is this a prime piece of real estate or not? A city of books would suggest yes. Negeb (desert) land would suggest no. The reference to it as a "field" suggests maybe. And so the worth of the land, like the worth of Achsah, is up for grabs.

The biblical text both preserves and undermines Achsah's worth. What do

35. Chris Weedon defines subjectivity as "the conscious and unconscious thoughts and emotions of the individual, her sense of herself and her ways of understanding her relation to the world." *Feminist Practice and Poststructuralist Theory* (Oxford and New York: Basil Blackwell, 1987), 32.

commentators do with her? Alberto Soggin, for example, never even mentions her name in either of his commentaries[36] (except in his translations, where her name is unavoidable). But several interesting things happen in Soggin's translations that illustrate the ease with which subjectivity can be erased. In his 1972 translation of the Joshua passage, he reads 15:18 as follows: "When she came to him, she decided to ask her father for a field; and she alighted from her ass, and Caleb said to her, 'What do you wish?'" His 1981 translation of the Judges passage (1:14) reads, however, "When he came to her, he prompted her to ask her father for a field. She dismounted from the ass/She clapped her hands and Caleb asked her, 'What do you want?'" Who is arriving to meet whom? The grammar seems clear enough: a preposition plus a *qal* infinitive construct plus a feminine suffix, the natural reading being, "Upon her arrival" or "When she came" (or some general equivalent). Yet Soggin would have us believe there to be some ambiguity of subject. Never mind that Achsah, mounted on her donkey, is the only one portrayed as traveling!

Soggin's renderings of the second clause ("she decided" [1972]/ "he prompted her" [1981]) pose not only the question of the subject but also the question of the verb. Someone is doing something to someone else, but who is doing what to whom? In terms of the subject, Soggin's change stands on somewhat stronger ground here. His emendation "he prompted her" (cf. REB and Boling's translation), while clearly not what the Masoretic text says, has the support of the LXX and the Vulgate. At least the move to remove the woman as subject has ancient tradition behind it. Ancient translators, too, were trained to read alike!

But let us detour to the verb itself, because how the verb is understood often governs how commentators identify the subject. Soggin translated this verb first as "decided" and then as "prompted." Other options include "moved" (J. Slotki), "persuaded" (H. Freedman), "nagged" (Boling), "urged" (M. H. Woudstra), and "induced" (REB; Tanakh) with commentators quick to explain that the word usually has the negative connotation of inciting or luring someone to do something evil.[37]

What is at stake here? As Paul Mosca unabashedly declares, it is the reputation of Othniel that is at stake. Not only does Othniel vie with Achsah to be the subject of the verb, he usurps her place as the subject of commentary. The critical question becomes, Is Othniel indeed heroic?[38] Here is the dilemma: If

36. Alberto Soggin, *Joshua*, Old Testament Library series (Philadelphia: Westminster Press, 1972), and *Judges*, Old Testament Library series (Philadelphia: Westminster Press, 1981).

37. See Bal, *Death and Dissymmetry*, 275, n.27.

38. Paul G. Mosca, "Who Seduced Whom? A Note on Joshua 15:18//Judges 1:14," *Catholic Biblical Quarterly* 46 (1984): 18–22.

Achsah is the subject of the verb, we get an Othniel who is easily manipulated by his wife (God forbid!). We are also left with the question, When does Othniel get around to asking for the land? If, reading with the LXX and the Vulgate (cf. REB and Boling), Othniel is the subject, we get a greedy hero who nags his wife to do something he is not willing to do himself. Some hero! In the end we see how interpreters are preoccupied with how the biblical text models men. Women are not considered to be subjects worthy of interest. Ideological investment incites (!), provokes yet other texts to deconstruct the texts originally under consideration.[39] And one should remember that the ideological investment has institutional sanction. Academic institutions decide who can offer critical readings. Consequently, scholars like Soggin are given permission to ignore, to erase, whatever is Other in the text.

However, no matter how hard commentators work to erase Achsah from the text, traces of her remain — more traces of her, we might say, than of Othniel! In fact, we might be wise to ask, is Othniel even part of these negotiations at all? What if he, indeed, is absent?[40] In that case we would have to be willing to allow Achsah to remain the subject of her own action. The "him" in "she persuaded him" would then turn out to be none other than her father Caleb. Mosca argues that *lish'ôl* (usually translated "to ask") is "a perfectly good gerund construction, attested in preexilic as well as postexilic texts," consequently rendering the sentence, "When she arrived, she beguiled him, asking from her father arable land."[41] Achsah's request for water then becomes the actual request for a decent piece of land.

If we have settled or unsettled the question of who persuaded whom, we might move on to the question of what Achsah does "from upon her ass" before making her request. The verb *tsanach* or *ṣānaḥ* is an elusive one, occurring only here (and in its Joshua parallel) and in Judges 4:21 in the context of Jael's murder of Sisera. What does the verb mean? Provided that we can bypass G. R. Driver's now-debunked argument that flatulence was involved, we are left with two contending readings (as is evidenced in Soggin's later translation). Either she dismounts from her ass before speaking to Caleb or she claps her hands from upon her ass before speaking to Caleb. Most translations and commenta-

---

39. Even Mieke Bal, so critical of ideological biases in others and despite the fact that she wants to underscore Achsah's subjectivity, argues (against the Hebrew text) that Othniel is the subject of the seduction in order to support her theory that the text is really about the conflict between virilocal versus patrilocal residence. See Bal, *Death and Dissymmetry*, 155–56.

40. Compare Martin Noth, *Das Buch Josua* (Tübingen: Mohr [Siebeck], 1953), 86; and Soggin, *Joshua*, 166.

41. Mosca, "Who Seduced Whom?" 21.

tors read "dismount," inferring from the two contexts that the basic meaning must be "descend." My colleague David Gunn and I have argued[42] for the meaning "dismount" because we think it makes the most sense in both contexts: Here Achsah dismounts from her animal; in Judges 4, where we understand the feminine subject of the verb to be Jael and not the tent peg, we see Jael dismounting Sisera after nailing his head to the floor.

Recently, Bal[43] has revived the reading "she clapped," a translation based upon a similar Arabic word meaning "to strike." She contends that Achsah's action was a symbolic gesture designed to get her father's attention, since his immediate response is to ask literally, "What to you?" or, we might say, "What's the matter?" (cf. Tanakh and Boling) or "What do you want?" (cf. NRSV and REB). Simply dismounting from the ass would merely be a sign of submission and could hardly be what motivates Caleb's surprise. The meaning "to strike," she argues further, is also appropriate to both contexts since striking is indeed what is going on in the case of Jael and Sisera. While Bal claims to make her argument on the grounds of philology, anthropology, and speech-act theory, we might also notice that she seems to have as much at stake in how the biblical text models women as many male commentators have in how the text models men.

If an assertive Achsah is the point of Bal's reading, however, she can surely find her without the linguistic strain.[44] An intertextual analysis would suggest that dismounting might indeed be the sort of emphatic gesture Bal thinks necessary to the episode. Read in connection with Genesis 24:64, where Rebekah alights unassisted from her camel to meet Isaac,[45] and in connection with Judges 19:28 (a natural closing frame for the book), where the Levite's wife lies across her donkey unable to move, Achsah's self-determined mobility need not be read as a mere sign of submission. She does, after all, dismount by herself, waiting for no man's help or permission. She refuses to be "hobbled," so to speak. By planting herself firmly on the ground, she communicates that she is willing to travel no further until she gets what she wants. And once on her feet,

---

42. Danna Nolan Fewell and David M. Gunn, "Controlling Perspectives: Women, Men, and the Authority of Violence in Judges 4 and 5," *Journal of the American Academy of Religion* 56 (1990): 389–411, see 394, particularly n.14.

43. Bal, *Death and Dissymmetry*, 151–55.

44. Some of the problems with Bal's reading are (1) the positing of metathesis from a foreign root; (2) the absence of the object "her hands" in the text in Judges 1:14// Joshua 15:18; and (3) the oddity in Judges 4:21 of a tent peg striking (if she takes the peg, as is traditionally assumed, to be the subject) without a clearly defined agent.

45. Although Genesis 24:64 also deconstructs itself with the use of the verb *npl*, usually translated "fall." Does Rebekah "fall" in the sense of "quickly dismount" or does she quite literally and unintentionally "fall" from her camel upon seeing Isaac?

she can confront her father face to face. The action could easily carry with it the implicit message, "If you want this marriage to proceed without incident, you had better make it worth my while."

Or, read in a less assertive vein, we might see her dismount as overcoming the distance between herself and her father. She physically enacts the meeting of minds that she hopes to achieve. She might be using physical closeness as a tactic of persuasion, designed to signify to her father their familial intimacy and to remind him of familial obligation. His response, then, would not necessarily be surprise, but rather recognition of her strategy. He reads her body language to mean that she is about to initiate a conversation and to make a request.

Then there's always submission, that bugaboo we feminists hate so much. It stands, like the other alternatives, as a viable interpretation of her action.[46] When coupled with Boling's rendering of her speech as a question ("The Negeb-land you have given me and you shall give me basins of water?"), a respectful dismount merely sets the stage for a tentative request. Suddenly our assertive Achsah dissolves into a deferential, unassuming young woman who would have never bothered her father with such an entreaty had she not been pushed into it by her husband. Boling caps off this warm familial interchange by having Caleb give her "her heart's desire,"[47] just as any loving father would do for his modest and respectful daughter. And therein lies the lesson of how families ought to operate!

Contexts, Intertexts, and the Shifting of Meaning, or, What about the Others?

In addition to its internal instabilities, the entire story has a way of slipping and sliding in its production of meaning. What is the story saying? What is it doing? And is it saying and doing the same things?

The story sits in the Book of Judges amidst a catalogue of military successes on the part of Judah (and to a lesser degree, Simeon) and failures on the parts of the other tribes. It is placed as though to illustrate Judah's foregrounded triumph.[48] A superficial reading suggests that Caleb and, by extension, Othniel as his kinsman and Achsah as his daughter are all associated with Judah. This is not the first time such an association has been made. When chosen by Moses to spy out the land, Caleb goes as a representative of Judah (Num 13:6). The

---

46. Compare Judah Slotki, "Judges: Introduction and Commentary," A. Cohen, ed., *Joshua and Judges* (London: Soncino, 1959), 160.

47. See n.26.

48. See Marc Brettler, "The Book of Judges: Literature as Politics," *Journal of Biblical Literature* 108 (1989): 395–418, who argues that this section of the text was edited to reflect a pro-Judean bias.

text never says explicitly, however, that Caleb is from the tribe of Judah. Rather, he and Othniel are called Kenizzites, and Kenizzites from early on are identified as foreigners. Of course, it should be noted that the translation of Kenaz as the personal name of an individual (cf. NRSV, REB, and Boling) obscures the problem of ethnic identity. In Genesis 36:11, 15, 42, Kenizzites are specifically classified as descendants of Edom. In Genesis 15:19, the Kenizzites are numbered among those to be dispossessed by the children of Abraham. Here is the question: Are Caleb, Achsah, and Othniel Israelites, or are they foreigners?[49]

The answer to this question affects how we see the story's function. Does the story illustrate the obedience and achievement of Judah, hinting that had the conquest been left to Judah it would have been more successful? We certainly do not get the impression that either Achsah or her kin would have been intimidated by a few iron chariots! Or does the story suggest that foreigners did what Judah was unable to do; that foreigners took what was allotted to Judah? In other words, does the story undermine Judah's, indeed all Israel's, supremacy? Does it applaud or does it mock Israel's attempt to take the land?

The story's placement complicates its meaning yet further. Because the story appears in two places, Judges 1 and Joshua 15, we can see how it interacts with its immediate contexts to produce different meanings. In Joshua, the episode appears in the midst of a long, detailed description of the tribal allotment of Judah. As part of the description it is anecdotal in its explanation of exactly how that portion of the land was taken. More precisely, however, it comes after Caleb approaches Joshua, reminding him of Moses' earlier promise. When Caleb and Joshua had returned with an encouraging report from the first espionage mission into Canaan, Moses had promised Caleb, "The land on which you have walked shall be an inheritance for you and your children forever because you have wholeheartedly followed YHWH my God" (Josh 14:9). Caleb's claim to the hill country around Hebron is confirmed. The capture of Kiriath-sepher, then, brings to conclusion Moses' promise. As the ending of Caleb's story, it completes his portrait as a man whose strength and determination shines even brighter in his later years, and it communicates that reward awaits those who are faithful to YHWH and his plans.

In the context of Judges, on the other hand, the taking of Kiriath-sepher is not an ending but a beginning. As such, it sets the tone for the remainder of the conquest and settlement, indeed for the remainder of the book. It stands as a model of courage to the (other) tribes of Israel. It introduces the first judge

49. Historians have long recognized the discrepancy. See, for example, the comments of Gray, *Joshua, Judges, Ruth*, 234, 237, and A. Graeme Auld, *Joshua, Judges, and Ruth* (Philadelphia: Westminster Press, 1984), 92.

of Israel as a great warrior. Of course, with its ethnically ambiguous characters and its erasure of a center of culture, it also undermines the us-them ideology that drives the conquest.

The inclusion of a female character also has multiple effects. In Joshua, where women are rarely mentioned and where the major concern is allotting patriarchs their patriarchal holdings, Achsah's request for fertile land is unusual indeed. Like the petition of the daughters of Zelophohad in Joshua 17:3-6, Achsah's bid for real estate stands as an exception to prove the rule, namely that women do not usually own property and it is not likely that this Israelite policy is going to change. In Judges, where women appear more frequently, Achsah's story invites intertextual comparisons. Her status as a daughter sets the stage for all the other daughters of Judges whose fates will be decided by their fathers and husbands. Hence her story introduces the theme of female vulnerability, which will reach painful crescendos with the fates of Jephthah's daughter, Samson's bride, the Levite's wife, the women of Benjamin, Jabesh-Gilead, and Shiloh. And yet, Achsah's situation suggests that even in patriarchy women can sometimes have power, especially when they are treated with esteem by the men in their family. Unfortunately, Achsah's endogamous marriage and her demand for a home on cultivable soil also serve to accentuate all the daughters who are sold to foreigners (Judg 3:6), who are, in fact, dispossessed from the landholdings of Israel. Consequently, as the story of a woman, Achsah's brief debut raises all sorts of unresolved issues about power, control, possession, personhood, and the social health of the Israelite nation.

We considered earlier the question of whether the story is literal or figurative: Does the story deal with individuals or does the story represent some sort of tribal settlement? In this same vein, we might also ask, Is the story some kind of theological allegory? We saw the slippery association of Achsah with the land. Might that not suggest an allegory at work? Does Caleb represent God, Othniel Israel, Achsah the land? Isn't God's promise of the land conditioned upon a successful conquest? Or perhaps Othniel and Achsah represent the ideal Israel who was meant to be courageous, determined, and undaunted by the obstacles to which the real Israel fell prey. Or is Achsah Israel's own self-perception: Having been given over to a situation not of her making, does she now find herself having to make additional demands of a God who has not carefully considered what all this story entails? Wasn't she promised milk and honey? And yet now she finds herself in a vastly overrated land having to insist on being blessed with the very basic necessity of life, water. And so we are left wondering, does the story offer a model for all Israel? Or does the story subvert the divine promise? And is the subversion of the divine promise such a bad thing? The fact that the promised land of milk and honey is, like the garden of

Eden,[50] imperfect might be its very attraction. An imperfect land, like an imperfect creation, may be what provides life its challenge. It may be what provides the plot for the ongoing story. It may be the very thing that will build Israel's (and God's) character.

What's the Meaning of This?

Such a simple story of the settlement has become unsettled and unsettling. Not only have individual words and narrative elements revealed themselves to be undecidable, the entire story as a cultural construct has shown that it, too, can change its stripes depending upon its contexts, its intertexts, and its readers. Like Achsah we have asked for water and have received more than we bargained for — two springs instead of one. Or, to turn the metaphor, we are perhaps more like Caleb, who is pushed into seeing that there is something more to be done with Achsah and Achsah's story than simply to surrender her and it to the possession of Whoever happens to be master in the City of Books.

What's really at stake here in all this reading and counterreading of Achsah and company? And what's the point of reading if the point of what you are reading is not forthcoming? Reflections on these questions are not easily separated. To begin with, the point is that there is no one point to a text. There are many points, and deconstruction refuses to allow any one point to prod the others into submission. This does *not* mean that a text can say anything the reader wants it to say. Texts have rights, too. Texts have constraints.[51] Deconstruction does not give the reader permission to violate those constraints. Nevertheless, within those constraints, a text can mean a lot of things. Within those constraints, a text can always be read Otherwise. And deconstruction would suggest that we have an ethical responsibility to read Otherwise.

How do deconstruction and reading and ethics relate? First of all, deconstruction insists that readers be up front about the limitations of their reading method(s). Don't pretend that your particular critical method will answer satisfactorily all the "important" questions about a text. Method plus text always equals a surplus of text. Don't even pretend you know what all the "important" questions are. Other readers will tell you otherwise — if, of course, academic institutions allow those other readers to speak. After all, who should be allowed

50. My thanks to John Havea for reminding me of this intertextual connection. This connection is more often explored in discussions of the Exile: the expulsion of the couple from Eden is a precursor to Israel's eventual expulsion from the land of promise.

51. See Robert C. Culley and Robert B. Robinson, eds., *Textual Determinacy* (Part One); *Semeia* 62 (1993); particularly Daniel Patte, "Textual Constraints, Ordinary Readings, and Critical Exegesis: An Androcritical Perspective," 59–79.

to read is a question that has all of Academia in a turmoil. We find ourselves back with the scribes in the City of Books dealing with the threat of erasure, suppression, (ex)termination. The issue of academic honesty has turned into one of academic freedom.

Deconstruction also asks, Who, what is allowed to be the subject of a reading? What has recognizing subjectivity to do with ethics? Why should we care whether or not a literary figure gets a hearing? Perhaps because the way we read literary texts has the power to shape our attitudes and values. Why anyone should care what happens to a girl named Achsah has as much to do with the crime reports in our newspapers as it does with the biblical text. What happened to the inhabitants of the City of Writing challenges our own military policies and our own educational practices and our own ethnic prejudices as much as it does those policies, practices, and prejudices of ancient Israel. Attending to the Other in our reading is a step toward attending to justice in our own neighborhood.

Why bother with deconstruction? What difference does it make how we read?

It may make all the difference in the world.

Further Reading

General

Places to Start

ATKINS, G. Douglas. *Reading Deconstruction: Deconstructive Reading.* Lexington, Ky.: University Press of Kentucky, 1983. Includes discussions of the works of Derrida, Hartman, and Miller as well as interpretive essays employing deconstructive criticism.

NORRIS, Christopher. *Deconstruction: Theory and Practice.* Rev. ed.: New York and London: Routledge, 1991. Traces deconstruction from its roots in structuralism and New Criticism through to its current critics. Devotes much attention to Derrida, Nietzsche, Marx, and the Yale School. Good bibliography.

For Teachers

ATKINS, G. Douglas, and Michael L. Johnson, eds. *Writing and Reading Differently: Deconstruction and the Teaching of Composition and Literature.* Lawrence, Kans.: University of Kansas Press. Collection of accessible essays by well-known critics on the topics of pedagogy, reading, writing, and criticism.

MARSHALL, Brenda K. *Teaching the Postmodern: Fiction and Theory.* New York and London: Routledge, 1992. Contains a helpful introduction to postmodern thought. Offers postmodern readings of current literary works, including Toni Morrison's *Beloved*.

For More Advanced Readers

CULLER, Jonathan. *On Deconstruction: Theory and Criticism after Structuralism.* London/Melbourne/Henley: Routledge & Kegan Paul, 1983. This has become perhaps the classic introduction to deconstruction and its critical consequences.

DERRIDA, Jacques. *Of Grammatology.* Translated by Gayatri Chakrovorty Spivak. Baltimore and London: Johns Hopkins University Press, 1974, 1976. Derrida's classic discussion of the problematic status of writing in the Western philosophical tradition. Translator's preface is one of the better introductions to Derrida's thought.

Deconstruction and Biblical Studies

The Broader Picture

BEARDSLEE, William. "Poststructuralist Criticism," in Steven L. McKenzie and Stephen Haynes, eds., *To Each Its Own Meaning: An Introduction to Biblical Criticisms and Their Applications.* Louisville, Ky.: Westminster/John Knox Press, 1993, 221–36. Situates deconstruction in the Western philosophical discussion, explains key terms, and offers a deconstructive reading of the first of Luke's beatitudes.

THE BIBLE AND CULTURE COLLECTIVE. *The Postmodern Bible.* New Haven: Yale University Press, 1995. Collaborative work on different, mostly postmodern, forms of criticism. Covers both Testaments.

CULLEY, Robert C., and Robert B. Robinson, eds. *Textual Determinacy* (Part One). *Semeia* 62 (1993). Essays focus on how meaning is determined by the interplay of texts and the reading process.

DETWEILER, Robert, ed. *Derrida and Biblical Studies. Semeia* 23 (1982). Contains three essays that move toward "a critical approximation of Derrida's style and tactic" plus an example of Derrida himself engaging in the interpretation of (among other things) biblical texts.

FEWELL, Danna Nolan, ed. *Reading Between Texts: Intertextuality and the Hebrew Bible.* Louisville, Ky.: Westminster/John Knox Press, 1992. Essays focus on how meanings are created as texts overrun their borders to connect with other texts and contexts.

JOBLING, David, and Stephen D. Moore. *Poststructuralism as Exegesis. Semeia* 54 (1992). Essays engaged in postmodern exegesis.

MOORE, Stephen D. *Poststructuralism and the New Testament: Derrida and Foucault at the Foot of the Cross*. Minneapolis: Fortress Press, 1994. A highly accessible, personal, and inviting introduction to poststructuralism and its impact on New Testament studies. Excellent glossary and list for further reading.

PHILLIPS, Gary A., ed. *Poststructural Criticism and the Bible: Text/History/Discourse*. *Semeia* 51 (1990). Essays devoted to critical method, theory, and exegesis.

Deconstructive Readings of First Testament Texts

BAL, Mieke. *Death and Dissymmetry: The Politics of Coherence in the Book of Judges*. Chicago: University of Chicago Press, 1988. While Bal does not label herself as a deconstructionist per se, she stresses throughout this trilogy "the ambiguities that the texts allow and contrast[s] them with disambiguated rewritings of various kinds." She sees herself as making "a case for difference."

———. *Lethal Love: Feminist Literary Readings of Biblical Love Stories*. Bloomington, Ind.: Indiana University Press, 1987.

———. *Murder and Difference: Gender, Genre, and Scholarship in Sisera's Death*. Translated by Matthew Gumpert. Bloomington, Ind.: Indiana University Press, 1988.

BEAL, Timothy K., and Tod Linafelt. "Sifting for Cinders: Intertextuality and Leviticus 10:1–5." *Semeia*, forthcoming. An intertextual reading of Leviticus 10 and one of Derrida's own texts.

CLINES, David J. A. "Haggai's Temple Constructed, Deconstructed and Reconstructed." *Scandinavian Journal of the Old Testament* 7 (1993): 51–77. Analysis includes a deconstructive phase.

———. "Reading Esther from Left to Right: Contemporary Strategies for Reading a Biblical Text." David J. A. Clines, Stephen E. Fowl, and Stanley N. Porter, eds., *The Bible in Three Dimensions*. Sheffield, Eng.: JSOT Press, 1990, 31–52. Includes deconstruction as one contemporary strategy for reading Esther.

FEWELL, Danna Nolan. *Circle of Sovereignty: Plotting Politics in the Book of Daniel*. Nashville: Abingdon Press, 1991. A detailed reading that focuses on the instabilities of divine and human sovereignty in the Masoretic text of Daniel.

FEWELL, Danna Nolan, and David M. Gunn. *Gender, Power, and Promise: The Subject of the Bible's First Story*. Nashville: Abingdon Press, 1993. An extended reading of Genesis through Kings that "changes the subject" from the Israelite patriarchs to the women, children, and foreigners who are usually relegated to the margins of the text and the reader's attention.

GREENSTEIN, Edward L. "Deconstruction and Biblical Narrative." *Prooftexts* 9 (1989): 43–71. Deconstructive analysis of Genesis 1; 11 and Leviticus 10.

GUNN, David M. "In Security: The David of Biblical Narrative," in J. Cheryl Exum, ed., *Signs and Wonders: Biblical Texts in Literary Focus*. Atlanta: Scholars Press, 1989, 133–51. Exposes the problematic in pinpointing the character of David in biblical portrayal.

JOBLING, David. "Deconstruction and the Political Analysis of Biblical Texts: A Jamesonian Reading of Psalm 72." *Semeia* 59 (1992): 95–128. Offers three divergent readings of Psalm 72, which focus on political modes of production and the social and semantic contradictions inherent in the psalm.

———. "'Forced Labor': Solomon's Golden Age and the Question of Literary Representation." *Semeia* 54 (1992): 57–76. Exposes how the depiction of the Solomonic golden age is contradicted by the traces of the "fallen," "real," present world contained within it.

MISCALL, Peter. *1 Samuel: A Literary Reading*. Bloomington, Ind.: Indiana University Press, 1986. Exposes the undecidability of the text of 1 Samuel.

———. *The Workings of Old Testament Narrative*. Chico, Calif.: Scholars Press, 1983. One of the first studies to incorporate deconstruction into biblical literary criticism. Analyzes the stories of Abraham and David.

7

IDEOLOGICAL CRITICISM: JUDGES 17–21 AND THE DISMEMBERED BODY

Gale A. Yee

Introduction

The latest approach to the interpretation of the Hebrew Bible is ideological criticism. The publication of Norman K. Gottwald's *The Hebrew Bible: A Socio-Literary Introduction* in 1985 can be seen as a major step toward this approach.[1] In 1990 the Society of Biblical Literature Consultation on Ideological Criticism of Biblical Texts conducted its first session. In 1992, a special volume featuring ideological criticism appeared in *Semeia,* an experimental journal exploring new methods of biblical interpretation. In addition to articles applying ideological criticism to biblical texts, this volume includes a fine introductory bibliography on ideological criticism.

Ideological criticism uses literary critical methods within a historical and social scientific frame in a comprehensive strategy for reading biblical texts. (See chapter 1 for a discussion of these critical approaches.) On the one hand, the social sciences and historical analyses help to reconstruct or "unmask" the material[2] and ideological conditions under which the biblical text is *produced.* On the other hand, literary critical methods address how the biblical text assimilates or "encodes"[3] these conditions in *reproducing* a particular ideology.

---

1. *The Hebrew Bible: A Socio-Literary Introduction* (Philadelphia: Fortress Press, 1985). Gottwald maintains that his socio-literary approach is "in deliberate continuity with older historical-critical scholarship" (xxvii), but it integrates the newer literary and social scientific approaches that have taken biblical studies in new directions.

2. The term "material" refers to the production and distribution of economic goods and the social relationships of owners and workers.

3. Ideology is a code people produce that helps them make sense of a confusing world; it is like a template keyed to a specific computer program, put over the computer keys to give the keyboard a specific pattern of meaning. The literary text "encodes" a particular ideological "worldview." It then transfers this constructed system of values and perceptions into its rhetoric. In many ways this code feature is similar to allegory.

For example, in Catholic high school religion classes in the late 1950s and early 1960s, female students read and discussed a book titled *Charm*. The book cover was bright pink and pictured an elegant, gloved woman in a full-skirted dress and a pillbox hat. The book offered instruction on such matters as makeup and clothes (which were very modest), posture, "charming" social skills, and etiquette in dating "boys." Concerning sexuality (although the word was never used), advice to a chaste young woman was never to venture beyond a goodnight kiss, and always "save herself" for her future husband. Today, instruction has changed rather dramatically. Magazines such as *Glamour* and *Sassy* targeted at adolescent girls feature very thin young women in various stages of undress and provocative sexual poses. The articles describe in detail "how to please your man in bed" and "how to convince your man to use a condom."

An ideological critic has a twofold task in analyzing the radically different messages encoded in these diverse texts. First, in an *extrinsic analysis,* the critic investigates the social and historical worlds in which these texts were produced: attitudes of the time regarding gender relationships, body image, sexuality, economic and social ideals, with particular reference to women, and so forth. The critic tries to determine which group produced the text and whose socioeconomic interests it serves. Then, in an *intrinsic* analysis, the critic focuses on what the text actually says (content) and how it says it (rhetoric). The critic's concern is to determine how the texts incorporate or "encode" the particular ideologies of their time regarding gender, class, race, and so forth, and thereby reproduce these ideologies.

To facilitate this twofold reading strategy, ideological critics of the Bible often appropriate the models developed by Marxist literary critics. (See entries for Terry Eagleton and Fredric Jameson in this chapter's further reading.) However these literary critics redefine Marx's relationship between *base* (socioeconomic relations) and *superstructure* (culture, ideology, politics, and legal system), the core insight remains that literature is grounded in historical, real-life power relations. Literature is regarded as an ideological production of social practices.

What Is Ideology?

To comprehend what ideological criticism does, one must understand what ideology is.[4] This is no simple task. "Ideology" has taken on popular connotations that give it a negative meaning. The term routinely appears in newspapers

4. For an introduction, see James H. Kavanagh, "Ideology," *Critical Terms for Literary Study,* Frank Lentricchia and Thomas McLaughlin, eds. (Chicago: University of Chicago Press, 1990), 306–20.

and television broadcasts. For example, presidential candidate Michael Dukak-is's acceptance speech at the Democratic convention on July 21, 1988, included this sound bite: "This election is not about ideology; it's about competence." Here, the word suggests some abstract system of extremist ideas at both ends of the liberal-conservative spectrum. Radical leftists or ultra–right-wingers "have" ideologies; the mainstream or majority — typically assumed to be "people like me" — do not. Ideology in this context is what "other people" have. This negative identification of ideology with extremist views is definitely *not* what is understood as "ideology" in critical theory.

Ideology is not simply a set of doctrines or ideas, although it certainly contains these. As a complex system of values, ideas, pictures, images, and perceptions, ideology motivates men and women to "see" their particular place in the social order as natural, inevitable, and necessary. According to the Marxist theorist Louis Althusser, "ideology is a 'representation' of the imaginary relationship of individuals to their real conditions of existence."[5] Ideology encourages people to internalize an "unreal" relationship to the "real" world. For example, slave owners made ideological use of biblical texts such as Ephesians 6:5 — "Slaves, be obedient to your earthly masters . . . as to Christ" — to keep African-American slaves from rebelling. Although many slaves resisted this message, many others internalized it. Ideology *constructs* a reality for people, making the oftentimes perplexing world intelligible; it is not, however, the actual state of affairs in its entirety. While helping people understand or make sense of the world, ideology concurrently masks or represses their real situation or standing in the world. All people have an ideology (or, more correctly, ideologies) that organizes and directs their lives. These ideologies "resolve" the contradictions and struggles in daily existence.

Marxist theory is primarily concerned with the network of economic class relations. It examines how ideology "explains" any unequal distribution of wealth, prestige, and control over the means of production — land, natural resources, factories, and so forth — in a given population. Dominant ideologies are produced primarily by the class in power (and internalized by the subordinate class) in order to reproduce particular sets of class relations. Yet ideology governs other social relations as well. Differences among genders, races, ethnicities, educational levels, and religion also exist and interconnect in complex ways.[6] Hence, there are ruling-class ideologies and lower-class ideologies, sexist

5. Louis Althusser, "Ideology and Ideological State Apparatuses (Notes towards an Investigation)," *Lenin and Philosophy and Other Essays* (New York and London: Monthly Review Press, 1971), 162.
6. In Euro-American society, for example, those who wield the most social, economic, and political power are usually white males, and those who possess the least are women of color.

ideologies and feminist ideologies, racist ideologies and Afrocentric ideologies, and so forth. These ideologies cooperate, confront, and often clash with one another in the "real" world. They articulate "reasons" for these differences and provide a basis for social control or social resistance when conflict erupts because of them. For example, in the antebellum South, racist, classist, and sexist ideologies cooperated in providing an excuse for the rape of black female slaves by their owners.

Ideological Strategies

Ideologies operate through a number of strategies to produce their desired social effects. They *unify* social groups. By linking the abstract level of ideas with the concrete level of social practices, ideologies are *action-oriented*. They *rationalize* certain interests, beliefs, or behaviors by providing credible explanations for them. Moreover, they *legitimate* these beliefs or interests by sanctioning them, by having people accept their authority. They *universalize* historically specific values, ways of acting, and so forth as the only valid ideals for everyone for all time. They *naturalize* them by identifying them with the "common sense" of a society, so that they become seemingly self-evident and "natural." Thus the Marxist literary critic Fredric Jameson regards ideologies as "strategies of containment," because they close off any critical questioning of the actual historical situation and repress both its contradictions and evidence of power struggles.[7]

What Is Ideological Criticism?

Ideological criticism presumes that the *text* (1) is a *production* of a specific, ideologically charged historical world that (2) *reproduces* a particular ideology with an internal logic of its own. One can understand the relationship among text, ideology, and history by comparing these relationships in a dramatic production. A staging of *Hamlet* does not mechanically "reflect," "mirror," or "express" Shakespeare's dramatic text of *Hamlet*. The staging manipulates the text of this play and performs it interpretively; it generates a unique production. Ideology, like the dramatic script, is a production of sociohistorical realities; the literary text, like the dramatic production, orchestrates and reworks this ideology to "re-produce" it in its own way:

$$\text{history/ideology} \rightarrow \text{dramatic text} \rightarrow \text{dramatic production}$$
$$\text{history} \rightarrow \text{ideology} \rightarrow \text{literary text}[8]$$

7. Fredric Jameson, *Political Unconscious: Narrative as a Socially Symbolic Act* (Ithaca, N.Y.: Cornell University Press, 1981), 53–54.

8. On this analogy between dramatic and textual production, see Terry Eagleton, *Criticism and Ideology: A Study in Marxist Literary Theory* (London: Verso, 1976), 64–69.

Ideological criticism entails, then, an extrinsic analysis that uncovers the circumstances under which the text was produced and an intrinsic analysis that investigates the text's reproduction of ideology in the text's rhetoric.[9] Because of the complex interrelation between production and reproduction, extrinsic and intrinsic analyses should be regarded as two sides of the same coin. A preliminary intrinsic analysis observes ideological gaps, contradictions, and competing voices in the text. Critics then read the text backward, so to speak, to determine the nature of the material-ideological power struggles the text's ideology tries to resolve. They then return to a more complete intrinsic analysis to ascertain precisely how the text encodes and reworks the ideological conditions of its production.

Extrinsic Analysis

Extrinsic analysis makes use of the social sciences and historical criticism to understand the complex social structures of specific historical groups and their interrelationships with other parts of the society. Its major focus is the *mode of production* dominant in the society producing the text. The term refers to the complete operation of social relations (family organization, status, class, gender, etc.) and forces (technological, political, juridical, etc.) of a society's material production. Three dominant modes of productions can be distinguished during the course of ancient Israelite history: a *familial* mode, a *tributary* (or tribute/tax-based) mode, and a *slave* mode. Each mode is undergirded by its own political economies, social structures and relations, power groups, and dominant ideologies.[10] These aspects of a society in their specific historical manifestations are what the ideological critic must uncover.

Certain explicit questions interest the ideological critic. What are the major social, political, and economic structures in a society at a particular time? Where are the sites of power located in these structures, and what kind of power do they exhibit? How do these groups break down according to class, race, gender, ethnicity, region, religion, occupation, and so forth? What control do they ex-

9. In addition to investigating the text's production and reproduction of ideology, ideological criticism can also study how the text is received/read in the *consumption* of that ideology. However, because of constraints on length, this essay focuses primarily on the twin tasks of extrinsic and intrinsic analysis of a text.

10. For discussion, see Norman K. Gottwald, *The Anchor Bible Dictionary*, vol. 6, s. v. "Sociology (Ancient Israel)," D. N. Freedman, ed. (New York: Doubleday, 1992), 82–87. What Gottwald describes as a "communitarian" mode of production, I refer to as a "familial" mode, along with David Jobling in "Feminism and 'Mode of Production,'" *The Bible and the Politics of Exegesis,* David Jobling, Peggy L. Day, Gerald T. Shepphard, eds. (Cleveland: Pilgrim Press, 1991), 241–43.

ert over the means of production? What are the conflicts, struggles, and contradictions among these various social arrangements? What are the ideologies produced by these groups? Which one is dominant? On whose behalf do these ideologies speak? Whose voices, what groups, do they exclude or distort? What is the social location of the author of the text? What ideology does this author hold in relation to the dominant ideology?[11]

Intrinsic Analysis

Intrinsic analysis determines how the text encodes in its rhetoric the oftentimes conflicting circumstances of its material-ideological production. It makes use of literary critical methods such as narrative criticism, structuralism, and deconstruction to accomplish this. The text is presumed to be a symbolic resolution of real social contradictions, inventing and adapting "solutions" to unresolved ideological dilemmas. For example, racist texts published by white supremacy groups such as the Ku Klux Klan present "solutions" to the real-life conflicts between the races. One such "solution" is shipping all blacks to Africa. The Final Solution, as the Nazis called it, to the "problem" of the Jews was the extermination of six million of them. Just as the dramatic production does not merely "express" the dramatic script, the literary text does not simply "express" the ideology of its time. The text can also confront and challenge this ideology in reproducing its own ideology. Intrinsic analysis therefore attempts to determine the precise relationship of the text to the ideology of its production.

Intrinsic analysis pays special heed to particular *absences* in the text. As Marxist literary critic Pierre Macherey states, "In order to say anything, there are other things *which must not be said.*"[12] In trying to articulate what it regards as the "truth," the text cannot express things that will contradict that "truth." In these silences, in the text's gaps and absences, the presence of ideology is most tangibly perceived. Already determined through extrinsic analysis are the social locations of power, their conflicts and their ideologies. Taking an opposing perspective, intrinsic analysis asks about those voices that are excluded: perhaps those of women, of other tribal groups, or of the poor. Intrinsic analysis uncovers competing voices, marginalized by the society's power structures, that are encoded in the text by their very absence. The text conceals and represses these voices in its attempt to resolve the contradictory opinions they pose.

---

11. These questions roughly follow Eagleton's "categories for a materialist criticism" (*Criticism and Ideology*, 44–63): (1) general mode of production; (2) literary mode of production; (3) general ideology; (4) authorial ideology; (5) aesthetic ideology; and (6) text.

12. Pierre Macherey, *A Theory of Literary Production*, trans. Geoffrey Wall (London: Routledge and Kegan Paul, 1978), 85. Italics his.

Moreover, intrinsic analysis requires an in-depth investigation of *rhetoric:* that is, a text's artful ability to persuade its audience to accept a particular ideology. Because it is a means of persuasion, a text's rhetoric is thus a form of power. The social strategies of ideology — how they universalize, rationalize, or legitimate certain values, behaviors, and so forth — have already been discussed above. The text reorganizes ideology and reinscribes its strategies in written form through the rhetorical features of persuasion. An important part of these features are the commonly recognized elements of structure, such as characterization, plot, repetition, point of view, symbolism, irony, foreshadowing, and framing. Hence, the various and often contradictory ways in which a text portrays individual characters, involves them in specific plots, presents the story from a certain point of view, makes ironic comments or dogmatic statements, and so forth, reveal its particular ideology.

Judges 17–21: An Extrinsic Analysis of the Dismembered Body

The provocative conclusion to the Book of Judges, Judges 17–21, provides an excellent occasion for illustrating ideological criticism. As stated above, an ideological critique begins with a preliminary intrinsic analysis by noting ideological absences, contradictions, and competing voices. The critic then reads "backward" in an extrinsic analysis to unmask the power struggles the text tries to resolve. To simplify the steps, however, I will assume the results of a standard intrinsic analysis. The most obvious ideological comment of Judges 17–21 is that the violence and anarchy of Israel's tribal period is explained by the absence of a king (17:6; 18:1; 19:1; 21:25). Determining when such an ideology could have been produced, then, is one of the first steps in an extrinsic analysis.

The dating and editing of these chapters have been disputed. (See chapter 1 of this volume regarding theories on the editing of Judges and the Deuteronomistic History.) Commentators usually regard these chapters as an "appendix" added during the exilic/postexilic period, years after the main body of the book took shape.[13] My thesis poses a challenge to this late dating. A strong case can be made for assigning Judges 17–21 to the preexilic Deuteronomist in the seventh century, the producer of the first edition of the Deuteronomistic History (Joshua–2 Kings). The prestate or tribal period (c. 1250–1020 B.C.E.), which the Deuteronomist describes in Joshua and Judges, operated under a *familial* mode of production. The Deuteronomist himself lived several centuries later. He worked in a society that functioned under a *native tributary* mode of produc-

13. For a review, see Barry G. Webb, *The Book of the Judges: An Integrated Reading* (JSOTSup 46; Sheffield, Eng.: JSOT Press, 1987), 19–40.

tion, in its specific historical configuration during or just after Josiah's reform (c. 627–609 B.C.E.). The conflicts between these two modes of production are quite evident in the Deuteronomist's editorial statement: "There was no king in Israel; every man did what was right in his own eyes."

As its name implies, the familial mode of production in Israel's tribal period was characterized by strong patrilineal, kinship- and village-based social groupings wherein the family was the basic socioeconomic unit. These family households collected into clans, which formed themselves into the largest social units, the tribes. (See chapter 3 in this volume.) The economy was based on highland agricultural and pastoral production. The tribal lineages owned and administered the land, which was the principal means of production. The tribes were self-sufficient, self-protecting entities, having mutual, family-based relations with one another, on the whole. Since "in those days there was no king in Israel," the tribes were tributary-free, that is, they paid no tribute or taxes to a king or ruling elite who appropriated their surplus wealth. Instead, this wealth went directly back into the tribe. Women were materially and ideologically subordinate to men. Nevertheless, they wielded considerable informal power and authority in family household management. Dividing lines between the so-called domestic sphere and the public sphere were blurred in such a family/kinship-based society.[14]

Because of a number of internal and external factors, Israel moved to a native tributary mode of production (c. 1020–587 B.C.E.).[15] Tribal government became centralized under a king. In contrast to the tribal period, the community was now characterized by the "haves" and the "have-nots."[16] The king and his ruling elite would make up a small percentage of the population at the top of the social pyramid, with the peasants, the bulk of the population, at the bottom. Peasant life was difficult under a tributary mode of production, since it was the peasant who bore the heaviest tax burden of the state. In order to finance a centralized bureaucracy, costly war efforts, ambitious building projects, and a luxurious lifestyle at court, the king and the ruling class extracted surpluses from the peasants, both in human and natural resources. After a generation, this heavy taxation would lead to the impoverishment and decline of the lower classes.

The changes in political system and mode of production had a negative effect

14. Carol Meyers, *Discovering Eve: Ancient Israelite Women in Context* (New York: Oxford University Press, 1988), 122–88.

15. In a *native* tributary mode of production the king and his ruling elite are indigenous to the land. In a *foreign* tributary mode of production, the land is administered by foreign colonizers or conquerors.

16. Norman K. Gottwald, "Social Class as an Analytic and Hermeneutical Category in Biblical Studies," *Journal of Biblical Literature* 112 (1993): 3–9.

on prestate Israel's tribal structure. In order to maintain his centralized political control, the king had to subvert and ultimately destroy the social solidarity and authority of the tribal "body": the family and lineage groups that had the potential for conspiracy and revolt. For example, in the politics of state centralization, Solomon tried to "dismember" tribal organization and kin group loyalties when he redivided his kingdom, cutting across tribal boundaries[17] to create twelve tax districts (1 Kgs 4:7-19). Moreover, a number of recent studies demonstrate how the sex and family laws of the Deuteronomic code slowly eroded the authority of the male head of the household in favor of the state.[18]

State formation would also have an adverse effect on the status of women in Israel. As power shifted from the family household to the state, with its male king and male political and religious bureaucracies, female power and prestige receded. When the family household became progressively more impoverished by the state, women would bear the greater burden. Hierarchical relationships among male and female family members intensified as society itself became more economically and politically stratified by the state.[19]

Although the monarchy with its tributary mode of production supplanted the tribal structure with its familial mode of production, it never completely erased popular tribal kinship loyalties and household economies and ideals. The familial mode persisted in rural areas, since the state did not have the technical and administrative apparatus to oversee the kingdom totally.

In its present form, edited by the Deuteronomist, Judges 17–21 tries to resolve ideologically the conflicts between the two modes of production (one dominant, the other subordinate but still stubbornly present) in their specific historical forms during King Josiah's time in the seventh century (c. 640–609 B.C.E.). Scholars usually regard the Deuteronomist's edition of the Deuteronomistic History as propaganda for Josiah's reform policies.[20] The Deuteronomist had only high praise for the ruler of the southern kingdom of Judah. Josiah was depicted as the ideal by which all the other kings were judged. Under his

17. Compare Joshua 13–21.

18. For example, Naomi Steinberg, "The Deuteronomic Law Code and the Politics of State Centralization," in *The Bible and the Politics of Exegesis,* David Jobling, Peggy L. Day, and Gerald T. Sheppard, eds. (Cleveland: Pilgrim Press, 1991), 161–70.

19. Meyers, *Discovering Eve,* 189–96. The effects of state formation on the position of women has been analyzed extensively by feminist anthropologists and historians. See, for example, Sherry B. Ortner, "The Virgin and the State," *Feminist Studies* 4 (1978): 10–33; Ruby Rohrlich, "State Formation in Sumer and the Subjugation of Women," *Feminist Studies* 6 (1980): 76–102; Barbara S. Lesko, "Women of Egypt and the Ancient Near East," in *Becoming Woman: Women in European History,* Renate Bridenthal, Claudia Koontz, and Susan Stuard, eds. (Boston: Houghton Mifflin, 1987, rev. ed.), 41–77.

20. Richard D. Nelson, *The Double Redaction of the Deuteronomistic History* (Sheffield, Eng.: JSOT Press, 1981), 121–23.

rule, the Book of the Law was discovered in the temple (2 Kgs 22:3-20). His first public response to the find was a covenant renewal ceremony, where he read this law to the people (2 Kgs 23:1-3). He then purified and centralized the cult by destroying what he considered "idolatrous" (2 Kgs 23:4-20, 24). Finally, he commanded the Passover to be celebrated in Jerusalem (2 Kgs 23:21-23).

Nevertheless, by examining the subtext of the narrative critically, one realizes that Josiah's cultic reform involved the ruthless destruction in God's name of all high places and local shrines except the Jerusalem temple. These native Israelite sanctuaries were licit under older laws, and ministered to a substantial portion of the population. The Deuteronomist glosses over the class conflicts Josiah's "religious" reform entailed. However, when the reform is viewed from an economic standpoint, these class conflicts are strongly foregrounded.[21]

For seventy-five years prior to Josiah's reform in 640 B.C.E., Judah was reduced to Assyrian vassalage. Its ruling classes squeezed all they could from their peasant economic base to pay the tribute to Assyria, while still preserving their privileged lifestyle. However, the balance of power shifted with the decline of Assyrian power during Josiah's time, especially after the death of Ashurbanipal in 627. Josiah saw an opportunity to intensify his hold on Judah and extend his control into the former northern kingdom of Israel. This expansion would considerably enlarge his tax base and stimulate the faltering economy of his state.

Josiah could not, however, finance this expansion by raising taxes on a peasantry already strained under current tariffs. Nor could he raise taxes on the wealthy, because his own political hold had been rather shaky since his controversial rise to power (2 Kgs 21:23-24). He could not afford to alienate either of these two groups.[22] He therefore initiated a "religious" reform that made his appropriation of peasant surpluses more efficient. He reorganized the collection of taxes, tributes, and fees *that were already assessed* so that they flowed directly into Jerusalem's coffers. He thus bypassed the local leaders, who had been collecting these revenues for him, but who also had been taking their cut.

Significant for understanding Judges 17–21 is that the local class, which was pocketing its share of peasant funds in the rural and remote areas of the kingdom, was largely composed of country *Levites* of the priestly house often called the Mushite.[23] These Levites ministered in the high places and sanctuaries in

21. For the argument that Josiah's reform had more socioeconomic than religious intent, see W. Eugene Claburn, "The Fiscal Basis of Josiah's Reforms," *Journal of Biblical Literature* 92 (1973): 11–22 and, more recently, Shigeyuki Nakanose, *Josiah's Passover: Sociology and the Liberating Bible* (Maryknoll, N.Y.: Orbis Books, 1993).

22. Nakanose, *Josiah's Passover,* 50.

23. Claburn, "Fiscal Basis of Josiah's Reforms," 17–21; Nakanose, *Josiah's Passover,* 59–60, 62–65.

Judah and in the former northern kingdom, and they competed with Jerusalem and its Zadokite priesthood for cultic revenues. They prospered from their tax collection, as well as from tithes on peasant sacrifices and pilgrimages to shrines. Rallying Judah under an ideology of cultic "reform," Josiah tore down the religious sanctuaries of the Levites in the areas surrounding Jerusalem and in Judah (2 Kgs 23:4-14). He then turned northward and destroyed their major shrine at Bethel and other holy places in the former kingdom of Israel (2 Kgs 23:15-20).

By destroying competing cult centers, neutralizing their priests, and promoting a religious ideology that made Jerusalem the only legitimate place to worship YHWH, Josiah sought to ensure that an enormous flow of cash would come into his capital city. The desire for this influx of funds lay behind the following law regarding pilgrimage festivals:

> Three times a year all your males shall appear before the Lord your God at the place that he will choose: at the festival of unleavened bread, at the festival of weeks, and at the festival of booths. *They shall not appear before the Lord empty-handed; all shall give as they are able,* according to the blessing of the Lord your God that he has given you. (Deut 16:16)

The command to celebrate Passover in Jerusalem illustrates another site of struggle between the tribal and tributary modes of production. In tribal Israel, Passover was a family-oriented feast celebrated in the local household (Exod 12). The feast promoted the communal values and kinship relations typical in a familial mode of production. The religious, social, and economic shift from the family to the state is evident in the directive to make a pilgrimage to Jerusalem to observe Passover. The religious (ideological) means that promoted the family values of the tribal mode of production were thus co-opted by the Jerusalem elite to exercise its social, economic, and ideological power over the people.[24]

The socioeconomic and ideological conflicts between the tribal body and the tributary mode of production, the competition between the Jerusalem priesthood and the rural Levitic priesthood, the fiscal ambitions of King Josiah, the destruction of regional sanctuaries, and the centralization of worship in Jerusalem all provided the material and ideological circumstances that produced Judges 17–21. It is these power struggles, ideological dilemmas, and social contradictions that the text tries to "resolve." We can move on to an intrinsic analysis of Judges 17–21 to determine how the text encodes these struggles in its reproduction of the deuteronomic ideology.

---

24. Nakanose, *Josiah's Passover,* 104–12.

Intrinsic Analysis of the Dismembered Body

Fascinated by absences and contradictions, an intrinsic analysis uncovers very significant ones in Judges 17–21. In a book devoted primarily to judges and heroes, no such individuals inhabit the concluding chapters. Instead one encounters a ragtag bunch of questionable virtue: a son who embezzles from his own mother; a corrupt Levite on the lookout for a fast buck; another Levite who sacrifices his wife to save his own hide; an assortment of idolatrous, inhospitable, and warmongering tribes. The notion of absence and contradiction can be extended to biblical scholarship—the *consumption* of the text by the academic—on and of Judges 17–21. As was pointed out, scholars regard these chapters as an exilic or postexilic "appendix" added after most of the book was formed. Mieke Bal likely is correct in arguing that the elimination of Judges 17–21 from the so-called authentic material depends on a politics of coherence that privileges a reading focused on male heroes, political nationalism, and military accomplishments.[25]

The most striking absence is textually explicit: "In those days, there was *no king* in Israel." This editorial comment is strategically repeated throughout these chapters (17:6; 18:1; 19:1; 21:25). Accompanying the first and last of these statements is the deliberately ironic note, "Every man did what was right in his own eyes."[26] What is "right" in men's eyes are a woman's rape and torture at the hands of a predatory mob, her ghastly dismemberment, an intertribal war that almost extinguishes one of Israel's members, the seizure and rape of more women to replenish this tribe. The orderly framework of apostasy, oppression, crying out, and deliverance that shapes much of Judges disintegrates by the end. Indeed, the complete absence of order in these final chapters culminates in the most brutal events in the book.[27]

The ideological thrust of the editorial remarks is straightforward: the ab-

25. Mieke Bal, *Death and Dissymmetry: The Politics of Coherence in the Book of Judges* (Chicago: University of Chicago Press, 1988), 9–16.

26. A literal translation of the Hebrew.

27. Literary studies have highlighted the breakdown of the Deuteronomist's theological framework as well as the redactional unity between Judges 17–21 and the beginning of the book: D. W. Gooding, "The Composition of the Book of Judges," *Eretz-Israel, Archeological Historical and Geographical Studies, Vol. 16; Harry M. Orlinsky Volume* (Jerusalem: Israel Exploration Society, 1982), 70–79; David M. Gunn, "Joshua and Judges," *The Literary Guide to the Bible* (Cambridge: Harvard University Press, 1987), 102–121; Alexander Globe, "'Enemies Round About': Disintegrative Structure in the Book of Judges," *Mappings of the Biblical Terrain*, V. Tollers and J. Maier, eds. (Lewisburg, Pa.: Bucknell University Press, 1990), 233–51, and J. Cheryl Exum, "The Centre Cannot Hold: Thematic and Textual Instabilities in Judges," *Catholic Biblical Quarterly* 52 (1990): 410–31.

sence of a king accounts for the chaos and cruelty of Israel's tribal period. Nevertheless, this explicit absence masks an imperceptible one. In order to extol the monarchy, the text must conceal the social hardships and contradictions of a society actually governed by a king and his ruling elite. Embedded ideologically in the text are the conflicts between familial and tributary modes of production. The text implies a positive appraisal of the latter at the expense of the former. Although diminished by the state, tribal and lineage loyalties were still evident during Josiah's time and were potential sources for rebellion. Judges 17–21 provides an ideological means of "dismembering" such allegiances and suppressing revolt. Characterizing the tribal period as anarchic and violent at the end of Judges, the Deuteronomist at the same time foreshadows the establishment of the Davidic monarchy in the next two books of his history (1 and 2 Samuel). He ultimately paves the way for his ideal king, Josiah (2 Kgs 22-23). Keeping these absences and contradictions in mind, we can proceed to an investigation of the text's rhetoric.

Judges 17–18: Cultic Chaos

The stories in Judges 17–18 underscore the disintegration of Israel's cult during the tribal period. Each chapter is filled with irony, humor, and ambiguity that ridicules this decline. Judges 17:1-6 introduces Micah, a resident of the northern hill country of Ephraim. He is just returning the eleven hundred pieces of silver he had filched from his unnamed mother. Possibly, she is Delilah, who, according to the preceding chapter, betrays Samson to the Philistines for precisely the same amount (16:5). No reason for Micah's confession is given; it may have been prompted by genuine contrition, a guilty conscience, or fear of his mother's curse upon the thief. The ambiguity highlights the cavalier attitudes these characters have toward the cult. The mother calls a blessing down upon the wayward but seemingly repentant son. Apparently forgetting the second commandment (Exod 20:4), she announces that she is consecrating the silver to YHWH to make a idol of cast metal for her son. She contributes, however, only two hundred pieces toward it. Evidently she pockets the rest, although the text is unclear. Along with this idol, Micah also boasts of a shrine. He installs one of his sons as its priest and has more cult objects made — an ephod and teraphim.[28]

Homemade idols of stolen silver, private shrines, personal priests, self-made sacerdotal gear: these are hardly the proper trappings of one whose name means "Who is like YHWH?" The repeated references to cult objects throughout

---

28. An ephod is a type of priestly garment worn over the breast. A teraphim is a cultic image of a household god.

Judges 17–18 emphasize an idolatrous worship practiced by sacrilegious men.[29] They highlight a wicked age when "there was no king in Israel; every man did what was right in his own eyes" (17:6). The Deuteronomist implies that a king like Josiah would rid the country of such cultic abuses.

In the next scene (17:7-13), a young Levite travelling from Bethlehem in Judah finds his way northward to Micah's house. He seeks a place in which to settle and make a living. Micah hires him on the spot, without asking for references: "Stay with me, and be to me a father and a priest, and I will give you ten pieces of silver a year, a set of clothes, and your living" (17:10). The freelancing Levite agrees to Micah's offer, but, ironically, he does not become a "father" to Micah. Instead, he becomes like one of Micah's sons in his house. The father-son relation becomes empty because it is reversible. With the Levite's coming, Micah's glee is palpable: "Now I know that the Lord will prosper me, because the Levite has become my priest" (17:13). Not only does Micah obtain a priest, but his very own *Levite* at that, who guarantees God's favor—or so Micah thinks.

Poor Micah discovers otherwise in Judges 18, when he and his Levite encounter the tribe of Dan. Just as the peripatetic Levite journeys northward in search of a place to settle, so too the landless tribe of Dan migrates north to find an "inheritance" to colonize.[30] Five Danites scouting potential territory accept hospitality in Micah's house (18:2). Once they recognize the Levite, they inquire about his circumstances. The Levite's broad hints to the Danites—"he hired me/I have become his priest" (18:4)—do not go unnoticed. However, unlike Micah, who requested no references, the Danites test the Levite's priestly skills: they want to know if their mission will succeed (18:5). The Levite's ambiguous reply reveals his shrewdness: "Go in peace. The mission you are on is *nokaḥ* YHWH." The rare Hebrew word *nokaḥ* apparently can signify both "in front of" and "opposite," so that the Danite's mission can be either "favorable" or "unfavorable" to God.

The Danites evidently understand their instant oracle in the former sense, because they continue their journey northward. Reporting to their comrades in the south, they urge the capture of Laish, a city inhabited by a peaceful, unsuspecting, and defenseless people (18:7-8). Six hundred fully armed warriors then set out. Along the way, they loot Micah's shrine, taking its idol, ephod, and teraphim; they are completely oblivious to his earlier hospitality toward

29. Judges 17:3, 4; 18:14, 17-18, 20, 30-31.

30. According to Judges 13–16, the tribe of Dan was settled around the southern coast near Philistine territory. Although scholars presume that the Danites had to abandon their homeland because of Philistine incursions, the text is ambiguous on the matter, in keeping with the lack of clarity throughout these chapters.

them. Witnessing this raid, the Levite makes a half-hearted attempt at protest (18:18). The Danites basically tell him to shut up and offer him the post of tribal priest. Thus, an idol of stolen silver gets stolen; a bought priest gets bought again, for an even bigger price (18:19-20). Micah pursues the Danites to recover his possessions, but his whining is rather pathetic: "You take my gods that I made, and the priest, and go away, and what have I left?" (18:24). Homemade gods and a callous priest. Indeed, Micah had nothing in the first place! And thugs that they are, the Danites threaten to set their "hot-tempered fellows" on Micah and his household.[31] Seeing himself hopelessly outnumbered, Micah returns home. The "mighty warriors" continue on to Laish and destroy the helpless town. They rename it Dan after their eponymous ancestor, and there they enshrine their purloined idol.

Finally, the narrative provides more information about the money-grubbing Levite who will service this idol. He is the grandson of Moses himself and his name is Jonathan! He and his sons will minister to the Danite shrine and Micah's idol "until the time the land went into captivity" (18:30).

The underlying grotesquerie of Judges 17–18 can be contextualized in the Deuteronomist's propaganda for Josiah's so-called religious reform. His ideological production legitimates Josiah's brutal demolition of the northern sanctuaries. A recurring theme in his edition of 1 and 2 Kings is a polemic against the ostensibly illicit cult and priesthood Jeroboam I established at Dan and Bethel. These northern shrines rivaled the royal cult in Jerusalem. The Deuteronomist reproaches Jeroboam for setting up the "two calves of gold" at these shrines (1 Kgs 12:25-33). In his opinion, Jeroboam's "idolatry" led to the fall of the North in 721 B.C.E. (2 Kgs 17:20-23). His reference to "the captivity" in Judges 18:30 most likely refers to this event.

Judges 17–18 anticipates this condemnation through a rehearsal of Dan's dubious beginnings. Although its partner in cultic crime, Bethel, is not explicitly named, it is certainly included in the censure.[32] The ideological critic needs to ask, "Why Dan and not Bethel?" in Judges 17–18. Assuming that he wanted to disparage the tribal system, the Deuteronomist focuses on Dan, thus reproaching the tribal name and therefore the tribal affiliation.

Furthermore, the portrayal of the Levite is significant. Tracing his origins to Moses encodes the priestly rivalry between the Mushite and Zadokite families. The Deuteronomist represents the Levitic competitors of the Jerusalem priesthood as unscrupulous opportunists. Both Micah and the tribe of Dan pay im-

31. Judges 18:25: lit., "men of bitter spirit"; translated "hot-tempered fellows" in the NRSV.

32. Yairah Amit, "Hidden Polemic in the Conquest of Dan: Judges 17–18," *Vetus Testamentum* 40 (1990): 4–20.

pressive fees for the Levite's "services," and so they guarantee his financial security. However, within the overall thrust of the Deuteronomist's propaganda, any hint of Josiah's own economic ambitions in neutralizing the country Levites and redirecting their revenues to Jerusalem is absent in this narrative. The centralization associated with a tributary mode of production is repressed in the text.

Tribal Israel certainly does not escape caricature either. It is depicted as uncivilized; no king ruled and cultic disorder was rampant. Furthermore, because this was a time when kinship relations were highly prized, the breakdown of these relations in the text is quite remarkable. A son betrays his mother. A "son" (the Levite) abandons his "father" (Micah). A shameless tribe violates the laws of hospitality and the host/guest relation. These themes will carry over into Judges 19–21, where another tribe ignores hospitality codes, a Levite delivers his wife to rapists, and tribal lineages nearly wipe each other out. The Deuteronomist shifts the history of tribal collapse back two generations to the prestate period itself. He completely suppresses the fact that the monarchy deliberately broke up the "tribal body" in order to establish and preserve a tributary mode of production.

Judges 19–21: Social Chaos

Significant issues of gender intersect with those of class in an ideological critique of Judges 19.[33] Class and gender interests are most apparent at the beginning of the chapter in the unequal power relations between the Levite and his wife. The Levite, as the extrinsic analysis observes, is one of the local cult leaders, who obtains his wealth from the revenues peasants offer at regional shrines. His woman is described as a *pilegesh,* a wife of secondary rank, usually translated "concubine" (19:1). For a man who already has children by his primary wife, one of her main roles is to provide sexual pleasure.[34] A *pilegesh* can also be taken in order to provide children when the primary wife is barren (cf. Gen 16, 30). While a primary wife is already subordinate to her husband, the *pilegesh* endures a double subordination in her position as secondary wife.[35] The inferior status

33. The violent story of the rape and dismemberment of the Levite's wife in Judges 19 has been a topic for a number of feminist biblical scholars. See chapter 4 on feminist criticism by Exum in this volume; also, J. Cheryl Exum, "Raped by the Pen," *Fragmented Women: Feminist (Sub)versions of Biblical Narratives* (JSOTSup 163; Sheffield, Eng.: JSOT Press, 1993), esp. 176–94.

34. See the discussion of secondary wives in chapter 3 by Naomi Steinberg in this volume.

35. See, for example, the treatment of Hagar in Genesis 16–21.

of the woman in our story is particularly foregrounded after her rape, when the text describes her husband as her "master" (*'adon;* 19:26-27).

Intrinsic analysis, acutely aware of absences in the text, notices furthermore that there is no textual mention of a primary wife. Her absence provides the first clue to the Levite's character. In contrast to Israel's patrilineal ideology, where men typically marry and have sons to carry on the family name, the Levite apparently eschews a primary wife and uses his secondary wife for sexual gratification.

While the Levite of Judges 17–18 came from Bethlehem in Judah to settle in the northern hill country of Ephraim (17:7-8), this Levite leaves Ephraim to pursue his wife, who had left him and returned to her father's house in Bethlehem. The Levite seemingly does not care for his wife, since he waits four months before going after her.[36] The reason the Hebrew text gives for the wife's departure is that she "fornicated" against her husband.[37] The literal sense of her action, that she actually had illicit sex with other men, presents interpretive problems. Why would her father accept such a shameless daughter and allow her to remain with him for four months? Why would her husband expend the time and effort to bringing her back? Under the law she must be put to death (Lev 20:10; Deut 22:22).

A stronger case can be made for considering her act figuratively. It is her very abandonment of her husband that the Deuteronomist describes as "fornicating" against her husband. Anthropological studies of women's resistance to male authority provide a helpful model. For example, disrupting the household by vacating it abruptly is one of a number of strategies women adopt to exercise autonomy in androcentric societies.[38] In a society that so rigorously supervises the sexuality of its women, the daring act of leaving a husband would be judged, as the Deuteronomist does in this case, as a metaphoric act of "fornication."[39]

---

36. Fewell and Gunn raise two other narrative possibilities regarding the Levite's inaction: his wounded pride holds him back, or, following Koala Jones-Warsaw, the concubine's secondary status does not rate an immediate response. (*Gender, Power, and Promise: The Subject of the Bible's First Story* [Nashville: Abingdon Press, 1993], 133.)

37. The Hebrew word used is *zanah,* usually mistranslated into English as "to play the harlot or whore, to prostitute oneself." See Phyllis Bird, "'To Play the Harlot': An Inquiry into an Old Testament Metaphor," in *Gender and Difference in Ancient Israel,* Peggy L. Day, ed. (Minneapolis: Fortress Press, 1989), 75–94.

38. Lila Abu-Lughod, "The Romance of Resistance: Tracing Transformations of Power through Bedouin Women," in *Beyond the Second Sex: New Directions in the Anthropology of Gender,* Peggy Reeves Sanday and Ruth Gallagher Goodenough, eds. (Philadelphia: University of Pennsylvania Press, 1990), 311–37.

39. Compare Exum's reading in this volume on this same point. The Septuagintal rendering of the Hebrew *zanah* in this text as "to become angry" particularly cor-

Besides bringing dishonor upon herself, the woman brings dishonor upon her husband, since it becomes publicly apparent that he cannot control her actions. Moreover, the extent of a man's disgrace correlates inversely with the status of the one who shames him: the lower the status, the greater the shame. That the deserting woman is a *pilegesh* therefore compounds the Levite's humiliation.

Feminist scholars have already pointed out that the biblical text primarily encodes male-male power relations. Women's voices are usually absent, muzzled, or mediated by the male narrator. Stories ostensibly about male-female relations are more often about the struggles among men for honor and status. Men frequently manipulate their relations with women in order to achieve certain goals in their relations with other men.

And so it is in Judges 19. The story shifts in vv. 3–9 from the Levite and his wife to the Levite and his father-in-law. Although it has been suggested that this narrative is about male bonding,[40] cross-cultural studies point out that the host-guest relationship is essentially one of unequal power relations. The flamboyant display of generosity by the father-in-law toward the Levite symbolizes the moral and conceptual subordination of the guest to the host.[41] Through this subordination, the Deuteronomist contributes to his carefully constructed portrayal of the Levite. Against the male ideology of his own time, an upper-class Levite seems to bypass a primary wife (and the procreative duties thereof) and takes for himself a secondary wife just for sex. He is doubly dishonored when his *pilegesh* abandons him, and he is taken down a few more social notches by his father-in-law's shrewd hospitality.

Following the pattern of Judges 17–18 (Levite-tribe), after his caricature of the Levite, the Deuteronomist launches into a negative portrayal of the tribes. The Levite finally resolves to quit his father-in-law's house and return north to Ephraim with his wife. It is significant that he refuses to spend the night in Jebus, which he scorns as a "city of foreigners who do not belong to the people

---

roborates the thesis that the woman's departure was an exercise of power. On women's quarrels, see Naomi Steinberg, *Kinship and Marriage in Genesis: A Household Economics Perspective*, (Minneapolis: Fortress Press, 1993), 103–6.

40. Phyllis Trible, "An Unnamed Woman: The Extravagance of Violence," *Texts of Terror: Literary Feminist Readings of Biblical Narratives* (Philadelphia: Fortress Press, 1984), 68.

41. Julian Pitt-Rivers, "The Law of Hospitality," *The Fate of Shechem, or the Politics of Sex: Essays in the Anthropology of the Mediterranean* (Cambridge: Cambridge University Press, 1977), 101–2; Michael Herzfeld, "'As In Your Own House': Hospitality, Ethnography, and the Stereotype of Mediterranean Society," *Honor and Shame and the Unity of the Mediterranean,* David D. Gilmore, ed. (Washington, D.C.: American Anthropological Association, 1987), 77.

of Israel" (19:12). Jebus, the author emphasizes in an editorial note, is in fact Jerusalem (19:10), the favored capital of the future monarchy, of King Josiah, and of the Deuteronomist. In an ideological plug for his royal city, the Deuteronomist implies that had the Levite overcome his prejudice and chose Jebus for his night's stay, he would have found safety and security. Certainly, the story would have been different for his wife. However, at sundown the Levite and his company reach the town of Gibeah, "which belongs to Benjamin" (19:14). Instead of a welcome from extended tribal kin, "no one took them in to spend the night" (19:15).

Eventually, the Levite is offered hospitality by an old man living in Gibeah as a resident alien (19:16-21). A gang of town thugs during their merrymaking encircles the house. They are not very subtle about their intentions toward the Levite: "Bring out the man who came into your house, that we may have intercourse with him" (19:22).

Homosexual rape should be understood in the context male-male power relations. The phallus serves as a weapon of aggression that establishes a relation of dominance and submission. A man who is raped by other men figuratively becomes emasculated and "feminized." The Deuteronomist progressively disgraces the Levite in this way. The shame caused by his wife's abandonment and the subordination by his father-in-law intersect here and become sexualized by this threat of gang rape. As noted above, the extent of a man's disgrace correlates inversely with the status of the ones who shame him. The rapists are described as a "perverse lot" (19:22).[42] Shamed and feminized by his secondary wife and her father, the Levite is in danger of becoming even more humiliated and emasculated by degenerate men.

The old man leaves his house to reason with the hooligans. Ironically, he addresses them as kin: "No, *my brothers,* do not act so wickedly. Since this man is my guest, do not do this vile thing" (19:23). He offers the would-be rapists his own virgin daughter and the Levite's wife as a substitute for his male guest (19:24). The rape of women—indeed of one's own daughter—is less repugnant for the old man than the rape of the Levite, which he describes as a "wicked act," a "vile outrage" (*nebalah*). The old man enjoins the mob to "Ravish them. Do to them *what is good in your eyes*" (19:24).[43] The violation echoes the Deuteronomist's censure of the whole tribal period, when "there was no king in Israel and every man did *what was right in his own eyes*."

The negative portrayal of the Levite becomes exacerbated. In a callous act of self-preservation, he seizes his wife and shoves her out to the mob. She is

---

42. The parallel story in Genesis 19:4-5 simply describes "men of the city" and does not add the qualifier, "perverse lot," lit., "sons of Belial" (Judg 19:22).
43. Compare Genesis 19:7, where the words "Ravish them" do not appear.

raped and abused the whole night. Released in the morning, she falls down at the door of the house where her "master" was safely ensconced (the text for the first time identifies the Levite as her "*'adon,*" 19:25-26). He leaves the house to continue his journey, and behold, his fallen wife blocks his passage. Oblivious to her pathetic, tragic, horrific condition, he orders her to "'Get up, we are going.' But there was no answer" (19:28).

The cultic chaos that the Deuteronomist lampoons in Judges 17–18 resurfaces in 19–20. The Levite puts the woman on his donkey and heads back to Ephraim. Upon entering his house, he takes *the* knife (i.e., a knife that is reserved for ritual purposes)[44] and "seizes" his wife again, just as he had "seized" his wife to throw her out to the crowd.[45] In a perversion of sacrificial ritual, he severs her body into twelve pieces (19:29-30). The possibility that the woman may still have been alive during her dismemberment—the Hebrew text does not say that she has died[46]—makes the Levite's brutal gesture even more harrowing. Undoubtedly, the Deuteronomist intends that the Levite's act be contrasted with 1 Samuel 11, where Saul, under the power of God's spirit, hacks a yoke of oxen to pieces. The first king of Israel then sends the pieces throughout the territory to summon the tribes to war against the Ammonites. As ideological propaganda for the monarchy, the depiction of Saul is positive in 1 Samuel 11. He heroically delivers the people of Jabesh-Gilead, who are besieged by the Ammonites. The Levite, however, whose profession should guarantee that the ritual is legitimate, becomes the agent of a grotesque antisacrifice that desecrates rather than consecrates. A woman's raped and battered body replaces the sacrificial animal.

Responding to the Levite's grisly communication, the tribes assemble at Mizpah, their members numbering four hundred thousand strong (Judg 20:2). By noting that they gather "as one man" and act "as one man" (20:1, 8, 11), the Deuteronomist highlights a corporate entity which will soon incur his reproach: "Every man did what was right in his own eyes."

The tribes ask of the Levite, "Tell us, how did this criminal act come about?" (20:3). But the Levite blatantly suppresses the truth of the matter. He states that the "lords of Gibeah" (20:5) rose up against him. "They intended to kill me," he declares. In fact, those who demanded the Levite were not "lords" but a "perverse lot." In the ideology of male prestige, it is infinitely preferable to be attacked by lords rather than by the local louts. It is certainly more compa-

44. Compare Genesis 22:10, where Abraham takes "the" knife (*hamma'akelet*), that is, a knife set aside for cultic purposes, in order to slay his son Isaac for a sacrificial offering.

45. Fewell and Gunn, *Gender, Power, and Promise,* 134.

46. Trible, "An Unnamed Woman," 79.

tible with the Levite's own upper-class station and his perceived importance. Furthermore, it was not the plan of these ruffians to kill the Levite. They intended what could be regarded among males as a fate worse than death; they wanted to rape him.

Brazenly glossing over the fact that he delivered his wife into the mob, the Levite then recounts that "they raped my concubine until [lit., "and"] she died." But, as noted above, the text allows for the disturbing possibility that the Levite killed her himself. The only truthful statement the Levite makes is that he took his wife and cut her into pieces and sent her throughout Israel's territory (20:6). And the truth is not honorable: instead of providing a decent burial—the least he could have done for his wife—the Levite hacks her up and sends her out in a clearly self-serving act. He thus prolongs the villainy against her. The tribes supposedly gather to hear *her* story, the one behind the bloodied arm, hacked leg, and battered head that they received. Her limbs cry out her agony, only to be censored and silenced by her husband's rhetoric.

The Levite concludes his speech by referring to the "vile outrage" the town of Gibeah has committed against Israel, and he enjoins the tribes, "Give your advice and counsel here" (20:6b-7). Commentators normally refer to this episode as the "outrage of Gibeah," but the object of the "outrage" is ambiguous. The Hebrew word for "outrage" is *nebalah,* which the Levite uses here to refer to his wife's rape. However, in 19:23-24, the word is used by the old man to depict the gang-rape attempt on the Levite. The Levite manipulates the *real* outrage against his wife (which he himself caused) to exact retribution for the *attempted* outrage against himself. He could not reveal to the tribes that he was almost raped by dissolute men. He would have incurred dishonor and loss of prestige. Instead, he manipulates his relationship with a woman in order to maneuver his male relations to accomplish his personal vendetta against Gibeah.

Having completed his humiliation and censure of the levitical class, the Deuteronomist removes the Levite from the scene. He next goes after the tribal body. The social chaos in Judges 20–21 parallels the cultic chaos described in Judges 17–18. Having been duped by the Levite, the tribes wage war against Benjamin. Noteworthy is the kinship language used to describe these intertribal relations (20:13, 23, 28; 21:6). In order to break down kin group relations among the tribes, the Deuteronomist depicts these "brothers" as engaged in a senseless internecine war. Four hundred thousand Israelites advance against twenty-six thousand Benjaminites. The Deuteronomist describes their confrontations in a slapstick manner. Despite their remarkable numeric advantage, the Israelite tribes are initially decimated by Benjamin. On day one, they lose twenty-two thousand men, almost the number of their opponents themselves

(20:21); on day two, eighteen thousand (20:25). But by day three, only thirty men are lost (20:31, 39), and the momentum turns in Israel's favor. They wipe out the tribe of Benjamin, leaving it only six hundred men (20:46-48).

Having intended the extinction of Benjamin, and thus having sworn not to give their daughters to its survivors (21:1), the tribes inexplicably have "compassion for Benjamin their kin" (21:6, 15). But where to get women to replenish Benjamin? The cycle of violence then continues, and the rape of one woman becomes the rape of six hundred. In contrast to 1 Samuel 11, where King Saul protects Jabesh-Gilead, tribal governance and familial allegiance destroy the citizens of that city. Four hundred virgins from Jabesh-Gilead are seized (21:8-12). Two hundred more are taken from the city of Shiloh, a local shrine where a deity cannot protect the people (21:19-23). To explain the anarchy of this period, the Deuteronomist concludes, "In those days there was no king in Israel; every man did what was right in his own eyes" (21:25).

Conclusion

An ideological analysis reveals that Judges 17–21 should be contextualized during the time of King Josiah as a literary production of the preexilic Deuteronomist. To support Josiah's so-called religious reform, which demolished popular cult centers that competed with Jerusalem, the Deuteronomist conducts a propaganda war against their clergy, the country Levites. According to Judges 17–18, they are corrupt opportunists intent on financial gain. In Judges 19–21, they become heartless individuals who foment civil war to avenge attempts to dishonor them. But repressed in the text are Josiah's own fiscal ambitions for the state and his redirection of the enormous revenues collected by the Levites into the Jerusalem treasury.

Moreover, Judges 17–21 is a systematic attempt by the Deuteronomist to break up the tribal body in service to the monarchy. It encodes the conflicts between the familial and tributary modes of production. It shifts the history of tribal collapse two centuries back to tribal Israel itself. It subverts tribal kin-group connections in order to centralize and stabilize monarchic sovereignty. The woman's fractured body becomes an ideological symbol of tribal disintegration.[47] As the Levite literally mutilates the body of his wife, the Deuteronomist narratively dis-members the "body" of the tribes.

---

47. Susan Niditch, "The 'Sodomite' Theme in Judges 19–20: Family, Community, and Social Disintegration," *Catholic Biblical Quarterly* 44 (1982): 371–73; Alice Keefe, "Rapes of Women/Wars of Men," *Semeia* 61 (1993): 85–86.

Further Reading

General

DAVIS, Robert Con, and Ronald Schleifer, eds. "Marxism and the New Historicism." *Contemporary Literature Criticism: Literary and Cultural Studies.* New
York: Longman, 1989, 369–428. An introduction to Marxist criticism and a
related approach, New Historicism, plus articles by Marxist critics Raymond
Williams, Mikhail Bakhtin, Terry Eagleton, and Fredric Jameson.

DOWLING, William C. *Jameson, Althusser, Marx: An Introduction to* The Political
Unconscious. Ithaca, N.Y.: Cornell University Press, 1984. Provides the student with the theoretical background on critics Marx and Althusser for
Jameson's *The Political Unconscious.* Contextualizes Jameson's difficult writing style in the wider field of critical theory and tries to render Jameson in
"plainer English."

EAGLETON, Terry. *Criticism and Ideology: A Study in Marxist Literary Theory.*
London: Verso, 1975. Particularly helpful are the chapters on the different
modes of production and the various ways they interrelate (chapter 2), and
the significant relations between history, ideology, and the text (chapter 3).

———. *Ideology: An Introduction.* London and New York: Verso, 1991, 33–61.
A lucid, often witty, introduction to the complexities of ideology. Includes
chapters on the definition and strategies of ideology, the major thinkers, and
the intricate relations among ideology, discourse, and power.

———. *Literary Theory: An Introduction.* A concise overview of New Criticism,
phenomenology, hermeneutics, reception theory, structuralism, semiotics,
poststructuralism, and psychoanalysis. Lays out the ideological underpin-
nings of each literary theory and concludes with a call for a politically committed criticism.

———. *Marxism and Literary Criticism.* Berkeley, Calif.: University of Califor-
nia Press, 1976. A brief look at four central topics of Marxist literary criticism
and relevant theorists: literature and history (Marx and Engels); form and
content (Lukács, Goldmann, Macherey); the writer and political commitment (Marx and Engels); the author as producer (Benjamin and Brecht).

JAMESON, Fredric. *The Political Unconscious: Narrative as a Socially Symbolic Act.*
Ithaca, N.Y.: Cornell University Press, 1981. A major, influential work by an
important Marxist literary critic. For the advanced student. See Dowling
entry above.

NEWTON, Judith, and Deborah Rosenfelt, eds. *Feminist Criticism and Social
Change: Sex, Class, and Race in Literature and Culture.* New York and London, Methuen, 1985. See especially the editors' introduction, "Toward a Ma-
terialist-Feminist Criticism," pp. xv–xxix, and Michèle Barrett's "Ideology

and the Cultural Production of Gender," pp. 65–85, which bring feminist issues into an area of critical theory traditionally associated with economic class.

SELDEN, Raman. "Marxist Theories," *A Reader's Guide to Contemporary Literary Theory.* Lexington, Ky.: University Press of Kentucky, 1989, 2d ed., 24–50. A very accessible introduction to Marxist literary theory, with bibliography.

WALHOUT, Clarence. "Marxist Criticism." *Contemporary Literary Theory: A Christian Appraisal,* Clarence Walhout and Leland Ryken, eds. Grand Rapids: William B. Eerdmans, 1991, 72–93. Analyzes Marxist criticism from a Christian point of view. A brief survey of some of the issues in Marxism, the critic Mikhail Bahktin, and the major differences between Marxist and Christian thinking.

Biblical

CERESKO, O.S.F.S., Anthony R. *Introduction to the Old Testament: A Liberation Perspective.* Maryknoll, N.Y.: Orbis Books, 1992. An accessible introduction to the Hebrew Bible that applies Gottwald's theory of Israel's social origins, emphasizing the dynamics of social power and conflict that are embedded in the texts and highlighting the political engagement of the reader who interprets them.

CLEVENOT, Michel. *Materialist Approaches to the Bible.* Maryknoll, N.Y.: Orbis Books, 1985. A helpful presentation of the "materialist" school of reading the Bible. The first half of the book deals with the Hebrew Bible.

COOTE, Robert B., and Mary P. Coote. *Power, Politics, and the Making of the Bible: An Introduction.* Minneapolis: Fortress Press, 1990. A brief survey of formation of the biblical tradition, canons, and ancient commentaries from the tribal period of Israel's history (c. 1250 B.C.E.) to the time of the Babylonian Talmud (c. 530 C.E.). Emphasis on the power struggles and conflicts among the elites who produced the Bible.

COOTE, Robert B., and David Robert Ord. *The Bible's First History.* Philadelphia: Fortress Press, 1989. Contextualizes the history of the Yahwist (J) as a social production of the court of David during the tenth century B.C.E.

GOTTWALD, Norman K., and Richard A. Horsley, eds. *The Bible and Liberation: Political and Social Hermeneutics.* Maryknoll, N.Y.: Orbis Books, 1993, rev. ed. An excellent collection of essays on both the Hebrew Bible and New Testament from liberationist, feminist, and third world perspectives.

————. *The Hebrew Bible in Its Social World and in Ours.* Atlanta, Ga.: Scholars Press, 1993. A convenient anthology of essays revealing the emergence and development of Gottwald's socio-literary thinking. One-third of the collection is comprised of previously unpublished works. Other articles were previously published elsewhere in sources not normally read by biblical scholars.

———. *The Hebrew Bible: A Socio-Literary Introduction*. Philadelphia: Fortress Press, 1985. An excellent introduction to the Hebrew Bible from a socio-literary perspective.

———. *The Tribes of Yahweh: A Sociology of the Religion of Liberated Israel, 1250–1050 B.C.E.* Maryknoll, N.Y.: Orbis Books, 1979. A monumental study of the origins of Israel, perhaps the first of its kind to incorporate a socio-literary method.

JOBLING, David, Peggy L. Day, and Gerald T. Sheppard, eds. *The Bible and the Politics of Exegesis*. Cleveland: Pilgrim Press, 1991. A fine collection of essays in honor of Norman K. Gottwald, incorporating his socio-literary approach to the Hebrew Bible.

JOBLING, David, and Tina Pippin, eds. *Ideological Criticism of Biblical Texts*. *Semeia* 59 (1992). A collection of essays arising from the SBL Consultation on Ideological Criticism of Biblical Texts. A talk by Fredric Jameson is reprinted in the collection. Excellent bibliography on ideological criticism.

MOSALA, Itumeleng J. *Biblical Hermeneutics and Black Theology in South Africa*. Grand Rapids: William B. Eerdmans, 1989. A materialist reading of biblical texts from a South African perspective.

NAKANOSE, Shigeyuki. *Josiah's Passover: Sociology and the Liberating Bible*. A socio-literary reading of 2 Kings 22–23, with practical application to basic ecclesial communities (CEBs) in Latin America.

PIXLEY, Jorge. *Biblical Israel: A People's History*. Minneapolis: Fortress Press, 1992. A brief survey of Israelite history from a socioeconomic perspective. Convenient charts on the modes of production and power relations in each period.

GLOSSARY

Actantial model—a proposal for organizing the character roles in a narrative event under six categories. A *sender* initiates the action, in order to transfer an *object* to a *receiver.* The action is carried out by a *subject,* who is aided and/or opposed by *helpers* and *opponents.* The entity occupying one of these categories is called an **actant.**

Androcentric—male-centered.

B.C.E.—before the common era or before the Christian era; the equivalent of B.C., but expressed without being Christocentric.

Bêt ʾāb—"house of the father"; the household, which was the smallest basic unit of social organization in ancient Israel.

Bilateral kinship—tracing one's descent through both one's mother's and father's relatives.

Binary opposition—a pair of concepts felt (within some human groups) to be opposed to each other, for example, male/female. Some structuralist theories hold that the human mind works by positing and mediating such oppositions.

Characters—people who participate in the events of a story, and are usually portrayed through their own actions or speeches, the speeches of other characters, or by the narrator's comments.

Chiasmus—a literary device that structures words, phrases, sections of a work, and so on by balancing them in an A B B' A' pattern. The artistic focus is usually on the center of the chiasmus, in this case, the B B'.

Deconstructive criticism—an act of reading that exposes the ways in which texts contradict themselves and accents the textual elements that traditional readings have overlooked or have intentionally ignored. A deconstructive reading is one that explores the complexity (even the conflictual nature) of a text's production of meaning, as opposed to a reading that reduces a text's meaning to a single or a dominant interpretation.

Deuteronomist(s)—the author(s) or editor(s) of the "Deuteronomic History," which, according to a hypothesis popular in biblical studies, forms a coherent and originally separate work.

Deuteronomistic History—the name given to the biblical books of Joshua, Judges, 1 and 2 Samuel, and 1 and 2 Kings.

Diachronic—literally, "through time"; a form of study that considers changes in some phenomenon over the course of time (contrast *synchronic*).

Direct discourse—refers to occasions where the narrator reports the speeches of characters in the story.

Discourse—the various symbolic and linguistic systems and narratives used in human communication, for example, newspaper articles, academic textbooks and articles, films, songs, paintings, poetry, stories, and so on.

Endogamy—marriage within boundaries established by the individual's group.

Ethnocentrism—projecting one's own contemporary notions of the world onto other social systems without considering whether or not this is an appropriate view of reality.

Exogamy—marriage outside boundaries established by an individual's group.

Familial mode of production—a kinship or lineage-based mode of production whose members own the principle means of production and do not pay tribute or taxes to an external ruling elite.

Focalization—a term some narrative theorists use to refer to the perspective from which a narrative event is presented. An event may be focalized by the narrator or by a character.

Form criticism—a method of exegesis that examines the literary forms of biblical genres and their life settings in a believing community.

Gender—the cultural definition of behavior considered to be appropriate to the sexes in a given society at a given time. Whereas sex is a biological given, gender is culturally created. For example, only women can give birth; thus giving birth is a sex role. Both men and women are capable of raising children, but most societies assign this role to women; it is therefore a gender role.

Ideological criticism—a method of exegesis that incorporates both sociohistorical and literary approaches to investigate the production and (re)production of ideology in a text.

Ideology—a complex system of meaning that constructs a "reality" for people and helps them understand their place in the world as natural, inevitable, and necessary. It is not the "reality" itself.

Intertextuality—the notion that texts are interrelated through direct citation or allusion, subtle influence, or by the very fact that all texts, as products of language, form a boundless network. Intertextual reading is reading that attends to how textual connections participate in any one text's production of meaning.

Langue—French for "language"; used in structuralism (in contrast to *parole*) to refer to language as a system of relationships and, by extension, to the system of relationships underlying any cultural phenomenon.

Lineage—a descent group that is composed of a number of residential groups.

Linguistics—the science of language.

Material/materialist—refers to the production and distribution of economic goods and the social relationships of owners and workers.

Mediation—used in a special sense by structuralists to refer to an attempt (for example, in myth) to hold together the two incompatible sides of a *binary opposition*.

Mode of production—the complete operation of social relations (family organization, status, class, gender, etc.) and the forces (technological, political, juridical, etc.) of a society's material production. Ancient Israel had three dominant modes of production at different historical times: familial, tributary, and slave.

Narrated discourse—refers to occasions where the narrator speaks and relates aspects of the story.

Narrative criticism—a literary method of analysis that focuses on plot, character, setting, point of view, and compositional techniques such as repetition and the use of narrated discourse or direct discourse.

Narratology—the theory of narrative.

Narrator—the person who tells the story; usually a third-person, omniscient narrator in biblical narratives.

Neolocal residence—the practice of newlyweds' taking up a new place of residence separate from both sets of parents after marriage.

Parole—French for "word"; used in structuralism (in contrast to *langue*) to refer to the individual linguistic utterance, and, by extension, to any individual cultural production.

Patriarchy/patriarchal—refers to both a social system and an ideology in which women are subordinated to men and younger men to older men.

Patrilineal descent—descent traced from fathers to sons.

Pilegesh—secondary wife.

Plot—the sequences of events related in terms of their causes and consequences.

Point of view—the perspective from which the story or portions of the story is told. Usually the vantage point of the third-person, omniscient narrator, but often the more limited viewpoint of a particular character.

Polycoity—a form of marriage in which a man takes women who are of lower status than his primary wife as his secondary wives.

Polygyny—a form of marriage in which a man may have more than one wife at a time, but in which the wives are of equal status to one another.

Redaction criticism—a method of biblical exegesis that analyzes the final written stages of a text by various editors. Many scholars currently accept the theory of a Josianic and/or an exilic deuteronomistic redactor for the final editing of the Book of Judges.

Repetition—multiple use of words or phrases, motifs or themes, or a sequence of actions for the purpose of indicating narrative structure, identifying key themes, or emphasizing central ideas.

Semantics—the study of meaning, particularly as a branch of *linguistics*.

Semiotics—the study of signs and signification. The object of study may be the ways that the natural world signifies things to humans, or the ways that humans signify things to each other.

Semiotic square—a visual representation of the system of logical relations generated by a *binary opposition*. If the terms of the opposition are A and B, the square relates A, B, their contradictory terms non-A and non-B, and more complex combinations.

Serial monogamy—a form of marriage in which an individual may have only one spouse at a time.

Setting—the locales where the narrative events take place.

Social scientific criticism—an approach that emphasizes collective, or group, organization rather than individual perspective.

Structuralism—a philosophical view according to which the mind apprehends reality as sets of relationships among items rather than as individual items. Also, methods of study in the human or social sciences based on this assumption.

Structure—in narrative criticism, refers to the organization of events into an ordered and coherent story.

Synchronic—literally, "at the same time"; a form of study that considers some phenomenon as a set of relationships existing at a given moment in time (contrast *diachronic*).

Tradition criticism—a method of biblical exegesis that studies the transmission and development of the oral and written stages of tradition before the final editing of the text.

Tributary mode of production—a mode of production characterized by a stratified, hierarchically ordered society where a king or ruling elite demand tributes or taxes from the lower classes. In a native tributary mode of production, the ruling elite are indigenous to the land. In a foreign tributary mode of production, the land is administered by foreign colonizers or conquerors.

INDEX OF TOPICS AND NAMES

INDEX OF ANCIENT SOURCES

CONTRIBUTORS

RICHARD G. BOWMAN is Associate Professor of Religion and Chair of the Department of Religion, Philosophy, and Classics at Augustana College, Sioux Falls, South Dakota. He received his doctorate from Union Theological Seminary in Virginia and is the author of "The Fortune of King David/The Fate of Queen Michal: A Literary Critical Analysis of II Samuel 1–8," in *Telling Queen Michal's Story,* David J. A. Clines and Tamara Eskenazi, eds. (Sheffield, Eng.: Sheffield Academic Press, 1991).

J. CHERYL EXUM is Professor of Biblical Studies at the University of Sheffield, England. She is the author of *Tragedy and Biblical Narrative: Arrows of the Almighty* (Cambridge University Press, 1992); *Fragmented Women: Feminist (Sub)versions of Biblical Narratives* (Sheffield Academic Press and Trinity Press International, 1993); and executive editor of *Biblical Interpretation: A Journal of Contemporary Approaches.*

DANNA NOLAN FEWELL is Associate Professor of Old Testament at Perkins School of Theology at Southern Methodist University, Dallas, Texas. She is the author of *Circle of Sovereignty: Plotting Politics in the Book of Daniel* (Nashville: Abingdon Press, 1991); with David M. Gunn, *Compromising Redemption: Relating Characters in the Book of Ruth* (Louisville, Ky.: Westminster/ John Knox Press, 1990); *Narrative in the Hebrew Bible* (Oxford: Oxford University Press, 1993); *Gender, Power, and Promise: The Subject of the Bible's First Story* (Nashville: Abingdon Press, 1993); and editor of *Reading Between Texts: Intertextuality and the Hebrew Bible* (Louisville, Ky.: Westminster/John Knox Press, 1992).

DAVID JOBLING is Professor of Old Testament Language and Literature at St. Andrew's College, Saskatoon, Saskatchewan. He is the author of *The Sense of Biblical Narrative, Vol. I* (Sheffield, Eng.: JSOT Press, 1978) and *The Sense of Biblical Narrative, Vol. II* (Sheffield, Eng.: JSOT Press, 1986), and co-editor of *The Bible and the Politics of Exegesis: Essays in Honor of Norman K. Gottwald on His Sixty-fifth Birthday* (Cleveland: Pilgrim Press, 1991).

NAOMI STEINBERG is Associate Professor of Religious Studies at DePaul University, Chicago, Illinois. She is the author of *Kinship and Marriage in Genesis: A Household Economics Perspective* (Minneapolis: Fortress Press, 1993).

GALE A. YEE is Associate Professor of Hebrew Bible/Old Testament and Director of the Women's Studies Program at the University of St. Thomas, St. Paul, Minnesota. She is the author of *Composition and Tradition in the Book of Hosea: A Redaction Critical Investigation* (Atlanta: Scholars Press, 1987) and *Jewish Feasts and the Gospel of John* (Zacchaeus Studies; Wilmington, Del.: Michael Glazier, 1989).